Also in the Variorum Collected Studies Series

NORMAN HOUSLEY
Crusading and Warfare in Medieval and Renaissance Europe

PETER W. EDBURY
Kingdoms of the Crusaders: From Jerusalem to Cyprus

BERNARD HAMILTON
Crusaders, Cathars and the Holy Places

DENYS PRINGLE
Fortification and Settlement in Crusader Palestine

JAMES A. BRUNDAGE
The Crusades, Holy War and Canon Law

PETER LINEHAN
Past and Present in Medieval Spain

GARY DICKSON
Religious Enthusiasm in the Medieval West: Revivals, crusades, saints

DAVID ABULAFIA
Mediterranean Encounters, Economic, Religious, Political, 1100–1550

DAVID JACOBY
Byzantium, Latin Romania and the Mediterranean

BERNARD S. BACHRACH
Warfare and Military Organization in Pre-Crusade Europe

CLIFFORD DAVIDSON
History, Religion, and Violence: Cultural contexts for medieval and renaissance English drama

KELLY DEVRIES
Guns and Men in Medieval Europe, 1200–1500: Studies in Military History and Technology

GORDON LEFF
Heresy, Philosophy and Religion in the Medieval West

VARIORUM COLLECTED STUDIES SERIES

Warriors and their Weapons around the Time of the Crusades

David Nicolle

David Nicolle

Warriors and their Weapons around
the Time of the Crusades

Relationships between Byzantium,
the West and the Islamic world

ASHGATE
VARIORUM

This edition copyright © 2002 by David Nicolle.

Published in the Variorum Collected Studies Series by

Ashgate Publishing Limited
Gower House, Croft Road,
Aldershot, Hampshire GU11 3HR
Great Britain

Ashgate Publishing Company
Suite 420, 101 Cherry Street,
Burlington, Vermont 05401–4405
USA

Ashgate website: http://www.ashgate.com

ISBN 0–86078–898–9

British Library Cataloguing-in-Publication Data
Nicolle, David, 1944–
    Warriors and their Weapons around the Time of the Crusades:
    Relationships between Byzantium, the West and the Islamic
    World. – (Variorum collected studies series: CS756)
    1. Weapons – Europe – History – To 1500 2. Weapons – Byzantine
    Empire – History – To 1500 3. Weapons – Islamic Empire – History –
    To 1500 4. Military Art and Science – History – Medieval, 500–1500
    5. Europe – History, Military 6. Byzantine Empire – History,
    Military – 527–1081 7. Byzantine Empire – History, Military – 1081–1453
    8. Islamic Empire – History, Military
    I. Title
    355'.02'094'0902

US Library of Congress Cataloging-in-Publication Data
Nicolle, David, 1944–
    Warriors and their Weapons around the Time of the Crusades: Relationships
    between Byzantium, the West and the Islamic World / David Nicolle.
        p.   cm. – (Variorum Collected Studies Series: CS756).
    Includes bibliographical references and index.
    1. Military Weapons – Mediterranean Region. 2. Armor, Medieval. 3. Crusades.
    4. Military Art and Science – Mediterranean Region. I. Title.
    II. Collected Studies: CS756.
    U810 .N52324 2002
    623.4'41'0918220902–dc21   2002074538

The paper used in this publication meets the minimum requirements of the
        American National Standard for Information Sciences – Permanence of
        Paper for Printed Library Materials, ANSI Z39.48–1984. ∞ ™

Printed by TJ International, Padstow, Cornwall

VARIORUM COLLECTED STUDIES SERIES CS756

CONTENTS

This volume contains xiv + 324 pages

INTRODUCTION

The articles in this volume are primarily concerned with the question of to what extent changes in military technology within one culture reflected influence from other cultures, and to what extent they resulted from internal developments. In most cases the conclusion is that, to some extent, they usually did result from outside influence or that at least outside influences played a part. More often than not this influence resulted from meeting another culture on the battlefield. Yet this was clearly not the only means whereby ideas and technologies were exchanged. Military equipment and the raw materials for its manufacture were traded over long distances during what Europeans know as the Middle Ages. Furthermore, soldiers crossed cultural as well as political frontiers, not only as raiders or conquerors but as allies, mercenaries or in the dual role of merchant-adventurers.

The first article in this anthology, *Medieval Warfare: The Unfriendly Interface*, attempts to provide an overview of the entire question of warfare as a channel for cultural-technological exchange during the medieval period. It also includes translations of a number of what might be called 'military texts' taken from training manuals, books of advice for rulers, and the like, several of which were here published in English for the first time. The technological relationship between the Byzantine and Islamic worlds was particularly close, and military-technological influences clearly flowed in both directions. This is, of course, the subject of the second and third articles, *Byzantium and Islamic Arms and Armour: Evidence for Mutual Influence*, and *No way overland? Evidence for Byzantine arms and armour on the 10th-11th century Taurus Frontier*. The evidence for mutual military and technological influence between Western Europe and the Islamic world is much less obvious, but I believe that the flow of ideas, fashions and military hardware was as important within this relationship as it was in the Byzantine-Islamic relationship.

One specific aspect of this proposed mutual influence forms the subject of the fourth article; *The Impact of the European Couched Lance on Muslim Military Tradition*. There were several places within medieval Western or 'Latin' Christendom where one might expect to find evidence for the proposed exchange of military styles, systems and technologies. The Iberian peninsula is perhaps the most obvious, while the ephemeral Crusader States in what are now parts of Turkey, Syria, Lebanon, Palestine including present-day Israel, and Jordan are the second most obvious candidates. Hence the fifth article, *Armes et armures dans les Épopées des Croisades*, looks for evidence of such mutual influence in both the poetic epics and the pictorial art of the Crusader States. This subject is continued in the sixth article, *Arms and Armour illustrated in the Art of the Latin East*. The subject of the seventh article is somewhat different, *Wounds, Military Surgery and the Reality of Crusading Warfare; The Evidence of Usamah's Memoires*, since it looks at the medical aspects of medieval warfare. But again the question of different approaches within Islamic and Christian cultures is considered.

The eighth article, *'Ain al-Habis. The cave de Sueth*, remains the author's only serious venture into the field of archaeology. In fact, not having been trained as an archaeologist, the author only published a study of the extraordinary 'cave fortress' at 'Ain al-Habis because he was lucky enough to be able to explore the site which, at the time and probably still today, lies within a sensitive military zone on Jordan's frontier with Syria. Articles nine and ten, *The Monreale Capitals and the Military Equipment of Later Norman Sicily* and *The Cappella Palatina Ceiling and the Muslim Military Inheritance of Norman Sicily*, both look at the military equipment of twelfth century Sicily. This is reflected in two highly distinctive pictorial sources; the carved capitals in the Cloister of Monreale Cathedral and the Islamic-style painted panels on the Cappella Palatina ceiling in Palermo. The ninth and final article, *Arms, Armour and Horse Harnesses in the Parma Baptistery Painted Ceiling*, looks at military equipment illustrated on a slightly later pictorial source in northern Italy where there might be evidence of Byzantine influence. This was originally written for a wide-ranging collection of articles on various aspects of the painted ceiling which was, unfortunately, never published.

The story of the varied influences upon the styles and development of arms and armour in the medieval Mediterranean world can be said to have begun with the *fabricae* or state-run armaments factories of the late Roman Empire. These were located in what would subsequently either become the post-Roman or Byzantine Empire, the most economically advanced regions of medieval Western Europe, and the western half of the medieval Islamic world. Hence their importance can hardly be ignored. Late Roman arms manufacture was, however, a mass-production system which would not be replicated in Western Europe for many centuries, though it did find parallels in some aspects of Islamic arms manufacture. Forty-four *fabricae* were, in fact, listed in the early 5th century while archaeological evidence suggests that smaller, unlisted, *fabricae* were attached to many provincial military units.

Some seem to have survived the fall of the western Roman Empire and it is similarly possible that Italian cities such as Pisa and Lucca retained their arms industries from Roman times well into the medieval period. The same may also be true of Liège, Soissons and other centres north of the Alps as well various locations in the Iberian peninsula. On the other hand most of the armourers of the Merovingian and early Carolingian centuries were migratory smiths, operating small mobile forges as they moved around the country, as was also the case in 5th and 6th century Celtic Britain. Several parts of Western Europe rose to prominence as centres of arms production by the 11th century. Over the next four hundred years a few of these outstripped all others in terms of volume production, the quality of their arms and armour, and as centres of fashion or new ideas. The most important were in northern Italy, southern Germany and western Germany. Meanwhile other regions continued to manufacture military equipment, largely for local use.

The situation was clearly different within the eastern rump of the Roman Empire which modern historians know as the Byzantine Empire. Here soldiers at first continued to receive their arms and armour from the state. In the case of 8th to 10th century élite *tagmata* troops these came from government stores, though some foreign recruits from what were called 'warlike peoples' brought their own weaponry with them. Otherwise military equipment seems to have been distributed to the men at the start of a campaign rather than remaining in their possession; a system which was still recorded in 12th-century Byzantine armies. Meanwhile the weaponry of provincial troops seems to have formed part of their 'estate' to be passed from generation to generation. As far as the Byzantine army as a whole was concerned, the bulk of its kit was manufactured by Byzantine armourers, yet there was also a steady flow of material from outside, either as official government imports, booty, tribute or diplomatic gifts. For example a substantial volume of Western European military equipment was captured from invading south-Italian Normans in the 12th century, and from similarly south-Italian invading Angevins in the 13th century. By then, however, the Byzantine Empire's shrinking resources meant that the government offered tax exemptions and other inducements to encourage the peaceful importation of Western European military equipment via places like Dubrovnik and Durrës on the Balkan Adriatic coast. Mid-13th-century Nicea (now Iznik) seems to have relied primarily on Genoa for both weaponry and horses, and during the 14th century Constantinople purchased iron and completed weapons from Dubrovnik, Genoa and Venice.

The importance of weapons smiths in medieval Western Europe is clearly indicated by the early appearance of separate armourers' guilds. In 13th century Venice the smiths were divided into ordinary smiths and specialist sword-makers; the latter being closely associated with scabbard, belt and armour makers. Even before the appearance of separate guilds these craftsmen were undoubtedly specialised, skilled and often highly paid according to the standards of their day. Most would have been local men, although a certain Richard the Saracen worked as an armourer in early 13th-century Paris while a Peter the Saracen worked for King John of England. Ordinary mass-produced items tended to be made where the basic materials were most easily available. For example, the largest centre for the manufacture of crossbow bolts in 13th century England was the castle of St Briavel in the Forest of Dean where iron, charcoal and wood were all abundant. Countries with less developed economies tended to fall back upon more primitive systems such as the imposition a form of tax to be paid in kind with arms, armour or horses. Nevertheless the skills involved could be highly sophisticated, as in the making of composite bows where the techniques were so complicated that they had to be learned from childhood.

Whereas the crude workmanship and simple design of much late Roman weaponry pointed to mass-production by low-skilled craftsmen, the quality of much medieval military equipment indicated very high levels of craftsmanship and sometimes hundreds of hours of work. The amount of iron involved may have been quite small, but the quantities of charcoal required to smelt the iron, and then to forge the finished items were remarkably high. Time was the main ingredient in the making of composite bows, since season and weather influenced the harvesting of suitable wood, while correct humidity and temperature were needed for each stage of construction. In fact it seems that a single bow took a year to make, so these weapons were normally manufactured in batches. Simple longbows were, by comparison, crude and easily made. Nevertheless they were manufactured in huge numbers under the pressure of conflicts such as the Hundred Years War.

Given a steadily increasing demand for military equipment during the medieval period, it is hardly surprising that an international arms trade developed. Arms and armour were, in fact, distributed in various ways and even in the late Roman period they could travel great distances. Several fine Roman swords have been found in 5th- to 8th-century Scandinavian and Baltic graves while most of the mail found in early medieval Scandinavian contexts is of eastern Mediterranean or Middle Eastern origin. Presumably it was acquired either as booty or trade or had been handed down through many generations. On the other hand some arms-manufacturing centres were catering for a wide market as early as the 6th century when, for example, Ostrogothic Italy may have exported distinctive helmets to surrounding countries. Elsewhere in early medieval Europe tribute from subjects to their rulers, and gifts from rulers to their followers, were probably a more important means of arms distribution.

An economic revival which began under Carolingian rule may have meant that the relative cost of weaponry went down between the 8th and 11th centuries. Changes in arms and armour, or at least in the amount of equipment that the military élite were expected to possess, may then have caused costs to rise again from the 12th to 14th centuries. During the 12th century inheritance remained a very important source of weaponry although battlefield loot also played an important role, especially for those of lower rank. Meanwhile new weaponry was undoubtedly purchased, usually by individuals although communes as well as governments were buying arms in bulk by the 14th century. The prices of specific items could fluctuate considerably but the main price differences reflected quality. In fact armour was clearly getting very expensive by the mid-13th century; full knightly equipment, plus a horse, often equalling the average annual revenue of a knight's fief. Perhaps as a result armour was often rented; the full price only being paid if it was lost.

Each part of Western Europe seems to have had its own recognised distribution centres, some of which were also places of manufacture. At the same time merchants acted as middle-men between manufacturers and their sometimes distant customers. Not surprisingly governments also tried to control such trade, especially in time of war. Nevertheless arms and armour of western European origin continued to spread widely, having been found among the pagan Lapps of the far north who exchanged such metal goods for furs, or deep in Siberia and even in Eskimo sites in the American Arctic. The exportation of Western European weaponry to Muslims was, of course, forbidden by Papal decree. Yet arms and armour still reached the Moroccan port of Ceuta, having apparently been camouflaged as other forms of trade-goods in Genoese financial records. Apart from a few exotic items, apparently brought back to Western Europe by travellers and by Crusaders, there seems to have been no exportation of arms from the Islamic world to Western Europe at this time.

During the 14th century the western European arms trade flourished as never before. Skilled armourers moved to whichever country paid them best and, partly as a result, new ideas and fashions spread rapidly. The role of

Italian arms merchants in the 14th century was clearly very important, though it may have been exaggerated by the very fact of the survival of the almost complete business records of Francesco di Marco Datini. Known as 'The Merchant of Prato', Datini purchased arms from northern Italy and Germany, traded in uncut sheet-iron for visors and arm-defences, tin studs for shields, received samples of armour and harness from Barcelona to check their quality, hired weaponry to those unable to pay the full price, bought captured equipment from the winning side then sold it second-hand, and sent agents to buy up weaponry when a temporary outbreak of peace during the Hundred Years War led to a glut on the market.

Merchants like Datini must have been found throughout most of Europe, dealing in Venetian arms in late 14th-century Albania as it faced the advancing Ottoman Turks, or providing new German equipment to German mercenaries serving in Serbian armies. Others probably carried Swedish crossbows to Teutonic Knights on the other side the Baltic Sea and perhaps transported wagon-loads of weaponry from northern or central Europe across southern Poland and Moldavia to the Black Sea ports. Much of the latter equipment then ended up in the Islamic armies of Persia and the Middle East.

David Nicolle
Woodhouse Eaves, 2002

ACKNOWLEDGEMENTS

Grateful acknowledgement is given to the following for permission to reproduce the articles in this volume: *Journal of Military History* (I); Institute for Graeco-Oriental and African Studies (II, III); The Arms and Armour Society (IV); *Zeitschrift für Französische Sprache und Literature* (V); B.Z. Kedar and Yad Izhak Ben-Zvi (VI); *The Journal of Oriental and African Studies* (VII); *Archéologie Médiévale* (VIII); *Gladius* (IX, X).

PUBLISHER'S NOTE

The articles in this volume, as in all others in the Collected Studies Series, have not been given a new, continuous pagination. In order to avoid confusion, and to facilitate their use where these same studies have been referred to elsewhere, the original pagination has been maintained wherever possible.

Each article has been given a Roman numeral in order of appearance, as listed in the Contents. This number is repeated on each page and quoted in the index entries.

I

Medieval Warfare:
The Unfriendly Interface

IN this context the term "medieval" is taken to mean the period from the fall of the western part of the Roman Empire to the fourteenth century, while "warfare" refers to active hostilities between states or groups of states linked by a shared religion, or between such entities and less structured tribal societies. It is not taken to include unfriendly coexistance between periods of active hostilities. Nor does it cover cultural, religious, or economic competition not involving organized violence. Contrary to a widespread popular impression, medieval Europe was no more warlike nor more violent than preceding or subsequent periods within Europe, nor indeed in comparison to most other societies during what Europeans call the medieval period. On the other hand, warfare as a social and political phenomenon was more widely accepted as "normal" within medieval Europe than it was in many other cultures, times or places.

As to the historical importance of warfare, certain factors applied to medieval conflict just as they did at any other time. Above all, warfare involved human beings, male or female, and their societies under extreme stress. Of course, this stress could be widespread or very localized. It could be persistent or brief. Nevertheless it is the stress, individual or social, caused by warfare which tended to highlight certain characteristics of the society involved.

These factors could be regarded as the internal stresses generated by conflict between political entities. There are also what could be regarded as external stresses: in other words those highlighted by the different ways in which different and usually rival cultures reacted to similar situations or challenges. These latter are more relevant when looking at warfare between rival cultures rather than merely competing states. A second, and one could almost say more positive, aspect of human conflict was the way in which warfare served as a channel for ideas across frontiers and between different cultures. The ideas involved were most obviously military, such as the technology of arms and armour, tactics, various aspects of military organization, and so on. Yet to some extent they also included motivation and, by extension, individual motivating beliefs. Nor is there any paradox in the fact that conflict helped the spread of minor artistic ideas, including flags, heraldry, and, in its most general sense, costume.

There seem to be three main reasons why one culture should adopt ideas from a rival or even an enemy. The first is obvious. War tended to bring societies, and their individual members, back to basics. It could range from a matter of survival to merely winning a temporary advantage. One way or another, of course, individual soldiers, armies, and societies fought to win. Despite the culture of chivalry, which supposedly placed honour above mere military success, this was as true of medieval Europe as of any other society, medieval or otherwise.

My interpretation of the historical evidence leads me to the conclusion that those on the receiving end of what appeared, at that historical moment, to be a superior military system would—all other things being equal—adopt the military technology of whichever side was winning. In reality, of course, all things were rarely equal. As a result, many apparently and actually superior military technologies and systems of organization were not copied by those on the receiving end. In many ways, this phenomenon is even more interesting than those cases where such technologies or systems were adopted. Failure to adopt such "best practice" could not only lead to death or injury but could undermine existing political structures or belief systems. Of course, it did not always have this result, but then the reasons for an individual's survival, or that of an entire culture, depended any many factors in addition to the merely military equation.

The second and third of what could be regarded as the main reasons for copying an enemy are similar to one another. They tended to apply to the more superficial social or cultural aspects of military history such as costume and identifying motifs. Here the military elite rather than the ordinary soldiers of a particular culture often adopted some of these supposedly superficial aspects of their enemy's culture.[1] In the simplest terms, there were two reasons for this. The first was a conscious, or often almost unconscious, mark of respect for a worthy opponent. After all, it has been said that imitation is the most sincere form of flattery. Secondly, there was the adoption of aspects of, for example, costume as a means of showing political allegiance—usually temporary—across a cultural frontier. For reasons which are not yet entirely clear, such symbolism was particularly clear amongst those who were obliged to accept

1. H. Seyrig, "Armes et costumes Iraniens de Palmyre," *Syria* 18 (1937): 4-30.

Medieval Warfare: The Unfriendly Interface

influences upon the development of new types of protection in late thirteenth- and early fourteenth-century Europe.[10] This was clearly a time of greater change in armour than had been seen since the fall of the western Roman Empire.

To take just two examples: the bascinet helmet and the coat-of-plates. Both appeared quite suddenly in the late thirteenth century; the bascinet firstly in Italy,[11] the coat of plates either in Spain, Italy, or Germany, all of which were to some degree on the cultural frontiers of medieval western Europe.[12] The bascinet may have reflected Byzantine influence, but it seems more likely that the most powerful stylistic influence came from the Muslim Middle East. It could have resulted from trade contacts as much as warlike contacts in the eastern Mediterranean. The European coat-of-plates was structurally different from the Islamic *lamellar jawshan* and seems to have been closer to the armour used by the Chinese-influenced elite Mongol heavily armoured cavalry.[13] Yet this was not merely a matter of technological copying. The sudden appearance of primitive forms of the coat-of-plates in western Europe was, to a significant extent, also an acceptance of the broader concept of a semiflexible form of body armour loosely based upon those used by Muslim or Mongol rivals.

10. There had been strong resistance to this concept amongst earlier scholars of European arms and armour. It seems as if only those from the geographical fringes of Europe have taken the idea seriously, amongst them being Dr. Ada Bruhn de Hoffmeyer in Spain, *Arms and Armour in Spain, a Short Survey*, 2 vols. (Madrid: Instituto de Estudios sobre Armas Antiques, 1972–82); B. Thordeman in Sweden, *Armour from the Battle of Wisby, 1361*, 2 vols. (Stockholm: Kugl. vitterhets historie och antikvitels akademien, 1939–40); M. Scalini in Italy, *Armamento difensivo trecentesco* (Florence: Museo Nazionale del Bargello, 1984); T. Kolias in Greece, *Byzantinischen Waffen* (Vienna: Österreichischen Akademie der Wissenschaften, 1988); and several Russian scholars, most notably A. Kirpitchnikoff, *Drevnerusskoe Oruzhie IX-XIII vv.* (Medieval Russian arms, 9th–13th centuries), in Russian with French summary (Leningrad: Izdatelstvo "Nauka," 1971), and *Voennoi Delo na Rusi*, in Russian (Leningrad: Izdatelstvo "Nauka," 1976); M. Gorelik, "Kulikovskaya Bitva, 1380: Russki i Zoloturkuinskii Vojni," *Tseikhgauz* 1 (Moscow, 1991): 2–7; "Voini Kievskoi Rusi, IX-XI bb," *Tseikhgauz* 2 (Moscow, 1993): 20–25; "Bitva na Vorskle, 1399," *Tseikhgauz* 3 (Moscow 1994): 21–25. Currently A. Medveev of St. Petersburg is studying Mongol armour and its influence upon various neighbouring cultures.

11. The earliest reference to a bascinet or *bazineto* was in Padua in 1281, when it was worn by infantry. Bascinet-type helmets had, however, appeared in Italian art since before 1260.

12. A. V. B. Norman, "An Early Illustration of Body Armour," *Zeitschrift für Historische Waffen- und Kostümkunde* 18 (1976): 38–39.

13. One of the most remarkable results of the research currently being undertaken by Alexander Medveev (see note 10) is the fact that Mongol armies included a much larger number of heavily armoured close-combat cavalry than hitherto realized, and that they played a major role in Mongol successes on the battlefield.

Two obvious examples in weaponry are the composite bow and the sabre. The composite bow had been known in the Mediterranean region since ancient times and was even used in Britain by Roman archers.[14] It survived in the Iberian peninsula, possibly in Italy, and certainly in the Byzantine world throughout the Middle Ages. It was also, of course, a standard weapon in the Islamic world, Central Asia, and China but not in medieval India or Japan. The basic form of the weapon did not change much, though there were numerous minor changes in its construction, overall shape, size, and so on. To some extent, these reflected the way the compositite bow was used, either on horseback or on foot. Yet these relatively small changes are interesting because they seem to mirror the movement of militarily significant and usually dominant peoples, most obviously the Turks. Considerable research has been done into the way such changes improved or modified the composite bow's performance.[15] What has not apparently been considered, except by historians of "material culture" in what was the Soviet Union, is the way in which the acceptance of new variants of composite bow resulted from mere fashion. This may have been an extension of a copying of the weaponry of militarily successful people, whether or not the changes themselves brought any real military advantage.

But what about a movement of military ideas across the frontiers from western Europe to its neighbours in the era before a widespread use of firearms? This is remarkably difficult, since the evidence overwhelmingly points to the West as the recipient rather than the exporter of ideas. One highly visible, though far from successful, example of an Islamic people copying their Christian neighbours can, however, be found in the Iberian peninsula. This is also one of the clearest medieval examples of imitation as the sincerest form of flattery. From the late eleventh to early fourteenth centuries, the armies of al-Andalus, or at least those recruited from the indigenous elite, adopted relatively heavy

14. J. C. Coulston, "Roman Archery Equipment," in M. C. Bishop, ed., *The Production and Distribution of Roman Military Equipment,* Proceedings of the Second Roman Military Equipment Research Seminar, British Archaeological Reports, International Series 275 (Oxford: B.A.R., 1985), 220–366.

15. Y. S. Khudyakov and Y. A. Plotnikov, eds., *Voennoe Delo Drevnego I Srednevekovogo Naseleniya Severnoi i Tsentralnoi Asii* (Military affairs of the ancient and medieval peoples of northern and central Asia), in Russian (Novosibirsk: Akademya Nauk CCCP, 1990), 44–60, 81–96; Khudyakov, *Vooruzhenie Eniseiskikh Kirgizov VI-XII bb* (Arms of the Yenesi Khirghiz 6th–12th centuries), in Russian (Novosibirsk: Sibirskoe Otdelenye Izdatelstvo "Nauk," 1980), 66–117; Khudyakov, *Vooruzhenie Srednevekovikh Kochevnikov Yuzhnoi Sibiri i Tsentralnoi Asii* (Armaments of the medieval nomads of southern Siberia and central Asia), in Russian (Novosibirsk: Sibirskoe Otdelenye Izdatelstvo "Nauk," 1986), passim; A. I. Solovyev, *Voennoe Delo Korennogo Naseleniya Zapadnoi Sibiri* (Warfare of the aborigines of western Siberia), in Russian (Novosibirsk: Sibirskoe Otdelenye Izdatelstvo "Nauk," 1987), 19–49.

armour, the couched lance, the deep saddle, long stirrup leathers, and the armoured cavalry shock tactics associated with such equipment.[16] There was also a parallel development of crossbow-armed infantry which proved more positive. These centuries were, of course, the years when the *Reconquista* was at its most dramatically successful. Not surprisingly, perhaps, those on the receiving end of the *Reconquista* tried to counter its military effectiveness by using much the same military systems. They failed and it is interesting to note that fourteenth-century Moorish-Arabic commentators now applauded the fact that the armies of the remaining Muslim state of Granada were abandoning the heavy cavalry tactics which had failed to save thirteenth century al-Andalus.[17]

When it comes to identifying the migration of ideas or concepts in fortification, it is easier to look at small details than the overall plan. Perhaps the easiest is the "bent gate" which was designed to force a mounted attacker to expose his less shielded right side. This again spread from east to west during the medieval period.[18] Once again western Europe, and in this instance also the Middle East, were learning from cultures further east. The bent gate is believed to have first been developed in Khurasan and Transoxania, a wartorn yet culturally and militarily sophisticated borderland between the Iranian- and Turkish-speaking worlds. If this interpretation is correct, and if the bent gate did not originate in the Chinese world, then we have one of several examples of aspects of military technology first appearing in this region. On the other hand, so much seemed to reach the west from the east that it is tempting to assume that it all started in China. In several cases, however, it clearly did not. This leaves the rather amorphous region of Central Asia as the birthplace of several, perhaps more than several, significant aspects of military history.[19]

Costume is not strictly military, except for uniforms. Yet a study of the costume worn by military elites, whether or not they are also political elites, can provide clear examples of both the acceptance and the rejection of influence from "the other side." Some aspects of dress, particularly headgear, were explicitly rejected because they indicated respect for, political subjection to, or cultural affiliation with, a neigh-

16. De Hoffmeyer, *Arms and Armour in Spain,* 1: 98–114; 2: 115, 125–126, 142–146, and passim; A. Soler del Campo, *La evolucion del armamento medieval en el reino castellano-leonés y al-Andalus* (Madrid: Servicio de publicaciones del E.M.E., 1993), passim.

17. De Hoffmeyer, *Arms and Armour in Spain,* 2: 222–50.

18. K. A. C. Creswell, "Bab," in *Encyclopedia of Islam,* 2d ed., vol. 1 (Leiden: E. J. Brill, 1960), 830–32.

19. B. Rubin, "Die Enstehung der Kataphraktenreiter im lichte der choresmischen Ausgrabunden," *Historia* 4 (1955): 264–83; B. Brentjes, "Zu den Reiterbildern von Kurgan-Tepe," *Iranica Antiqua* 25 (1990): 173–81.

bouring culture or political entity. Similarly, such items were worn as a highly visible expression of such respect, subjection, or affiliation.

Heraldry, particularly in its highly formalized western European form, was equally obviously used to express both identity and affiliation. Yet such expressions were almost entirely within the basic cultural context—in this case Christian western Europe. More unusual aspects of western heraldry can be found on the cultural frontiers. Here there were examples, albeit rare, of outside influence. For example there was the use of written script in Italy and Iberia, which is generally believed to reflect Islamic influence.[20] Then there is the still not fully understood appearance of pseudo-Kufic Arabic on shields in Byzantine art; shields which were carried by "good" as well as "evil" or alien figures.

Military recruitment patterns, almost by definition, did not lend themselves to outside influence since they so closely reflected the social structure, cultural or even religious attitudes of the society in question. Nevertheless there is scope for interesting research when it comes to various apparently unusual or unorthodox systems of military recruitment in cultural frontier zones, one example being the Turcopoles of the Crusader States and later medieval Byzantium.[21] Then there are the origins of the Islamic system of slave-recruited *mamluks* which, though it has been studied in considerable depth, has not yet been adequately explained.[22] The Russian *druzhina* is another military formation which could do with a broader study looking at the origins of the system rather than merely at how it operated once up and running.

The payment of troops was an extension of this question of recruitment. It also takes the military historian into the very interesting area of the place of the military in society, their status, loyalty patterns and so on. The relatively higher pay offered to soldiers in professional Islamic armies, when compared to Byzantine and western European forces around the same time, is well established but again not adequately

20. E. Pardo de Guevara, *Manual de Heráldica Española* (Madrid: Gráficas Mar-Car, 1987), 11–12, 88; W. Leaf and S. Purcell, *Heraldic Symbols: Islamic Insignia and Western Heraldry* (London: Victoria and Albert Museum, 1986), 72–74.

21. J. Richard, "Les Turcopoles: Musulmans Convertés ou Chrétiens Orientaux," *Revue des Etudes Islamiques* 54 (1986): 259–70.

22. D. Ayalon has written extensively on this subject, most succinctly in his "Preliminary Remarks on the Mamluk Military Institution in Islam," in V. J. Parry and M. E. Yapp, eds., *War, Technology, and Society in the Middle East* (London: Oxford University Press, 1975), 44–58, while D. Pipes has gone into greater depth in his *Slave Soldiers and Islam: The Genesis of a Military System* (New Haven, Conn.: Yale University Press, 1981). Their interpretation of the early *mamluk* system's purely military characteristrics has been criticised by Shihab al-Sarraf in his "Furusiyya literature of the Mamluk period," in D. Alexander, ed., *Furusiyya*, vol. 1, *The Horse in the Art of the Near East* (Riyadh: King Abdulaziz Public Library, 1996), 118–35.

explained.[23] Nor has the pay of Muslim soldiers apparently been compared to that of the Muslim world's eastern neighbours.

The question of transport and above all of shipping has received a great deal of scholarly attention over recent decades.[24] Yet it can still provide a fertile field for those with a military interest. This is all the more true because marine technology—including the construction of ships, their sails, rigging, and arrangement of oars—seems to be the area where new ideas spread most rapidly and with least resistance. Perhaps the reasons are obvious. Ships were made to go from one place to another. Seas provided many of the frontiers between major cultures, and ships crossed them, or at least went round their edges, taking their new technological characteristics with them. Sailors did not want to drown, ship's masters did not want to lose their vessels, and merchants did not want to lose their cargoes. Small wonder that shipwrights seemed to copy successful new ideas so quickly. Some of these new ideas, like the *tarida* or specialized horse-transporting galley, had a specifically military rather than solely mercantile application.[25] If, however, the marine community was already mentally open to new ideas, this could help explain why the *tarida* of Arab-Islamic origin was copied so enthusiastically on the northern side of the Mediterranean just as the Chinese hinged stern rudder was copied in the Arabian Gulf in the twelfth century, if not earlier.[26]

23. E. Ashtor, *Histoire des Prix et des Salaires dans l'orient médiévale* (Paris: Touzot, Ecole des Hautes Etudes en Sciences Sociales, 1969), 70–72, 91–111, 229–65, 369–80, 538, and passim.

24. J. H. Pryor, various works, including: "The Naval Architecture of Crusader Transport Ships: A Reconstruction of Some Archetypes for Round-Hulled Sailing Ships," *Mariner's Mirror*, 1983, 171–219, 275–92, 363–86; "The Medieval Muslim Ships of the Pisan Bacini," *Mariner's Mirror*, 1990, 99–113; "The Mediterranean Round Ships, ca. 1000–1300," in R. W. Unger, ed., *A History of Ships*, vol. 4, *Cogs, Caravels, and Galleons* (London: Conway Maritime, 1994), 59–76; "From Dromon to Galea: Mediterranean Bireme Galleys, ca. 700–1300," in J. Morrison, ed., *The Age of the Galley* (London: Conway Maritime, 1995), 101–16, 206–16.

25. J. H. Pryor, "Transportation of Horses by Sea during the era of the Crusades, Eighth Century to 1285 AD," *Mariner's Mirror*, 1982, 9–27, 103–26; "The Naval Architecture of Crusader Transport Ships and Horse Transports Revisited," *Mariner's Mirror*, 1990, 255–72; V. Christides, "Some Remarks on the Mediterranean and Red Sea Ships in Ancient and Medieval Times, I: A Preliminary Report," *Tropsis* 1 (1989): 75–82; Christides, "Some Remarks on the Mediterranean and Red Sea Ships in Ancient and Medieval Times, II: Merchant-Passenger vs. Combat Ships," *Tropsis* 2 (1987): 87–99; Christides, "Naval History and Naval Technology in Medieval Times: The Need for Interdisciplinary Studies," *Byzantion* 58 (1988): 9–322.

26. V. Christides, "The Transmission of Chinese Maritime Technology by the Arabs to Europe: Single Rudder, Greek Fire, Barrels," *University of Kuwait Papers* (forthcoming); D. C. Nicolle, "Shipping in Islamic Art: Seventh Through Sixteenth Century AD," *American Neptune* 49 (1989): 168–97.

Appendix

Some English Translations of Documents on the Medieval Military

1. Leo VI, Emperor of Byzantium, *Taktika*, trans. M. Joly de Maizeroi, as the *Tactica* (Paris, 1771).

This Taktika *is perhaps the most famous of Byzantine military manuals and was either written by, or in the name of, Emperor Leo VI known as "The Wise," who ruled from 886 to 912 AD. The Taktika draws heavily upon the early seventh century* Strategikon *which was in turn attributed to Emperor Maurice, as well as subsequent experiences of warfare including those of Leo's father, the warrior-ruler Basil I, and of military events during the first years of Leo's own reign. One of the most interesting sections deals with the Byzantines' Arab-Islamic enemies, who consisted of the Ṭūlūnids of Egypt and Syria and the ʿAbbāsid Caliphate of Iraq and the Jazîrah (upper Mesopotamia).*

Saracen Armies

Saracen armies normally use camels for baggage, rather than oxen, donkeys or mules, because these animals frighten [attacking] cavalry. They also use cymbals and kettle-drums to scare the enemy's horses; their own horses having been accustomed to these. They normally have camels and other baggage animals in the centre of their army, and they attach flags and pennons to them.[1] They enjoy war and are accompanied by many "priests."[2]

They are hot blooded and do not like cold weather. Their infantry is composed of "Aethiopians"[3] who carry large bows.[4] They are placed ahead of their cavalry while these [cavalry] prepare to attack. The cavalry also carry the infantry on their cruppers when the expedition is not close to their own frontier. They[5] are armed with swords, spears, axes,[6]

1. Flags attached to the backs of camels are, in fact, illustrated on Islamic ceramics of this period.
2. It was a chacteristic of most Islamic armies that they were accompanied by numerous religious figures, including scholars, lawyers, Koran reciters, and others.
3. Infantry troops of African, or more specifically, Nubian, origin played a major role in early medieval Egyptian armies up to the late twelfth century. This suggests that here the *Taktika* is referring to Ṭūlūnid rather than ʿAbbāsid forces.
4. Arab sources also noted that the Nubians were skilled archers using "simple" noncomposite or multiple wood "partially composite" bows.
5. Presumably the cavalry.
6. The *ṭabarzîn* "saddle axe" was a distinctive Islamic cavalry weapon, probably of Iranian origin.

and also arrows [as horse-archers]. They are armoured in helmets, cuirasses, lined half-boots, gauntlets, and other things which are also normal amongst the "Romans."[7] They like to embellish their belts, their swords, and their horses' harness with silver ornamentation.[8]

Once they fall into disorder it is difficult to rally them, because they think of little but their lives. The hope of victory increases their courage but reversals undermine their courage. They believe that the outcome is [entirely] in the hands of God, like everything else. Hence they accept setbacks without complaint and wait for better times in battle. They do not need much sleep and for this reason they are formidable when fighting at night, particularly when invading enemy territory. To guard against surprises they fortify their camps and maintain a good watch all night.[9]

Their order of battle is a long square, reinforced all around and very difficult to cut into. They maintain this form on the march and in battle. They copy many other "Roman" manners in their usages of war and in their methods of attack they are much like us.[10] When they are arrayed and ready they do not hurry to make a charge. They receive [instead] the first shock like iron,[11] and when battle is joined they do not break off easily. When the ardour of their enemy relaxes they push [forwards] excitedly and more vigorously. In their battles at sea they use, as do their infantry [on land], closed ranks defended by their shields. They use all the [same] habits[12] as their foes but when they are exhausted and tired they fall into our hands. For that reason, they fight against us with great caution. Their maxims and methods in warfare evaluate all that is best in other, more experimental nations.[13] This is what we have found from our envoys, from the reports of our generals and from our respected father [Emperor Basil I] who was involved in war before us.

The rigours of winter, cold, rain, and many other torments reduce their forces. For these reasons, it is best to attack them in rainy or humid weather and in these circumstances we are most often successful. In

---

7. This phrase could be very misleading. The Byzantines referred to themselves as "Romans" and their military equipment was indeed similar to that of their Middle Eastern Islamic neighbours. But this similarity no longer reflected Byzantine influence in Arab-Islamic armies. In fact, both Arabs and Byzantines had been influenced by Iranian and Central Asian Turkish military styles for several centuries.

8. This is again confirmed in Arab-Islamic sources.

9. Again this emphasis on fortified camps within enemy territory is confirmed by contemporary Islamic sources which also suggest that techniques of field fortification were based upon both Romano-Byzantine and Sassanian-Iranian traditions.

10. This is a further example of the typical Byzantine assumption that they and their Graeco-Roman predecessors were the fountainhead of military fashions.

11. In modern terminology, "like a rock."

12. Probably meaning combat techniques.

13. Arab-Islamic sources confirm this eagerness to learn from others, but also indicate that the Muslims were very experimental in their own right.

such conditions, the cords of their bows are damp and they stretch, and are almost useless. [On the other hand,] It is primarily in the great heat of summer that they march out of Tarsus and the other cities of Cilicia to attack the "Romans."[14] As I have already said, it is very risky to engage them in general battle unless they are in very small numbers. It is best to remain hidden in a suitable place from which to attack their line of march. When they come in winter to raid and plunder the countryside, one might find a chance to attack them unexpectedly because this is a great ruse of war.

They do not form their armies by enlistment nor by conscription. Instead large numbers come from Syria and Palestine, presenting themselves voluntarily; the rich out of zeal for their country, the poor in hope of plunder. This lure attracts their young men who are at their strongest age[15] and whom the women take pleasure in arming.

14. Tarsus, the strongest and most important of the fortified frontier bases on the Islamic side of the southern Anatolian frontier, fell to Byzantine attack in 965 AD. Its remarkable military organization was described by an Arab scholar just a few years before it fell. (C. E. Bosworth, "Abū ʿAmrʿ Uthmān al-Ṭarsūsî's *Siyar al-Thughūr* and the Last Years of Arab Rule in Tarsus (Fourth/Tenth Century)," *Graeco-Arabica* 5 [1993]: 183–95.)

15. This phrase is not clear.

2. **Muḥammad Ibn Walîd Abū Bakr al-Ṭurṭūshî, ed. anon., *Sirāj al-Mulūk* (Cairo: n.p., n.d.); trans. M. Alarcón, *Lámpara de los Príncipes* (Madrid, 1931).**

> *The Sirāj al-Mulūk was written near the end of the eleventh century by a scholar of Andalusian Muslim origin. It is, however, unclear whether his description of a typical battle array in his country applied to his own day, when al-Andalus had just fallen to the North African Saharan Murābiṭūn, or to the preceding period when al-Andalus was ruled by its own native princes. The tone of the introduction rather suggests that the author was advocating the tactics of the previous era for the benefit of new, foreign, rulers who had little experience of warfare against the Christians of northern Iberia.*

Chapter 61. Treatise on War, Its Organization, Tactics, and Methods *(ed. anon, pp. 308–9; M. Alarcón trans. pp. 332–33; partial trans. by E. Lévi-Provençal,* Histoire de l'Espagne Musulmane, *tome III,* Le Siècle du Califat de Cordoue *(Paris, 1967), p. 100.*

Here is the order of battle which we use in our country and which has shown itself to be the most effective in our encounters with our enemies. The infantry with "complete shields" [*al-daraq al-kāmilah*],[1] long spears [*al-rumāh al-ṭuwāl*] and pointed, piercing javelins [*mazārīq*],[2] arrange themselves in several ranks [*saff*].[3] The butt of the spear is thrust into the earth with its front part pointing forwards towards the enemy and held against the man's chest [*wa yarkuzū marākazhum wa rumāhhum khāf zahūr fi'l-ard wa sudūrhā shārʿah ilā ʿadūhum jathian fi'l-ard*].[4] Each man has his left knee on the ground and holds the grip of his shield in his hand.

Behind these foot soldiers are the elite archers [*al-rumāt al-mukhtārūn*] whose arrows [*sahm*] can pierce mail hauberks [*durūʿ*].[5] Behind the archers are the cavalry. When the Christians charge against the Muslims, the infantry remain in their positions, with their knees on the ground. When the enemy arrive at a short distance the archers shoot a cloud of arrows after which the foot soldiers throw their javelins and receive them [the enemy] on the points of their spears. After that the foot soldiers and the archers open up their ranks in an oblique movement to the right and to the left and, through the spaces thus made, the Muslim cavalry fall upon the enemy and put them to flight, if God has decided that this will be the case.

1. The term *daraqah* was normally used for leather shields. Here the addition of the word *kāmilah* suggests that the shields were larger than the ordinary *daraqah*, either being a large round defence shield or being comparable to those tall but round-based shields shown in twelfth-century Christian Iberian art. These are often placed in the hands of "Moors" and may still be of leather construction.

2. The *mizrāq* was a standard form of javelin which could also be thrown from horseback. It was heavier than other forms of javelin associated with bedouin Arab infantry. The continued use of relatively heavy javelins by disciplined infantry drawn up in ranks could be regarded as the clearest example of a continuation of Romano-Byzantine infantry tactics in the Arab-Islamic world. Such tactics also survived in the equally disciplined and "professional" Byzantine armies, but had, of course, long been abandoned in Western Europe, where most infantry forces were little more than a despised rabble.

3. The term *saff* was normally only used for men on foot.

4. This is quite clearly the infantry tactic which would, in late medieval and early modern Western Europe, be regarded as that of the pikeman.

5. The *dirʿ* (singular) was the standard *hauberk* or coat of mail, also worn by Christian Western European warriors of this period.

3. Murḍā Ibn ʿAlî Murḍā al-Ṭarsūsî, *Tabṣirah arbāb al-lubāb fî kayfîyah al-nujā fî'l-ḥurūb*; partially ed. and trans. C. Cahen, "Un traité d'armurerie composé pour Saladin," *Bulletin d'Études Orientales* 12 (1947–48): 108–26.

> The Tabṣirah *is the best known or at least most accessible of medieval Arabic military treatises, large parts of it having been translated into French. Like all other extant Islamic military manuals its contents have not, however, been fully analysed. They clearly include information dating from earlier periods in Islamic history and the entire document should be seen as reflecting the military scholarship of the preceding Fāṭimid Caliphate rather than that of Saladin's own reign. Another feature of the* Tabṣirah *is its clear description of sophisticated infantry tactics, particularly when facing cavalry. These include concepts supposedly developed in Western Europe several centuries later but which had, of course, been fundamental to Islamic military thinking since the eighth or even seventh century AD.*

The Arraying of an Army
(Bodleian Library Oxford, Ms. Hunt 264, ff. 190v–191v; Cahen, ed., pp. 125–26, trans. pp. 148–49)

Place the infantry ahead of the cavalry to make a firm fortress [*ḥisn*].[1] In front of every foot soldier place a pavise [*januwîyah*][2] or kite-shaped shield [*ṭāriqah*],[3] or a screen [*sitārah*][4] as a protection against those who attack with sword, spear, or arrow. Behind each pair of men

---

1. The use of the term "fortress" to describe a battle formation is characteristic of early Islamic military writing, and was also used for military formations during ceremonial parades, displays, and manoeuvers. It reflects the somewhat static and defensive philosophy of early medieval Islamic warfare in which infantry continued to play an important though, by the twelfth century, a declining role.

2. The *januwîyah* was a tall shield, more like a mantlet or a later medieval western European *pavise*. It had a flat base so that it could more easily be rested on the ground, perhaps even being propped up at the back like a true mantlet. The name *januwîyah* might indicate that the form was originally imported from Italy via the major trading and arms-exporting port of Genoa. It appears occasionally in Islamic art of this period, as well as that of Armenia and, more significantly, of Italy. It does not yet, however, appear in other European art.

3. The *ṭāriqah* is described elsewhere in al-Ṭarsūsî's *Tabṣirah* as the kite-shaped shield with a rounded top and pointed base characteristically used by Crusaders and Byzantines. It had, of course, also been known in the Islamic world for many years where, however, it was regarded as an infantry as much as a cavalry protection.

4. Such a "screen" would presumably have been more like a parapet made of available materials, perhaps like the *zariba* (Arabic, *zarîbah*) learned by nineteenth century British troops from their various Muslim foes.

place an archer with a crossbow [*jarkh*][5] or with heavy arrows [*nabālah*].[6] Their role is to drive back the attackers.

The cavalry and "defensive cavalry" [*abṭāl*][7] to the rear are separated from danger by the archers. Meanwhile the "offensive cavalry" [*shujʿān*][8] wait to deliver a charge. Troops are grouped together into units with a prearranged separation between them. These they open up as properly coordinated units, thus making a passageway for the [cavalry] charge. This must be done in a calm and tranquil way, while praying to God for victory in silence and with lowered eyes. When the cavalry return from their charge, and flow back towards their point of departure, the infantry return to their original places, reassembling like the elements of a building. . . .

On the field of battle it is necessary to arrange the ranks [*maṣāffāt*][9] gathered into squadrons of soldiers [*ajnād karādīsan*],[10] and with the cavalry grouped flag [*alam*] by flag and battalion [*khamîs*] by battalion. [This should be done] when it is the enemy's habit to charge in a mass and to rely for impact on separate detachments of their force, as is the case with the evil Franks [Crusaders] and those neighbours who resemble them. In fact the [correct] array is the essence of the disposition of battle and this disposition stupifies and embarrasses this [sort of] enemy

5. The *jarkh* was a heavy form of crossbow suited to static warfare. In its earliest form, it may have been mounted upon a pedestal. The fact that it seems to have first been recorded in the Persian-speaking east of the Islamic world, where it was known as the *charkh,* might indicate some Chinese military-technological influence. The Persian term *charkh,* also suggests that the weapon was spanned, or pulled back, by means of a pulley or windlass. On the other hand, the whole question of the early history of the crossbow in the Islamic world and Middle East remains open. All that can be said with certainty is that the weapon did not arrive from Western Europe.

6. This is the plural of *nabl,* the heavier form of arrow with a wooden shaft normally associated with infantry, as distinct from the *nāshib* lighter form of arrow with a shaft wholly or partly of reed normally associated with cavalry. Meanwhile, the term *sahm* meant arrows in general. Here the use of *nabl* would indicate the presence of infantry archers, probably using larger bows of the so-called "Arab" type as opposed to the shorter so-called "Turkish" cavalry bow.

7. The term *abṭāl* had a double meaning of both "champions" and "thwarting." It was given to cavalry units equipped and trained for a defensive role. As such, they were the military descendants of the Romano-Byzantine *defensores*. Their tactics, as described in al-Ṭarsūsî's *Tabṣirah*, were also essentially the same as those of the *defensores*.

8. The term *shujʿān* meant "courageous" or "audacious." It was given to cavalry units equipped and trained for an offensive role. As such, they were the military descendants of the Romano-Byzantine *cursores*, their tactics, again, being essentially the same.

9. The term *maṣāffah,* "row" or "line," was normally used for ranks of infantry rather than horsemen.

10. The term *kurdūs* is usually translated as "squadron," though here it is used in an adverbial form as "in a squadron-like manner."

because, when they launch their charge against one rank and come near to it, the other units can attack it [the enemy] from both sides and so surround it. The fighting comes at them from all directions, bombarding all their senses. These things lead to success. The seriousness of the action imposed upon them [the enemy] leads to their weakness and defeat, all of which is made possible by this battle array.

---

4. Muḥammad Ibn Manṣūr Faḵhr al-Dîn Mubārakshāh, ed. A. S. Khwānsārî, *Ābab al-Ḥarb wa al-Shujāʿah* (Tehran, 1969).

> *This text was written by a Persian scholar living in the Punjab region of northern India, working for the last Ghaznawid and first Ghūrid rulers of this area.* His Abab al-Ḥarb wa al-Shujāʿah *is dedicated to Sultan Shams al-Dîn Iltutmish of Delhi and was probably written in the early 1230s AD. It draws upon a large number of wide-ranging sources of information, not only including the traditional Islamic Arab and Persian ones, but also Hindu Indian sources and, more distantly, those of China, Turkish Central Asia and even pre-Islamic South Arabia.*

Chapter 19, pp. 330–32: How to array an army and deploy it for battle

Know that for this purpose it is necessary to have the first rank consisting of armed infantry with broad shields[1] [*siparhā-yi farākh*] and spears [*ḥarba*][2] and archers[3] [*tîr-āndāzān*]. This is because their role is defensive. The second rank should be of infantry wearing a lamellar cuirass [*jawshan*] and tunic [*khaftān*],[4] and be armed with sword [*shamshir*], shield [*sipar*] and spear [*nîzah*]. The third rank should be of infantry armed with sword [*shamshir*], quiver[5] [*tarkash*], "iron bound staves"[6] [*chūbhā-yi āhan-bastah*] and large daggers [*kārdhā-yi buzurg*]. The fourth rank should consist of junior officers [*ʿarîfān*] with infantry

---

1. Mantlets, or perhaps meaning "abundant shields."
2. Often translated as a form of heavy javelin, but more probably a short infantry spear or staff-weapon.
3. Literally "arrow throwers."
4. A large coat which might sometimes be quilted and thus serve as an arming-coat beneath the cuirass.
5. Perhaps indicating that they have the supplies of arrows used by the archers in the front rank since the latter are not specifically stated to have quivers, while these men in the third ranks are not specifically said to have bows.
6. Probably a form of long-hafted mace rather than a stake to drive into the ground.

armed with small shields [*daraqah*],[7] swords [*shamshir*] and mace [*'amūd*].[8]

Between such ranks there should be a wide space so that each rank of soldiers is able to see what is happening, so that there may be a way through for the cavalry, and so that the warriors in the forefront [alternatively meaning "the champions"] can go forward and get through.

Warriors are in four groups. The first are the daredevil warriors in the forefront or champions [*mubārizān*] who seek fame in the battle. These should be placed on the right wing. The second group are the outstandingly firm and steadfast troops in battle. These should be placed in the rearguard. The third group are the archers, who may be necessary as a supporting force and who carry a shield as protection for themselves and who get down on their knees to loose their arrows.[9] These troops should be placed on the left wing. The fourth group comprises the noncombatant[10] element of the army, such as standard-bearers [*alamdārān*], those holding short spears [*miṭrad*],[11] warriors with kettle drums of the *duhul* and *tabîra* kinds, frames of bells [*zangiyāna*],[12] trumpets [*būq*], war-drums [*ṭabl*] and suchlike. There should also be a unit of valiant and hardy men who can inspire the troops with bravery,[13] make them keen to throw themselves into battle and give heart to the army so that it becomes intrepid and fearless. The baggage and impedimenta, the treasury, the army-bazaar, and the artisans should be kept in the rear but near to the centre and the two wings [of the main body of the army].

When the Caliph is established in his place with his leading commanders, the arrangement should be that each group should be deployed in its allotted place with its field officers [*sarhangān*] and with its complete array of weapons. In particular, the cavalry troop commanders, and the grooms and attendants [*chakirān*], all fully armed, should be in their designated places. The generals [*ḥājibān*] and royal guards [*khāṣagān*] must stay very close to the ruler [*pādishāh*] and the army's commander-in-chief [*sipahsālār*]. The guides [*rahbarān*] who police and keep the roads open, with their aides, should be at the right side of the centre. The archers [*tîr āndāzān*], the troops operating various mechanical

---

7. Usually of leather.

8. One of various forms of mace used throughout the Islamic world.

9. The shield may have served as a mantlet or pavise as was normal practice amongst later medieval western European infantry crossbowmen.

10. Literally "ornamental" or "auxiliary," *ārāyish*.

11. Literally or originally a form of short spear or staff weapon, but now used as a metallic standard or insignia.

12. Unclear, possibly a form of musical instrument or a manuscript corruption of *zangyājah* "little bells" which could have been an early version of the Turkish *çevgen*, subsequently known in European military bands as a Jingling Johnnie.

13. Probably indicating elite guards.

devices [ḥîlat ġarān][14] and fire throwers [naft-āndāzān][15] should be at the left side of the centre. The men who lead the baggage train, the men who lead the strings of remounts, and the experts with lassoes [kamand āndāzān][16] should be close at hand. The guard pickets [harasbānān], the men carrying calthrops [khasak dārān],[17] the crews operating mangonels [manjanîq] and ballistas ['arādah dārān], the men with scaling ladders and ropes [kamand ḥalqah āndāzān] and the outstandingly bold troops [jigar āndāzān][18] are stationed on the right [of the centre]. The animals, herds of horses, sheep, and oxen, should be held away from the army. The riding camels dispersed [at pasture], the beasts carrying fodder and other loads and baggage, should be placed furthest back of all, with trusty, strong, and fully armed men looking after them.

The great generals and senior field officers, the long experienced veterans of the army, the religious scholars, the physicians, the ruler's boon-companions and the astrologers should remain near the monarch and the supreme commander of the army. Servants [khādimān][19] and slaves, both those of the ruler's personal retinue and those in general, should be placed at the right hand [of the preceding group], together with the wazîr[20] and two knowledgeable, sharp-witted and experienced men from amongst the ruler's trusted confidants [amînān]. A second [group] of the ruler's personal guards [jāndārān][21] and protectors [nigāhibānān] should also be stationed on the army's right. The ruler's womenfolk [ḥaram], treasury and armoury [silāḥ][22] should always be near the centre, together with the ruler's personal kitchen. The rearguard remains stationed behind the ranks of the [front-line] troops with its back to the main body of the army[23] so as to protect and watch over the army and the baggage train.

If the opposing army appears in front of the left wing, the following deployment should be made in the manner in which they [the experienced commanders] usually make for the battlefield and for war and for drawing up the ranks of troops. A field officer or general moves from the centre to the right and left flanks in order to arrange and deploy the

14. Unclear, but not meaning heavy siege equipment as this is mentioned below. Perhaps this confirms the presence of mechanical antipersonnel weapons such as frame-mounted crossbows and what would later be known in Europe as espringals.

15. Those using or equipped with naft: "Greek Fire."

16. Or those with scaling ropes.

17. Or grapnel men.

18. Literally "those who hazard their lives."

19. Could also mean eunuchs.

20. Senior civilian goverment minister.

21. Originally meaning professional soldiers, now sometimes indicating a militia.

22. Literally "weapons."

23. When drawn up in battle array.

troops for battle and he goes around the scouts [*ṭalāya*]²⁴ and the four fronts of the army [i.e. the centre, the two wings and the rearguard].

If the danger of attack is coming from the front, one should throw forward half of the left wing towards the [opposing] line of troops, and the other half from the right wing so that the centre is just behind them. In this way the right and left wings and the centre remain compact and close together and remain in their battle order. If battle then has to be joined, the right wing must first give battle in that place and then the rest [of the army joins in]. If the danger of attack comes from behind the army's centre, it is necessary to adopt the same procedure as described above. If it is unclear where the threatened attack will come from, or from what direction, the army should remain silent and calm and scouts should be sent out. In any case the ruler and the supreme commander who deploys the army should remain in the centre, with the treasury in front of him, and experienced cavalry and infantry drawn up behind him, so that the ruler can see over all his troops.

On the day of battle, an issue of two days' rations of fodder, hay, bread, and meat should be given out. Every cavalryman intending to give battle should carefully check his saddle [*zīn*], bridle [*ligām*], and weapons [*silāh*] for if some failure of these should occur in the middle of the combat he will be thrown into a dangerous state and pay for it with his life. He should ensure that five things are firm and strong: the leather straps of the reins [*duwāl-i ʿinān*], the stirrup straps [*duwāl-i rikāb*], the girth [*tang*], the *pushtak*²⁵ and the surcingle [*hayāsa*], for a cavalryman's effectiveness depends on these things. If a crupper-strap [*pārdum*] or a collar [*bār-band*] is faulty this is not usually a serious problem. A cavalryman should never be without a cobbler's awl [*dirafsh*], a pack-needle [*juwāldūz*], a sewing needle [*sūzan*] and thread [*rîsmān*], plus a length of leather strap and an [extra] piece of thread so that if any damage occurs to any of these pieces of equipment he can speedily put it right and sew it up. Also if the leather straps are not long enough, he can take some hair from the horse's tail, twist it together and sew with that.

[The rest of this chapter deals with the care of saddle-sores and similar problems while on campaign.]

24. Presumably those ranging ahead of the army.
25. Unclear, probably indicating the breastband.

I

5. Don Juan Manuel, *Libro de los Estados*; ed. J. M. Castro y Calvo, *El arte de gobernar en las obras de Don Juan Manuel* (Barcelona, 1945).

Don Juan Manuel was born in 1282, the son of the Infante Don Manuel. He has been described as a typical man of his time and place. At the age of twelve he took part in his first combat with the "Moors" or Muslim Andalusians from the remaining Islamic Iberian state of Granada. He also lived at a time when the Christian Iberian kingdoms spent more time warring with each other than against the Moors. Don Juan Manuel wrote on several subjects and clearly knew the works of Vegetius but his own military writings are firmly based upon the military circumstances of early fourteenth century Spain.

Estado LXII

If you come close to the enemy, and he is in "groups" [*haz*],[1] you must face him in "troops" [*tropel*].[2] Put the horses who are equipped with horse armour in the front with the commander [*señor*] in the middle, close to his banner [*pendón*], with the head of the horse of the second in command [*alférez*] immediately to the right of the commander.[3] In this way he will not become separated when they reach the fight, and those he commands must follow him towards the enemy's banner, and fight bravely because this is what God finds good.

Estado LXIII

If you see that the enemy looks as if they are going to attack, you must meet them in a formation known as the "point" [*punta*]. This is led by three horses [horsemen], followed by twelve, and after them twenty. They are followed up by good cavalrymen so that when the "point" enters the [enemy's] "troop" [*tropel*] those at the back of the formation are not surrounded.

Estado LXXIV

Whether your forces are large or small, if you see that the enemy is about to attack "troops," the leader must arrange his men in four or five "groups" [*haces*]. These must be closely packed so that the horses' heads are close to the rumps of the others [horses ahead of them]. The commander [*señor*] and the banner [*pendón*] must move from the rearmost

---

1. Literally bundles or sheafs.
2. Troops or squadrons designed to make a charge. Western European armoured cavalry, even in Islamic-influenced Iberia, attacked in a very close formation generally known as a *conrois*.
3. Literally "at the right leg of."

"troop" into the middle of all the "troops." He must spread his men twice as wide so that the flanks can attack those enemy "troops" who penetrate the centre of the "groups" formation.

Estado LXXV

The warfare of the Moors is not the same as that of the Christians. In war they can fight at close quarters, or skirmish amongst their orchards, or attack in raids [*cabalgadas*] or "hit and run" [*correduras*] assaults against the communications and "rear areas" of their enemies, or they fight in single combat. In fact [their warfare] is very fragmented [varied] in one way or another.[4]

4. This is a remarkably accurate reflection of the traditional Islamic, as well as specifically "Moorish" Granadan, way of warfare. Unlike the knightly armies of medieval Europe, the commanders of medieval Islamic armies were concerned with success and minimizing casualties, rather than with glory or, as the medieval knight would see it, with "honour." Individual honour, insofar as the medieval Islamic warrior was concerned, could be won throught single combat.

Byzantine and Islamic Arms and Armour; Evidence for Mutual Influence

The technology of warfare is an area in which cultures have readily copied their neighbours or rivals. The reasons are obvious. In war survival generally depends on success and so, thoughout history, effective weapons or tactics have been widely copied. Only the most deep-rooted constraints, such as the availability of raw materials or certain fundamental sociological characteristics of the recipient culture, have been able to inhibit this kind of diffusion. Even non-essential military fashions, including clothing and the decoration of horse-harness, have moved with remarkable ease across the most hostile frontiers. It remains a fact that imitation is the highest form of military compliment.

Byzantine and Islamic civilizations seem to have been particularly adaptable in military matters. This almost certainly enabled Byzantium to survive for so long, surrounded by powerful and predatory foes. Byzantine military adaptability and willingness to learn from, as well as to recruit, those that the Greeks regarded as barbarians stood in stark contrast to Byzantine conservatism in so many other fields. Perhaps the fact that war was here regarded as a barbarous necessity, rather than being idealised as in so many medieval societies, enabled Byzantium to behave in this uncharacteristic manner.

The reasons for Islam's military eclecticism are more complicated. Unlike Byzantium, early Islam was generally not on the defensive and thus had no obvious reason to imitate the arms, armour, tactics and military organisation of a successful foe. Eclectism and openness seem, however, to have been characteristic of Arab-Islamic culture in almost all fields except, of course, religion. Added to this was the fact that, from the 7th to 11th centuries, three major ethnic groups enjoyed varying degrees of successive military dominance in the eastern and central Islamic lands; namely the Arabs, Iranians and Turks. Of course ethnicity or "race" has nothing to do with military skill, but the martial traditions of these three peoples did differ. A process of imitation and diffusion could also be seen within the widespread and militarily varied Muslim world during these five centuries.

Before looking for direct military-technological diffusion between Byzantium and Islam, it is important to emphasise the fact that both these great civilizations were under persistent military influence from the nomadic peoples of the Eurasian steppes. Indeed the overwhelming weight of evidence indicates that it was from the north, rather than from each other, that they received most new military ideas. Meanwhile Western Europe contributed little or nothing that was original until the 12th century while the evidence for specifically Indian military influence upon Islam remains unclear. The role of China as an initiator of technological change may prove crucial but was, of course, felt in both Islam and Byzantium via the medium of Turco-Mongol steppe peoples. Berber military traditions, as far as they are yet understood, had only minor local influence in North Africa, the Iberian Peninsula and perhaps Egypt. The rôle of Armenia was probably crucial, as one would expect given its geographical position, metallurgical wealth and warlike traditions. Unfortunately, very little study has as yet been made of this aspect of medieval Armenian culture.

The present paper focuses on the archaeological and pictorial records rather than documentary sources. On the Islamic side the latter are moderately straightforward, whereas medieval Greek literature is often consciously archaic, stylized and potentially misleading.[1] Similar problems apply to Byzantine art which is full of archaism, conventional models and stylized weaponry. This is not to say that such pictorial sources cannot be used in the study of Byzantine arms and armour. They merely have to be treated with extreme caution. Generally speaking it appears that the artistic creations of Constantinople and the Imperial heartlands are the most difficult to interpret whereas the cruder works of provincial and frontier regions tend to reflect current reality more closely. Perhaps the first discipline that needs to be learned is that of disregarding almost anything that harks back to a Classical past. By thus mentally "blacking out" large parts on an illustration one may be left with a number of interesting military features such as curved swords or helmets related to those of neighbouring cultures. These vestigial elements sometimes also find echoes in the meagre archaeological record.

The problems associated with pre-Saljūk Islamic art stem not so much

---

1. C. Mango, "Byzantine literature as a distorting mirror" in *Byzantium and its Image* (Collected Studies, London 1984).

from archaism as from a stylization that can almost reach abstraction, the repetition of relatively few models and, in most areas, the extreme rarity of such illustrated sources. On the other hand the specifically Islamic artistic record can be supplemented by that of the many Christian communities who flourished within the Muslim world. Their art naturally reflected that of Byzantium and other Christian areas outside Islam, but such communities did develop distinctive styles during the five centuries under consideration. It is also becoming clear that, in Egypt and the Fertile Crescent for example, there was a considerable degree of mutual influence between Christian and at least the secular Muslim visual arts. A similar process could be seen in Iran and Transoxania. One has only to look at the portrayal of military figures and their equipment within the Muslim world to see, on one hand, similarities between Christian and Islamic courses and, on the other, dissimilarities with Byzantine art. Once again, however, the art of border regions such as Cappadocia, Armenia, Ādharbayjān and the Jazīrah betray influences from both sides of the frontier.

Surprisingly, perhaps, the archaeological record is richer on the Islamic side than on the Byzantine, though neither could be described as abundant. Chance has presumably played its part but the relatively large number of surviving military artifacts from early medieval Islam also reflects a greater archaeological concentration on that side of the cultural divide. It may also stem from medieval Islam's relatively greater wealth in metals and its remarkably far-flung, flourishing patterns of trade. Where Byzantium is concerned one gets the maybe misleading impression that nothing was ever wasted, that damaged weaponry was always retrieved, repaired or recycled. Abundant or otherwise it is, nevertheless, from these archaeological records that any study must begin.

THE SINGLE-EDGED DAGGER

The large knife or dagger is one of the simplest forms of weapon. Surviving examples from the early medieval period have been found throughout much of Europe and Asia. The single-edged form was particularly widespread, so much so that it cannot be regarded as characteristic of any one society or area. However the presence of a small crosspiece or hilt-plate between the tang and the blade on two such knives from Jordan is worth nothing. These small hilt-plates were probably not guards or quillons but served to protect the base of perhaps wooden grips. These were, in turn, probably of the "whittle" type in which a hole was drilled into the handle or grip for the tang.[2] That on a dagger from an early Byzantine site near the Dead Sea (fig. 1b) has a bronze hilt-plate whereas that on a dagger from Pella, datable to the early or mid-8th century, is of iron. Two or perhaps three daggers are shown being used to dismember animals following a successful hunt on the Umāyyad wall paintings at Quṣayr 'Amra (figs. 11c-e). The fact that these have hilt-plates which are, in one case quite clearly, green on the paintings could suggest a bronze construction.[3] As far at the Umāyyad-period Pella dagger is concerned one can safely assume a continuity of design and structure from the preceding Byzantine period.

THE BROAD-BLADED, ROUND-TIPPED DOUBLE-EDGED SWORD

Straight swords were almost universal in both the Islamic and Byzantine regions during the period under consideration. The double-edged type could be long and slender, as in late Sassanian Iran,[4] but here we are considering relatively short and broad blades. Indeed Arab infantry took pride in the small size of their presumably handier weapons.[5] These had more in common with, and may have been descended from, the Roman *gladius*.[6] It is also worth noting that the Arabic word *sayf* was almost certainly derived from the Greek *xiphos*. The Arab infantry's delight in short swords was, however, expressed in comparison with the weapons of the Khurāsānis and Turks, not in comparison with Byzantine weapons.[7] A number of such blades may survive from the early Islamic and immediate pre-Islamic periods. Among those highly contentious swords associated with leading early Islamic figures, now in the Topkapi Reliquary, are some broad, double-edged and basically blunt-tipped

---

2. J. Cowgill, et al., *Medieval Finds from Excavations in London: 1. Knives and Scabbards* (London 1987), p. 9.

3. D.C. Nicolle, "Arms Production and the Arms Trade in South-Eastern Arabia in the Early Muslim Period," *Journal of Oman Studies* V/2 (1983), pp. 231-8.

4. For a list of ten such swords see: B.J. Overleat, "Contribution to Sasanian Armament in Connection with a Decorated Helmet," *Iranica Antiqua* XVII (1982), pp. 196-7.

5. Al Jāḥiz, *Al Bayān wa'l Tabyīn*, edit. H. al-Sundūbī (Cairo 1947), p. 14; Al Jāḥiz, *Rasā'il al Jāḥiz*, edit. 'Abd al Salām Muḥammad Hārūn (Cairo & Baghdad 1965), p. 26, also trans. by C.T. Harley-Walker, "Jahiz of Basra to Al-Fath ibn Khaqan on the Exploits of the Turks ans the Army of the Khalifate in General," *Journal of the Royal Asiatic Society* (Oct. 1915), p. 651.

6. J. Schwarzer & E.C. Deal, "A Sword Hilt from the Serçe Liman Shipwreck," *MASCA Journal* IV/2 (Dec. 1986), p. 53.

7. Al Jāḥiz, *Al Bayān...*, *loc. cit.*

weapons with and without *fuller* grooves down their blades (figs. 2b-c). All the weapons in the Reliquary have, of course, been given much later hilts while some have had later decoration added to their blades. Non-Muslim scholars may be permitted to query their association with specific early Islamic leaders but the previous tendency to dismiss all these weapons as products of a later period is now being questioned in the light of recent archaeological evidence. The partial remains of a similar blade have been founded at Nishāpūr (fig. 2a), though in a poorly stratified possibly 9th or 10th century context. The fact that this blade is approximately 6 centimetres wide is particularly interesting given the similar dimensions of a similarly dated iron sword-hilt from Saudi Arabia (fig. 3a). Another comparable weapon was found in Oman and has been provisionally dated to the late Sassanian period. Rather different is a sword from a 10th century western Islamic shipwreck (fig. 2e). Its pointed blade has much in common with similarly dated western European swords. However its strongly curved quillons would not appear in Europe for more than a century and the distinctive top of its tang, presumably to go inside a similarly shaped pommel, has no parallel in Europe. Meanwhile the artistic record of Byzantium and its cultural satellites, and of the Islamic world, provide numerous illustrations of straight swords. Many are broad, symmetrical and thus probably double-edged while most, though by no means all, are relatively blunt-tipped (figs. 13, 15d, 19, 25, 28, 30, 34, 36a-b, 40, 45, 46a-b, 47, 48a-f, 50a-b, 51, 54a & 60a-b). I am, however, inclined to regard the widespread use of these weapons in both the Byzantine and Islamic world as reflecting a common Romano-Byzantine heritage reinforced by continuing Byzantine and possibly Western European influence.[8]

THE STRAIGHT SINGLE-EDGED "PROTO-SABRE"

Though it is wrong to make simplistic generalisations about the developing technology of weapons, it does seem that the slender, single-edged straight sword came into use before the truly curved single-edged sabre. Such straight "proto-sabres" were common among Central Asian peoples long before they were seen in the Middle East.[9]. On the other

---

8. Al Kindī, "Al Suyūf wa ajnāsuhā," edit. A.R. Zaki, *Bulletin of the Faculty of Letters, Fouad I University* XIV/2 (1952), pp. 11-12 & 33; Al Birūnī, *Kitāb al jamāhir fī ma'rifat al jawāhir,* edit. F. Krenkow (Hyderabad 1936), p. 248; Al Tarṣūṣī, trans. C. Cahen, "Un Traité d'Armurerie Composé pour Saladin," *Bulletin d'Etudes Orientales* XII (1947-8), p. 127; M. Lombard, *Les Métaux dans l'Ancien Monde du Ve au XIe siècle* (Paris 1974), pp. 174-80.

9. A great deal had been written in the Soviet Union in recent years on the archaeology

hand they appear to have reached Byzantium and Iran before the coming of Islam. Such a blade is shown, for example, in the still somewhat mysterious but probably 7th century *Ashburnham Pentateuch* (fig. 35). Thereafter "protosabres" were illustrated with varying degrees of clarity in the arts of both Byzantium and the Muslim world (figs. 15a-c, 21, 57 & 58). The latter two examples are only tentatively identified as they are within their scabbards. Particular caution must be taken with the earlier of the two (fig. 57) as this weapon's hilt is very similar to those of long, slender but double-edged swords from the late Sassanian period.[10] Two surviving weapons might also fall within this category, though both pose problems. One is the so-called sabre of the Prophet Muḥammad (fig. 6a) which has a very slight curve and perhaps the weakest association with its supposed owner. The other is an extraordinary, recently excavated and as yet unpublished sword of truly massive length – approximately 1.8 metres judging from an available photograph. It comes from Aphrodisias in western Anatolia and is only assumed to be single-edged on the basis of apparently differing degrees of corrosion down each side. Even if this huge sword had a purely symbolic or decorative function, its form indicates that such weapons were known at the time it was manufactured. Meanwhile there is little evidence to suggest that Byzantine, Sassanian or Islamic armies had any influence upon each other in the adoption of "proto-sabres". It is to those Central Asian peoples who were caught up in the Great Migrations (5th-7th centuries) that we must look for the diffusion of this design, primarily to the Huns, Avars and Magyars.

THE TRUE CURVED SABRE

How and when the true sabre appeared in Islam and, by extension, among some of Islam's western neighbours, has long been debated. While it may still be true that such weapons were not widespread until the coming of the Saljūk Turks in the 11th century, it now seems reasonably certain that a few sabres were known earlier. There cannot, however, be any doubt that the idea still stemmed from Turco-Mongol Central Asia. In addition to a little known but originally splendid sabre found in a possibly 9th or 10th century context at Nishāpūr (fig. 6c), there exists a slightly

---

of medieval Central Asia and the Eurasian steppes, primarily by Yu. S. Khudyakov, N.A. Mazhitov, A.I. Solovjev, A.P. Derevyanko and V.E. Medvedyev. Much of this new material is incorporated into a larger survey by S.A. Pletnyeva, *Stepi Evrazii v Ehpoxu Spednevekovya (The Eurasian Steppes in the Middle Ages)* (Moscow 1981).

10. See Note 4.

later wall painting from the same city (fig. 17a) as well as more debate-able written references.[11] Judging by the fragmented remains of a scab-bard a true sabre may also have been present among weapons aboard the late 10th-early 11th century Serçe Liman shipwreck.[12] Curved blades do not seem to appear in Byzantine and Mediterranean Christian art until the 12th century onwards (figs. 32a, 41 b-c & 59) and then only in the hands of "infidels". Outside the special circumstances of Hungary, the sabre was nowhere adopted in western Europe until after the Middle Ages while it only seems to have entered the Byzantine armoury in the mid-14th century. Even here it is more likely to have reflected the influ-ence of Turco-Mongol peoples from north of the Black Sea rather than that of the Muslim Ottoman Turks.[13] Thus the non-diffusion of this par-ticular military development across the Byzantine-Islamic frontier is itself worthy of note.

THE SLEEVE OR COLLAR EXTENDING BENEATH A SWORD'S QUILLONS

Only occasionally can a minor feature of hilt design be clearly identified in both the archaeological and artistic evidence. This is, however, the case with a distinctive form of collar that, extending below the quillons or crossguard of a sword, enclosed part of the blade. Its purpose is not clear though it might have served as a form of *ricasso*. This was, in turn, nor-mally associated with a style of fencing in which a swordsman placed his forefinger over one quillon and around one edge of the blade. Dr. A.B. De Hoffmeyer has suggested that such a fencing technique entered Europe from Islam[14] and there is also pictorial evidence to suggest that it was used in pre-Islamic Iran. Such collars are found on surviving Islamic hilts (figs. 3a & 5). They appear in art from the Islamic region from at least the 8th century onwards (figs. 20[uncertain], 46a[uncertain], 47 & 60b[uncertain]), and in more varied forms in Byzantine or strongly Byzantine-influenced art from the 9th century onwards (figs. 34[uncertain], 36a-b & 40). These *ricasso*-col-lars may, therefore, betray influence from Islam to Byzantium and may

---

11. D.C. Nicolle, *The Arms and Armour of the Crusading Era 1050-1350* (New York 1988), *passim*.

12. *Ibid,* pp. 37 & 48-52.

13. J. Schwarzer, in conversation at the *Third International Congress on Greek-Arabic Studies* (Athens 17-20 July 1988).

14. A.B. De Hoffmeyer, "Introduction to the History of the European Sword," *Gladius* I (1961).

have been more readily adopted because the Byzantines employed a similar style of fencing.

THE "D-SHAPED" SWORD-GUARD & ITS ASSOCIATED HILT

Another hilt form that can be found in both art and the archaeological record could be described as having a "D-spread" guard. A fine surviving example comes from the late 10th-early 11th century Serçe Liman shipwreck (fig. 4c). It is made of bronze, the lead of which was almost certainly mined in northern Iran or northern Turkey.[15] Though the decoration of this hilt derives from Indian art of roughly the same period,[16] the basic shape probably finds its closest parallel on an Armenian relief carving of a very similar date (fig. 30). A remarkably similar, and again bronze, grip or hilt was found in a pre-Islamic Arabian site (fig. 4a) while comparisons may be drawn between the pommel of the Serçe Liman hilt and one bearing the name of a 10th century west Iranian Būyid prince (fig. 4b). Other less clear artistic parallels may be found elsewhere in the Middle East, from the pre-Islamic period to the 11th century and beyond (figs. 19, 22, 28[uncertain], 46b, 48a-f & 55[uncertain]). Though most are from Islamic areas or those close to the Muslim frontier, Dr. Schwarzer has offered a strong case in favour of a Romano-Byzantine origin for at least the relatively light sword associated with such hilts.[17] Perhaps the specifically "D-shaped" guard was developed in the central Islamic regions, partially as a result of its suitability to the bronze casting techniques used in all or part of so many Islamic sword-hilts. Here again there seems to have been relatively little Byzantine adoption of this Islamic style, though further archaeological finds could change the picture dramatically.

THE CARRYING OF A SWORD ACROSS A WEARER'S BACK

In the Middle East there are a number of illustrations of swords apparently being worn across a warrior's back. This habit seems to have been even more common in the Far East, particularly in China and Japan, where it was primarily an infantry fashion. Most such Middle Eastern illustrations come from Egypt but date from both the Byzantine and

---

15. Schwarzer, "A Sword Hilt...," *op. cit.,* pp. 55-6.

16. *Ibid.,* pp. 54-5.

17. *Ibid.,* pp. 52-4; J. Schwarzer, "The 11th century weapons from Serçe Liman," paper delivered at the *Third International Congress on Greek-Arabic Studies* (Athens 17-20 July 1988).

Islamic periods (figs. 23, 44a-b & 45). It also appears in early Islamic Jordan (figs. 11b^{uncertain} & 20). Whether these pictures reflected the iconographic influence of Coptic art or represented a truly Arab infantry or camel-mounted military habit remains unclear. A very similar fashion is, however, shown among specifically Arab warriors in the detailed art of 14th century Iran while an identical way of carrying a sword appears in even clearer detail on certain 14th and early 15th century Iranian and perhaps Transoxanian pictures in one of the *Fātiḥ Albums*,[18] I have found no evidence for this habit in strictly Byzantine art.

THE TWO-PIECE OR "RIDGE" HELMET

Helmets of two-piece construction, joined by a strip of metal running fore-and-aft from the brow to the nape of the neck and often including a slightly raised comb, had become standard equipment in the Roman army by the 5th century A.D.[19] A very damaged and unpublished helmet of even simpler construction was found at Hadīthah in Jordan during an uncontrolled excavation (fig. 7a). It seems to have come from an early Byzantine site, perhaps even dating from immediately prior to the Islamic conquest when the Byzantine defences were drawn further north and west than they had been prior to the Sassanian invasion.[20] Such a system of construction certainly survived into early medieval Europe (figs. 7b-e) and may even have influenced a mysterious, unpublished, supposedly early Islamic helmet from Tunisia (fig. 7f). The artistic record strongly suggests that this late Roman style persisted for many centuries in Byzantium (figs. 12, 25, 32b, 38, 42, & 43) and may also have survived in some western Islamic areas (fig. 14^{uncertain}). Here, however, it is difficult to separate the true "ridge" helmet from the "Parthian Cap" type.

THE "PARTHIAN CAP" HELMET

The so-called "Parthian Cap" helmet, which had a pointed profile when seen from the front and a parabolic outline when viewed from the

---

18. *History of the World by Rāshid al Dīn,* Tabriz 1306-14 AD (ex-Royal Asiatic Society, ff. 3r, 7r & 52r); *Fātiḥ Album* (Topkapi Lib., Ms. Haz. 2153, ff. 3v-4r, 138v & 148v, Istanbul, Turkey).

19. S. James, "Evidence from Dura Europos for the Origins of Later Roman Helmets," *Syria* LXIII (1986), pp. 107-34.

20. P. Mayerson, "The First Muslim Attacks on Southern Palestine (A.D. 633-634)," *Transactions and Proceedings of the American Philological Association* XCV (1964), pp. 165 & 179.

side, was perhaps the most characteristic form of Sassanian helmet. It also provided the probable inspiration for the late Roman "ridge" helmet.[21] Some surviving examples have an essentially four-piece framed structure while those with particularly pronounced rivets stem not from north-western Iran, the provenance of most "Parthian Cap" helmets,[22] but from Iraq (fig. 8a). Like a very similar four-framed "Parthian Cap" helmet from Nineveth in the National Museum, Baghdad, its dating is conjectural. Given that an early Islamic date has recently been suggested for an associated but structurally different Iraqi helmet (fig. 8b)[23], might not both come from the post-Sassanian period? Might not the extraordinarily pronounced rivets of these Iraqi helmets be the reality behind the peculiarly spikey outline of a helmet worn by a guard figure on the Qusayr 'Amra wall-paintings (fig. 11a)? There is, after all, artistic evidence for the survival of the parabolic outlined "Parthian Cap" helmet in early Islamic Iran (figs. 29a-b & 54a-b). Similar helmets, with their pendant mail aventails, appear to have been associated with Sassanian Iran in the minds of Byzantine artists as late as the early 7th century. This thesis assumes, however, that S.H. Wander is correct in identifying the "David Plates" from Lampousa as a celebration of Heraclius' victory over the Persian general Razatis on the river Zab in 627 A.D.[24] Helmut Nickl has already pointed out that, on the largest of these plates, Goliath uses a typically Iranian method of hanging a scabbard.[25] Wander, of course, believes that Goliath represents Razatis. What has apparently not yet been noted is that the only figures to wear framed helmets with aventails are those of Goliath's immediate followers (fig. 50e). There is, however, as yet no evidence to suggest that the "Parthian Cap" style of helmet was itself used in Byzantium, either as a result of Sassanian or of early Islamic influence.

THE DIRECTLY RIVETED FRAMELESS SPANGENHELM

This form of helmet, which is generally characterised by a tall and very pointed outline, was of Central Asian origin. Its use spread during the Migration Era and it remained popular throughout much of eastern

---

21. James, "Evidence from Dura Europos...," *op. cit.,* pp. 113-7, 128 & 131-4.

22. *Ibid.,* pp. 117-20.

23. James, "Evidence from Dura Europos...," *op. cit.,* pp. 118-9.

24. S.H. Wander, "The Cyprus Plates: The Story of David and Goliath," *Metropolitan Museum Journal* VIII (1973), pp. 89-104.

25. H. Nickl, "About the Sword of the Huns and the 'Urepos' of the Steppes," *Metropolitan Museum Journal* VII (1973), p. 131 note 3.

Europe (fig. 8c) until at least the 13th century. A lack of surviving examples from Byzantium and the islamic world makes its use in these regions less clear. One such helmet from Iraq, of mixed bronze and iron construction, may have an early Islamic rather than late Sassanian origin but in either case probably indicates influence from Transoxania or K̲h̲urāsān (fig. 8b). This particular example includes vertical reinforcing strips but no brow band and thus does not have a real frame. Pictorial evidence suggests that similar helmets were used in Byzantine areas from at least the 7th century (figs. 51 & 52) while other illustrations show suitably pointed helmets without indicating their vertical segments (figs. 36c & 37a-b). Islamic sources show comparable helmets less frequently and, as far as I can tell, only in those eastern regions closest to Turkestan from whence the style probably orginated (figs. 17b & 33). Perhaps this somewhat primitive form of helmet never achieved wide popularity in the central Byzantine and Islamic lands, remaining an essentially Turkish or Germanic feature associated with tribal or slave recruited troops in frontier regions. It certainly provides no evidence for mutual Byzantine-Islamic technological influence.

THE ONE-PIECE HELMET

The large-scale production of iron helmets forged from a single piece of metal represents a major technological revival during the early medieval period. One-piece iron helmets had been made in Imperial Rome,[26] but their production appears to have lapsed during the later Roman period, perhaps as a result of a need to mass produce simple helmets made by less skilled *fabricenses*.[27] Their reappearance suggests a return to relatively stable and prosperous conditions, perhaps under a new empire. But was this empire the Byzantine, the Muslim or even the Ottonian? So far the evidence seems to point to an early Islamic centre for this revival. One surviving helmet with a single-piece bowl and purely decorative strips laid across is thought to have been made in a western Islamic workshop[28] (fig. &c). However, very much the same idea is seen

26. H.R. Robinson, *The Armour of Imperial Rome* (London 1975), pp. 42-61 & *passim*.

27. S. James, "The Fabricae: State Arms Factories of the Later Roman Empire," in *Military Equipment and the Identity of Roman Soldiers: Proceedings of the Fourth Roman Military Equipment Conference,* edit. J.C. Coulston (BAR International Series 394, Oxford 1988), pp. 257-331.

28. E.A. Gessler, "Der Kalotten-Helm von Chamoson," *Zeitschrift für Historische Waffen- und Kostümkunde* III (1930), pp. 121-7; D. Hejdová, "Der Sogenannte St.-Wenzels-Helm (part 3)," *Zeitschrift für Historische Waffen- und Kostümkunde* (1968), pp. 16-17.

in a lesser known helmet from Bulgaria (fig. 9a) which may have had a Byzantine origin or derivation. It again has a single-piece bowl with decorative cross-pieces but these are all fastened to a very wide brow-band. The fact that helmets with comparably deep brow-bands have been found in 12th century Moldavia[29] and 13th century Russia[30] might reflect the fuller archaeological record of these areas compared to that of Byzantium. On the other hand Dr. M. Gorelik believes that the broad brow-band type of helmet generally dates from the late 13th-early 14th centuries and displays Mongol influence.[31] To further complicate the issue the remains of a very different but still one-piece helmet of probable Khazar origin also survive (fig. 9b), as does a second one-piece helmet from Bulgaria (fig. 9d). This latter specimen is so unusual and in many respects so advanced in both form and construction that a 14th century European origin might be proposed instead of the published 9th or 10th century Byzantine date.[32] Meanwhile pictorial sources can only hint at the existence of such one-piece helmets (figs. 16, 36c, 37a-b, 39, 41a & 60b).

THE ONE-PIECE HELMET WITH FORWARD-TILTED CROWN

During the 12th century a distinctive development of the true one-piece helmet became widespread in western Europe. This had its pointed crown slightly tilted forwards, probably as a result of leaving the front portion of the bowl thicker than the sides and rear during the forging process. Such a style was so typical of 12th century westerners that it appears to have been used as an identifying feature in a small Fāṭimid drawing showing combat between Muslims and Crusaders (fig. 49). A few other pictorial sources suggest, however, that this form of helmet had been known in Byzantium and the Muslim world at an earlier date (figs. 18, 31 & 36d). The earliest of these (fig. 36d) may show a cap being worn over an ordinary helmet while there is some evidence for the forward-tilted crown also being known in 11th century western Europe, for example in the Bayeux Tapestry. Nevertheless, I am inclined to believe that the style emerged in Byzantium and could be linked with the develop-

---

29. From Vatra Moldovitei-"Hurghişca", in V. Spinei, *Moldavia in the 11th-14th centuries* (Bucharest 1986), p. 244.

30. Provenance unknown, in Moscow State History Museum, *The Battle of Kulikovo: 600 years* (Moscow 1980), fig. 13.

31. Dr. M.V. Gorelik in private correspondence 1987.

32. Hejdová, *op. cit.*, pp. 16-17.

ment of close-rank, couched-lance cavalry tactics with their associated long kite-shaped shields, tall saddles and relatively straight-legged riding position. This occurred under Nicephoros Phocas in the 10th century.[33]

THE WEARING OF A CAP OR HOOD OVER A HELMET

One fashion that could certainly show Islamic or eastern influence upon Byzantine military styles would be the wearing or a cap or hood over a helmet, as there is no evidence for this fashion in the preceding Roman period. The *bashliq* cap (fig. 24) of felt or leather had been an aristocratic form of headgear in the Iranian world since at least the 3rd century BC, the addition of a diadem being a mark of royalty. Certain elements of this headgear clearly survived into the late Sassanian era[34] (figs. 26a-b). A comparable cap was found in an 8th-9th century grave on the northern slopes of the Caucasus (fig. 10). Such headgear may, perhaps, provide an explanation of certain pictorial and sculptural sources from the early Islamic era (figs. 14, 27a, 30[uncertain], 53 & 56) though it is also clear that looser headcloths in essentially Arab style were also worn (figs. 11a, 13, 20[uncertain] & 30[uncertain]). More remarkable is the possibility that some peculiarly elaborate or neck-covering supposed helmets in Byzantine art could, in fact, be based upon caps or headcloths, either worn over helmets or worn alone (figs. 36c-d, 38, 41d, 42, 50c-d & 60a-b). Since these include representative of both "good" and "infidel" figures, one may tentatively suggest that here at least is an example of the Byzantine military élite adopting fashions from their eastern foes, both Sassanian and Islamic.

---

33. D.C. Nicolle, "The Impact of the European Couched Lance on Muslim Military Tradition," *Journal of the Arms and Armour Society* X (1980), pp. 11-12.

34. Overlaet, *op. cit.,* pp. 191-2.

ILLUSTRATIONS

1. a – Iron dagger with iron guard found on victim of 747 AD earthquake at Pella, Umāyyad, Jordan (R.H. Smith, "Pella of the Decapolis", *Archaeology* XXXIV/5 Sept.-Oct. 1981); b-c – iron daggers, one with a bronze guard, from Hadīthah on the eastern shore of the Dead Sea, Romano-Byzantine c. 324-635 AD (Castle Museum, Karak, Jordan).

2. a – Remains of double-edged straight iron sword from Nishāpūr, 9-10 century, width approx. 6 cms. (Archaeological Museum, Tehran, Iran); b – Sword attributed to the Khalīf 'Alī (656-661 AD) with later hilt (Topkapi Museum Reliquary, Istanbul, Turkey); c – Sword attributed to Zayn al 'Abidīn (early 8 century) with later hilt (Topkapi Museum Reliquary, Istanbul, Turkey); d – Sword excavated in Oman, possibly Sassanian or early Islamic (drawing after Carl Philips, present whereabouts unknown); e – Sword from shipwreck of Islamic North African origin off Agay, southern France, 10 century (after A.G. Visquis, "Présence Sarrazine en rade d'Agay au Xme Siècle", *Rencontre d'Archéologie Sous-Marine de Fréjus, Saint-Raphael,* St. Raphael 1975 (Mus. of Underwater Archaeology, St. Raphael, France).

3. Weapons fragments from al-Rabadhah, central Arabia 8-9 century; a – iron sword-guard, blade width 6.1 cms.; b – iron chape, width 3.2 cms.; c – iron chape or sheath, length 22.5 cms. (Dept. of Archaeology, King Sa'ūd Univ., Riyadh, Saudi Arabia).

4. a – Bronze sword-grip from *Qaryat al-Fau: A Portrait of Pre-Islamic Civilization in Saudi Arabia,* London 1982); b – Sword pommel inscribed with name of the Buyid Prince Abī'l Ghanā'im Manṣūr Billāh, western Iran 10 century (exhibited at Sprinks Gallery, London, April 1977; present whereabouts unknown); c – Bronze sword hilt from Islamic (?) ship-wreck off Serçe Liman shown here with calcium carbonate encrustation and scabbard fragments removed, probably Armenia or western Iran, late 10-early 11 century (Castle Museum, Bodrum, Turkey).

5. Bronze sword-guard and pommel inscribed with Sura 112 of the Qur'ān, probably from Fāṭimid Egypt 9-10 century (Louvre Museum, Paris, France).

6. a – Sabre attributed to the Prophet Muḥammad, probably of Central Asian or Avar origin (Topkapi Museum Reliquary, Istanbul, Turkey); b – Oversized single-edged sword from Aphrodisias, perhaps symbolic, Byzantine, Avar or Sassanian origin late 6-early 7 century (Aphrodisias Site Museum, Turkey); c – Sabre from Nishāpūr, Turkish or Khurāsāni 9-11 century (Metropolitan Museum of Art, no. 40.170.168, New York, USA).

7. a – Iron helmet from Hadīthah on the eastern shore of the Dead Sea, Romano-Byzantine c. 324-635 AD (Castle Museum, Karak, Jordan); b – Helmet from St. Vid (Narona), late Roman or barbarian 4-5 century (Waffensammlung, St. Vid no. 3, Vienna, Austria); c – Helmet from Prag-Stromovká, Slav or Germanic 7-8 century (Historical Institute, National Museum, Prague, Czechoslovakia); d – Helmet from Prag-Stromovká, Slav or Germanic 7-8 century (Historical Institute, National Museum, Prague, Czechoslovakia); e – Helmet from Gnezdovo, Russian 10 century (State Historical Museum, Gnezdovo No. 1, Moscow USSR); f – Helmet from central Tunisia Fāṭimid 10-11 century (?) (after M. Brett, Local Museum, Kayrawan, Tunisia).

8. a – Copper or bronze-covered bronze and iron helmet from Niveneh, Sassanian 6-early 7 century (British Museum, no. 22497, London, England); b – Copper or bronze-covered bronze and iron helmet from Nineveh, late Sassanian or early Islamic, 7-8 century (British Museum, no. 22495, London, England); c – Iron helmet with decorative copper fillets, Magyar-Hungarian 10-11 century (Archaeological Museum, Pécs, Hungary).

9. a – Iron helmet with broad rim-band and decorative strips across one-piece bowl, from Yasenovo, Bulgar or Byzantine 9-10 century (Archaeological Museum, inv. 200, Kazanlik, Bulgaria); b – Helmet from Murakaevskiye gravesite, southern Urals region, Khazar-Bulgar-Madjarian style 10-11 century (after M.V. Gorelik: also N.A. Mazhitov, *Kurgani Yuzhnogo Urala VIII-XII v.v.,* Moscow 1981); c – Helmet of possible Islamic origin, 9 century (?) (Schweizerisches Landesmuseum, Zurich, Switzerland); d – One -piece iron helmet with small brow-piece, from Ozana, Byzantine 9-10 century or Bulgarian 14 century (Archaeological Museum, inv. 199, Kazanlik, Bulgaria).

10. Silk-covered leather hood with metal finial from tomb at Moshchevaya Balka, northern Caucasus, Alano-Saltowe 8-9 century (Ethnographical Museum, Moscow, USSR).

11. Wall paintings, Umāyyad c. 740 AD *(in situ* audience-hall, Qusayr 'Amra, Jordan); a – "Guard figures, probably representing infantry" in audience hall; b – unidentified figure on central vault; c-e – "Slaughter of deer or onager following a hunt" in audience-hall.

12. "Martyrdom scene", Italo-Byzantine early 7 century *(in situ* Santa Maria Antiqua, Rome, Italy).

13. "Sacrifice of Jephthah's Daughter", wall painting, Coptic 7-8 century *(in situ* Church of Bema, Monastery of St. Catherine, Sinai, Egypt).

14. "Archangel Michael", wall painting from Faras Cathedral, Nubian c. 710 AD (National Museum, no. 234038MN, Warsaw, Poland).

15. Group of "Forty Martyrs", wall painting, Byzantine 963-969 AD *(in situ* "Dovecote Church", Çavusin, Cappadocia, Turkey).

16. "Joshua", wall painting, Byzantine 10 century *(in situ* Monastery of Hosios Loukas, Greece).

17. Wall paintings from Nishāpūr, eastern Iran 10 century (a – Archaeological Mus., Tehran, Iran; b – Met. Mus. of Art, New York, USA).

18. "Soldiers at the Crucifixion", wall painting, Byzantine 10-mid-11 century *(in situ* Pürenli Seki Kilisesi, Peristrema valley, Cappadocia, Turkey).

19. Sword of "Archangel Michael", wall painting, Georgian 1096 AD *(in situ* church, Iprari, USSR).

20. "Town Governor" (?), tesserae of figure removed and jumbled during an iconoclastic reform, 'Abbāsid period Christian mosaic late 8-early 9 century *(in situ* Church of St. Stephan, Umm al Raṣāṣ, Jordan).

21. Lustre-ware dish from Nishāpūr, eastern Iran 10 century (Museum of Oriental Art, inv. 2629/3258, Rome, Italy).

22. "Nergal" god of the underworld, bas-relief from Hatra, northern Iraq 2 century (National Museum, Baghdad, Iraq).

23. Figurine, Coptic 3-4 century (Coptic Mus., inv. 7286, Cairo, Egypt).

24. Statue of "King Uthal of Hatra", from Hatra 1 century (Archaeological Museum, no. MM8, Mosul, Iraq).

25. Bas-relief carving from Rushaydah area, probably Ghassānid 6-7 century (Local Museum, Suwayda, Syria).

26. Rock-reliefs, Sassanian 224-272 AD *(in situ* Naqsh-i-Rustam, Iran); a – "Ardashir I"; b – "Retainers of Shāpūr I".

27. Stucco statuettes from Khirbat al Mafjir, Umāyyad 724-743 AD (Palestine Archaeological Museum, east Jerusalem, Palestine); a – "Guards"; b – "The Khalīf (?)".

28. "Mounted Saint", bas-relief, Georgian mid-11 century *(in situ* church, Nicorzminda, USSR).

29. a – Stucco relief, Iran late 7-8 century (Metropolitan Museum of Art, no.

40.58, New York, USA); b – Stucco relief from Chal Tarkhān near Rayy, western Iran late 7-8 century (Royal Ontario Museum, no. 946.104.1-5, Toronto, Canada).

30. "Goliath", relief carving, early 10 century Armenian *(in situ* Church of Gagik, Aght'amar, Lake Van, Turkey).

31. "Caravan guard" on carved wooden panel, originally from Fāṭimid Khalīfal Palace doors, Cairo 11-early 12 century (Museum of Islamic Art, Cairo, Egypt).

32. Carved capitals, Siculo-Norman late 12 century *(in situ* Cloisters, Monreale Cathedral, Italy); a – "Moor"; b – "Sleeping Guards at Holy Sepulchre".

33. Ceramic plate from Nishāpūr, eastern Iran 10 century (Coll. of Sayid Motamed, Frankfurt, West Germany).

34. Carved wooden door lintel from Monastery of the Holy Apostles at Mouch, near Ahlat, Armenian 1134 AD (Mus. of Armenian History, Yerevan, USSR).

35. Sword of "Angel of Death", *Ashburnham Pentateuch,* Egypt or North Africa 7 century (Bib. Nat., Ms. Nouv. Acq. Lat. 2334 f. 65v, Paris, France).

36. Manuscript of *St. Gregory of Nazianzus,* Byzantine c. 880 AD (Bib. Nat., Ms. Gr. 510, Paris, France); a – f. 137r, "Massacre of the Innocents"; b – f. 215v, "Judgement of Solomon"; c – f. 170r, "Soldiers of Jairus, a ruler of the synagogue"; d – f. 226v, "Joshua; Angel appears to Moses and Joshua".

37. *Psalter,* Byzantine 9 century (Monastery of the Pantocrator, Ms. No. 61, Mt. Athos, Greece); a – f. 89r, "Bribing of Guards at Garden of Gethsemane", b – f. 109r, "Guards at the Holy Sepulchre".

38. "Philistines seizing Samson", *Bible,* Byzantine 9 century (Bib. Nat., Cod. Gr. 923, f. 107v, Paris, France).

39. "Israelite; David fighting Goliath", *Psalter,* Byzantine 10 century (Bib. Nat., Ms. Gr. 139, f. 4v, Paris, France).

40. "Massacre of the Innocents", *Studite Psalter,* Byzantine 1066 AD (Ms. Add. 19352, f. 123, London, England).

41. "Goliath" (?), *Smyrna Octateuch,* Byzantine late 10-11 century (Bib. Vat., Cod. Gr. 746, Rome, Italy); a – f. 471v, "Goliath" (?); b – f. 469v, "Jebusite defenders of Jerusalem"; c – f. 354r, "Sword of an angel"; d – f. 469v, "Jews besiege Jerusalem".

42. "Emperor's Protospathius", *Exultet Roll,* southern Italian 12 century (Bib. Casanatense, Ms. 724.B.1.13, Rome, Italy).

43. "Pharoah's Army", *Exultet Roll* from Gaeta, southern Italian 11 century (Cathedral Archives, Roll 2, Gaeta, Italy).

44. *Homilies* possibly from Monastery of St. Anthony in the Desert, Coptic 9-10 century (Vat. Lib., Ms. Copt. 66, f. 287v, Rome, Italy); a – f. 287v, "St. Mercurius, Abu'l Sufayn"; b – f. 194v, "St. Theodore".

45. "St. Theodore". *Synaxary,* from Touton, Fayūm, Coptic 10 century (Pierpont Morgan Lib., Ms. 613, f. 1v, New York, USA).

46. *Kitāb al Kawākib al Ṣufār,* 'Abbāsid Iraq or Fāṭimid Egypt 1009 AD (Bodleian Lib., Ms. Marsh 144, Oxford, England), a – ff. 325-6, unidentified figure; b – ff. 110-111, "Perseus".

47. "Perseus", *Kitāb al Kawākib al Ṣufār,* probably Fāṭimid Egypt 1130/31 AD (Topkapi Lib., Ms. Ahmet III 3493, f. 30r, Istanbul, Turkey).

48. *Gospels* from Dumyat, Coptic 1179/80 AD (Bib. Nat., Ms. Copt. 13, Paris, France); a – f. 79r, "The Betrayal"; b – f. 131r, "One of Pilate's guards"; c – f. 103r "Execution of John the Baptist"; d – f. 6v "Massacre of the Innocents"; e – f. 40v "Beheading of John the Baptist"; f – f. 79r "The Betrayal".

49. "Falling Crusader in picture of Muslim troops emerging from gate ('Asqalan?) to defeat European warriors (Crusaders?)," painted paper fragment from Fustat, Fāṭimid 12 century (British Museum, Dept. of Oriental Antiquities, London, England).

50. *The David Plates* from Lampousa, Cyprus, Byzantine 613-630 AD (Metropolitan Museum of Art, New York, USA); a – "Sword of Goliath"; b – "Annointing of David"; c – "David puts on Saul's armour"; d – "Goliath"; e – "Philistines".

51. Gilded browplate of helmet, 7 century Lombardic or Italo-Byzantine (Bargello Museum, Florence, Italy).

52. *Isola Rizza Dish,* repoussé silver, late 6-7 century Italo-Byzantine (Castelvecchio Museum, Verona, Italy).

53. "Horsemen besieging a castle", silver repoussé dish from Malo-Amkovaya near Perm, Transoxania or Semireçye 9-10 century (Hermitage Museum, Leningrad, USSR).

54. Coin of Yazīd Ibn al Muhallab, Curgan early 8 century (American Numismatic Society Coll., New York, USA); a – reverse; b – obverse.

55. Pendant of gold necklace, Iran 10 century (Art Museum, Cincinnati, USA).

56. Coin of Khalīf al Muqtadir Billāh, 'Abbāsid Iraq 908-932 AD (National Museum, Baghdad, Iraq).

57. Silver-gilt repoussée dish inscribed with name Puri Vahman (Persian from Arabic Ibn Raḥmān?), probably from eastern Iran 8-9 century (Hermitage Museum, Leningrad, USSR).

58. Reverse of gold medal of Būyid Prince, probably 'Adūd al Dawla, western Iran late 10 century (Freer Gallery of Art, Washington, USA).

59. "Sword of slain Diocletian", *Icon of St. George* from Seti, Georgian 11 century copy of 10 century original (Local Museum, Mestia, USSR).

60. Ivory chess-pieces from so-called *Charlemagne's Chess Set,* southern Italy or Fāṭimid Egypt 11-12 century (Cab. des Medailles, Bib. Nationale, Paris, France).

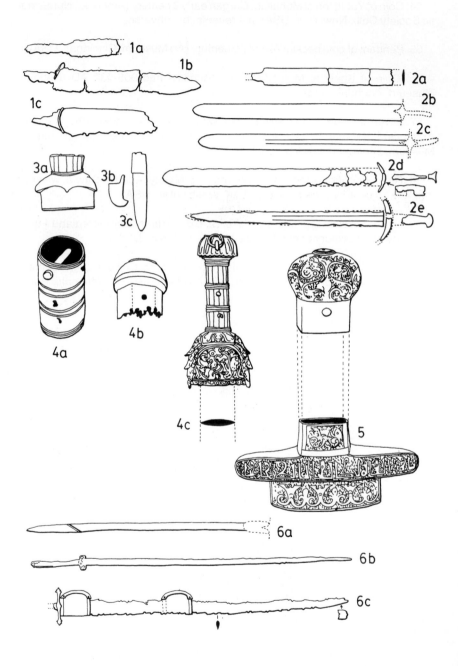

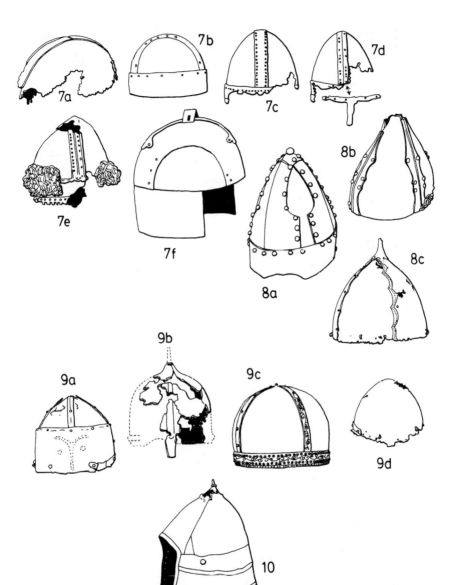

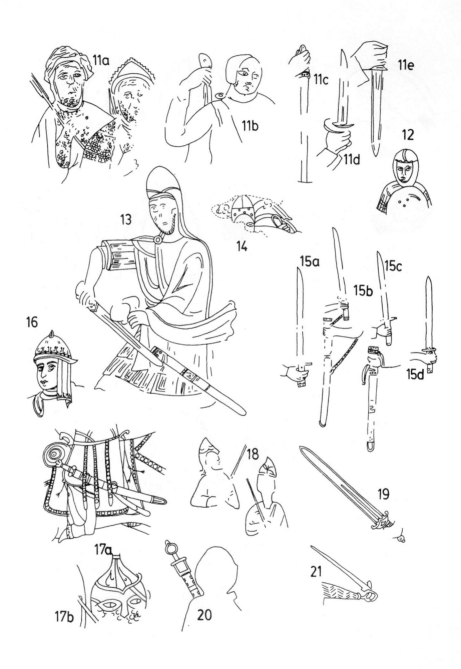

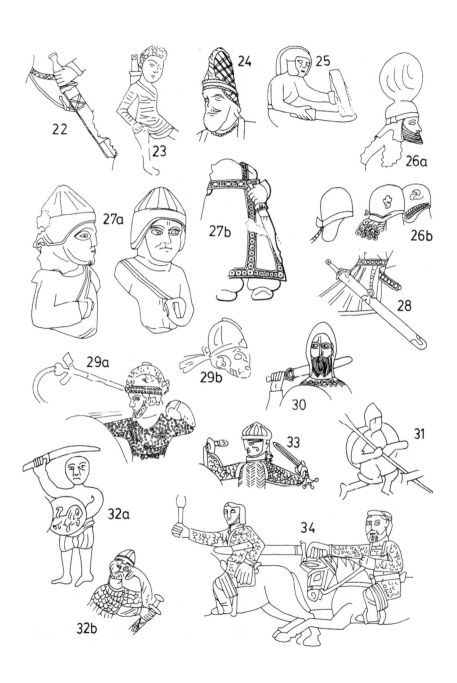

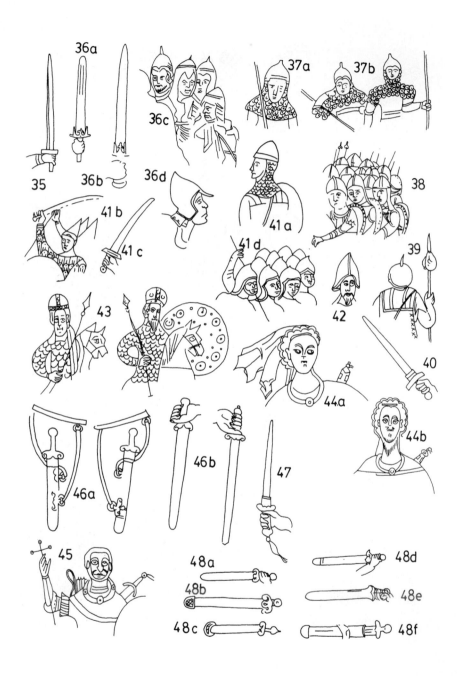

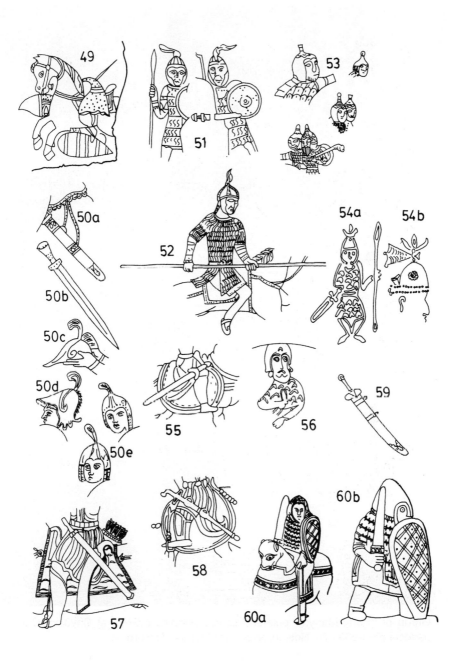

Group of "Forty Martyrs" painted in the *Dovecote Church* at Cavusin, Cappadocia (963-969 AD). Note three different types of sword.

"Guard figures", probably representing Arab infantry, painted in the audience hall at Qusayr 'Amra, Jordan (c. 740 AD). Note the spikey outline of the right-hand figure's helmet.

III

No way overland? Evidence for Byzantine arms and armour on the 10th-11th century Taurus Frontier.

This paper is based up two pieces of primary evidence, a decorated shield-boss in the Aleppo Museum and some military figures on wall paintings in the so-called "Dovecote Church" at Çavuşin in Cappadocia. The former will be presented as evidence of deep-seated conservatism within the design and decoration of Byzantine arms and armour. The second will be put forward as evidence of a contrasting but even more significant willingness to accept innovation on the part of the Byzantine military elite.

The gilded bronze shield-boss (pl. 1) comes from 'Ain Dārā in northern Syria and is now in the Aleppo Archaeological Museum, Syria. At one time it was labelled as a Byzantine helmet and although its shape does suggest a form of helmet later known in Europe as a *chapel de fer* or "iron hat" its size makes such a function quite impossible. Internally it is only 11 cms long, 9,8 cms wide, and 8,5 cms deep. Externally, including the brim, it is 19,5 cms long.[1] This object was found in the Byzantine level during excavations of a *tel* twelve kilometres from 'Ain Dārā on the right bank of the 'Afrin river, close to Syria's border with Turkey.[2] The site, which the Syrian Anti-

---

1. K. Toueir, Syrian Ministry of Antiquities, Damascus (private correspondence 1990-91), & S. Shaath, Curator of the Aleppo Museum (private correspondence 1990).
2. F. Seirafi, A. Kirichian & M. Dunand, "Recherches Archéologiques à Ayin-Dara (Preliminary Report) ", *Les Annales Archéologiques de Syrie XV/2* (1965), pp. 3-5.

quities Department started excavating in 1960, lies on the old road from Antioch to Gaziantep and was of considerable strategic importance, being strongly fortified during the Hellenistic and Byzantine periods. It is also close to the medieval Islamic castle of Bāsūṭā. The Byzantine level at 'Ain Dārā dated from the 10th to 11th centuries and was destroyed by fire, almost certainly during the Seljuk Turkish invasions.

The second piece of primary evidence consists a series of military figures painted on the lower register of the north wall of an underground church at Çavuşın (pls. II-IV). This is popularly known as the "Dovecote Church" and its wall paintings are believed to date from between 963 and 969 AD. The church is just outside the village of Çavuşın, about seven kilometres north-west of Ürgüp in the province of Nevşehir in central Anatolia. While the two horsemen on the far right of the north wall are believed to portray John Tsimiskes and a soldier identified as Melito (Melias in Greek) who was the youngest of the Forty Martyrs of Sebastea. The standing figures represent the Forty Martyrs of Sebastea themselves, although they may also mirror John Tzimiskes' east Anatolian army. The painting as a whole perhaps commemorates John Tzimiskes being raised to the rank of *Domesticus* and made commander of the Byzantine armies in Anatolia. John Tsimiskes was also a member of a leading Armenian aristocratic family; a fact of possible significance where his armour is concerned.

The 'Ain Dārā Shield-Boss

First of all it must be made clear that shield-bosses have, throughout the history of arms and armour, varied considerably in shape, size and decoration, as well as in the materials from which they were made. Shields could also be made without any bosses at all or they could have several large rivets to secure the *enarmes* holding straps, the heads of such rivets often looking like small bosses on the outer surface of a shield. Only rarely, however, have shield-bosses been studied in detail as a means of understanding technology, military methods and even social attitudes of early medieval societies. A notable and significant exception is the recent study of early Anglo-Saxon shields by Tania Dickinson and Heinrich Härke.[3] The 'Ain Dārā shield-boss (fig. 1) has several obvious characteristics. It is made of bronze and the surface was originally entirely gilded. It also has a very broad flange. This still holds the remains of one very large spherical-headed rivet or nail, eight of which would orginally have fastened the flange to the body of the shield. The remaining part of the flange is decorated with engraved animals, a hunting dog and a deer which run in a clockwise direction. These features seem to be found, though not all together, on most surviving late Roman and early Byzantine shield-bosses.

A number of such surviving earlier shield-bosses can be compared with the 'Ain Dārā example. Firstly there is a mid-3rd century Roman specimen from Dura Europos (fig. 2) overlooking the Euphrates in north-eastern Syria. It is a simple bronze shield-boss, probably for use in war rather than being a decorative object for parade purposes. It has neither gilding nor any other form of decoration apart from a slightly scalloped edge. The Dura Europos shield-boss does, however, have a broad flange and the rusted remains of one quite large rivet.

Several much more magnificent shield-bosses of a slightly later date have been found north of the Black Sea. One has a gilded bronze boss with a facetted dome and large gilded rivets grouped in threes (fig 3). It comes from a 4th or 5th century Hunnish grave-site on the western steppes of what is now the Ukraine. It was probably either made within the late Roman Empire or at least reflected late Roman military equipment. Apart from the gilding, the size of the near-spherical rivet-heads is worth noting. Another and very similar gilded bronze boss with a broad flange and large spherical-headed rivets grouped in threes (fig. 4) was excavated at a Romano-Byzantine or perhaps Goth site in the Crimea dating from around 400 AD. A third equally magnificent gilded bronze shield-boss was again found in a Romano-Byzantine or perhaps Goth site in the Crimea, once more dating from around 400 AD (fig. 5). Here eight very large rivet-heads

---

3. T. Dickinson & Heinrich Härke, "Early Anglo-Saxon Shields" *Archeologia* CX (1993).

are equally spaced around the wide flange. They are, however, semi-spherical rather than completely round. The somewhat pointed dome of this particular shield boss is also very similar in outline to the 'Ain Dārā example. It is also worth noting that this boss from the Romano-Byzantine Crimea was found within the remains of an shield of late Roman form.

The most magnificent shield-boss in this sequence was found in what is now believed to have been a 7th century Lombardic grave in Italy (fig. 6). The shield-boss itself is, however, generally considered to be of Byzantine manufacture. Its gilded bronze is cast rather than beaten into shape. It has a broad flange, five very large low-domed rivets, and is decorated with scenes of infantry combat. The dome itself is also quite pointed. The final comparative example is a much plainer and more functional object (fig. 7). It again comes from a Lombardic grave in Italy, this time dating from the late 7th or early 8th centuries. It appears to be of iron and clearly has a broad flange with the remains of seven large round rivet-heads.

As already mentioned, the decoration on what remains of the flange of the 'Ain Dārā shield-boss consists of a dog chasing some kind of antelope or gazelle (fig. 8a-b). There would presumably have been another two animals on the missing part of the flange. The workmanship might be simple but it is certainly not crude, and the animals are portrayed accurately in vigorous motion. One does not have to look far to find predecessors and contemporaries in other pieces of late Roman and Byzantine art, particularly art, from the eastern parts of the Empire.

Many such running animals, both hunters and hunted, are to be found in 6th century Byzantine mosaics. One representative example made in 531 AD is seen at Mound Nebo in Jordan (fig. 9). Not far away are others in the early 8th century Umayyad Islamic wall paintings at Qusayr 'Amra (fig. 10). Even within the more limited field of early and middle Byzantine metalwork there are plenty to be found. For example there is a late 6th century gold medallion found at Mersin in southern Turkey (fig. 11). More immediately relevant to the 'Ain Dārā shield-boss is a 6th to 9th century Byzantine bronze dish found in Daghestan in the eastern Caucasus (fig. 12a-b). Here the overall designed has been greatly influenced by Sassanian art. A second similarly dated but more obviously Byzantine bronze plate was found in Danghestan (fig. 13). Then there are a series of magnificent silver-gilt bowls that have been found in various parts of Russia and the Ukraine. They are generally considered to be of 11th to 13th century Byzantine or Georgian origin. The engraved animals beneath the rim of the example selected here (fig. 14a-b) are remarkably similar to those on the 'Ain Dārā shield-boss, both in style and technique.

It is obviously foolhardy to read too much into one small archaeological object, but I think it is fair to suggest that the 'Ain Dārā shield-boss does represent continuity in design and decoration within Byzantine arms and armour.[4]

The Çavuşın Wall Paintings

Among the "Forty Martyrs of Sebastea" painted on the north wall of the rock-cut "Dovecote Church" at Çavuşın are several soldiers wearing variations of a perhaps archaic form of body armour given to Byzantine warrior saints throughout the history of Byzantine art (pl. II). One man, however wears a more interesting form of cuirass (fig. 15). This appears to be of scales, perhaps fashioned from hardened leather. It is also divided at the waist, maybe for ease of movement when riding. Could this be the *lorikion alusidoton* or the *klibanion* armour of horn or leather scales mentioned in some Byzantine sources?[5] The same form of armour is worn by John Tzimiskes (pl. III & fig. 16) and Melito/Melias (pl. IV & fig. 17), both of whom are mounted. They look very different to the ordinary hero-warriors or soldier-saints portrayed in so much other Byzantine art. Both even appear to wear Arab-style head-cloths. Such a garment is, interestingly enough, also given to rulers and princes in some Armenian art. Their long cavalry spears clearly have bamboo hafts, again reflecting Arab rather than normal Byzantine, Persian or Turkish practice.

Several other representations of long apparently scale cuirasses are to

---

4. G. T. Dennis, *Three Byzantine Military Treatises* Washington (1985), pp. 53-7.
5. T. G. Kolias, *Byzantinische Waffen,* Vienna (1988) pp. 46-50; T. G. Kolias, *Die Schutswaffen der Byzantinischen Armée* (Doctoral thesis, Vienna 1980), pp. 45 & 50-1; J.F. Haldon, "Some Aspects of Byzantine Military Technology from the Sixth to the Tenth Centuries, " *Byzantine and Modern Greek Studies I* (1975) pp. 27-9 & 34-5.

be found elsewhere in Byzantine art or in the art of neighbouring Christian peoples influenced by Byzantium. They are usually worn by cavalrymen and most come from the eastern regions. They are nevertheless much rarer than illustrations of the short cuirass worn by most of the foot soldiers in the Çavuşin wall paintings. Taking some examples in chronological order; the first is a 9th century carved wooden panel from the Coptic church of Abū Sārga in Cairo (fig. 18). It should, however, be pointed out that many of these highly stylized figures could be interpreted as wearing lamellar cuirasses or even crudely represented mail armour. For example both the soldiers in a 9th century Byzantine manuscript a Psalter from Mount Athos (fig. 19) are "enemy" figures and might therefore have been given what the artist regarded at alien or Islamic equipment. Their armour might be of scale construction but is more likely to be a representation of long mail hauberks.

The clearest illustration of all is on a detailed low relief carving of Goliath on the early 10th century Armenian church of Gagik at Aght'amar (fig. 20). The Philistine giant is wearing a long scale cuirass with short sleeves. He also has mail over his shoulders and laminated arm defences made in the same way as those seen in several 7th to 8th century wall-paintings from Pianjikent and other sites in Transoxania. In fact this illustration of Goliath portrays, I believe, the kind of well-armoured soldier who formed the military elite of both sides of the Byzantine-Islamic frontier in eastern Anatolia in the 10th century.

Similar but less realistic is a long scale or lamellar hauberk worn by a horseman on an 11th century Byzantine ivory box now in the Bargello Museum in Florence (fig. 21). Similarly problematical, though for different reasons, is a "knight" in the so-called "Chess Set of Charlemagne" (fig. 22). Most scholars agree that this chess set was made in southern Italy, probably in the 11th century, but they disagree on whether it should be called southern Italian, Italo-Norman, Byzantine, or even Siculo-Islamic. This may not matter a great deal where the knight's armour is concerned for he is equipped in an essentially Mediterranean or Byzantine manner and appears to wear a full-length scale or lamellar cuirass. On the other hand this may again be a highly stylized way of representing mail.

One has to travel eastward to find the origins of the medieval scale or lamellar cuirass. It almost certainly first appeared in Turkish Central Asia and is seen in its characteristic early form on a 9th century stucco statuette from Karashah in what is now Chinese Turkestan. (fig. 23). It also appears slightly later and slightly further west on a magnificent silver-gilt plate showing the siege of a castle, which was found near Perm in Siberia. There is a great deal of debate about the exact dating and place of origin of this plate but the most convincing thesis suggests 9th-10th century Transoxania, and more specifically Semirečye south of Lake Balkash. One rider (fig. 24a) appears to be wearing a short shirt over a lamellar cuirass which covers his legs. Another (fig. 24b) wears a full-length scale or lamellar cuirass, while a third (fig. 24c) has full-length armour this time perhaps of mail. A final example of an eastern artistic source is a 10th century Manichaean wall-painting from Bezeklik in eastern Turkistan (fig. 26). It shows the ruling family of Idigutskai, now called Koço, and the ruler himself wears a long sleeveless lamellar cuirass.

Islamic art of this period tends to be highly stylized. Nevertheless several 10th century ceramic bowls from Nīshāpūr portray cavalrymen wearing long sleeveless lamellar or scale cuirasses, sometimes over long-sleeved mail shirts (fig. 26).

Archaeological evidence can add some reality to the often stylized representations of armour in Byzantine, Islamic and Central Asian art, largely as a result of the work done by Russian and other ex-Soviet scholars over the past few decades.[6] Taking this evidence in chronological order it is interesting to note how technological changes in Central Asian armour often precede, by a century or less, changing military fashions in the Byzantine and Muslim Middle East.

---

6. Those which have been of most immediate relevance to this study are: Yu.S. Khudyakof, *Vooruzhenie Srednevekovikh Yuzhnoi Sibiri i Tsentralnoi Asii (Arms of the Medieval Nomads of Southern Siberia and Central Asia),* in Russian (Novosibirsk 1986); Yu.S. Khudyakov, *Vooruzhnie Eniseickikh Kirgizov VI-XII vv. (Arms of the Yenesi Kirghiz 6-12 cents),* in Rusian (Novosibirsk 1980); & V.E Medvedyav & Yu.S. Khudyakov, *Voennoe Delo Drevnego Naceleniya Severnoi Asii (Military affairs of the ancient peoples of northern Asia),* in Russian (Novosibirsk 1987).

Reconstructions of two very different armours excavated at Kenkol on the borders of what are now Kirgizia and Kazakhstan demonstrate the variety within Central Asian scale cuirasses from the 1st to 5th centuries AD (fig. 27a-b). This was an iron-rich region and the armours are probably of nomad Iranian (Tajik) rather than nomad Turkish origin. One (fig. 27b) is remarkably similar to the armour shown on the Çavuşin wall painting. Its laminated arm defences appear to be virtually identical to those on the Armenian carving of Goliath at Aght'amar. The next example is a 9th to 10th century Kirgiz cuirass (fig. 28) and even more like those in the Çavuşin wall-paintings. It is somewhat lighter than the preceding armour and may thus reflect the gradual tendency to wear less heavy protection seen between the 7th and 13th centuries. This trend was characteristic of western Turkestan, the Muslim Middle East and of the Byzantine Empire but apparently not of eastern Turkestan and Mongolia.

A further reconstruction of a 9th to 10th century Kimak Turkish sleeveless cuirass (fig. 29) comes from an area to the north of the previous examples. It may represent another step in the trend towards lighter armours, particularly among the nomads of Central Asia but also among those neibouring settled peoples whom they influenced militarily. This particular scale cuirass would probably have been more typical of nomadic warriors of the northern steppes rather than those in closer cultural contact with Muslim Iran, the Middle East and Byzantium. In fact the Kimaks and their military styles may have had more in common with the 12th century Seljuk Turks.

Summary

To sum up, I therefore suggest that the 'Ain 'Dārā shield-boss is an example of the Byzantine Empire clinging to its treasured Roman heritage in the ceremonial aspects of arms and armour. I similarly suggest that the cavalry cuirasses portrayed in the Çavuşin wall paintings are an example of the Byzantine Empire's willingness, even eagerness, to learn from whoever seemed best able to teach when it came to the practical aspects of arms and armour. As such the scale armours in the Çavuşin wall-paintings perhaps reflect a Byzantine willingness to adopt military ideas even from their most deadly foes; in this case troops of Turkish origin who formed the elite of 10th century Muslim armies along Byzantium's Anatolian frontier.

pl. 1

pl.2

pl. I. Shield-boss from 'Ain Dārā, Byzantine 10-11 cents. AD
(National Museum, inv. nr. 1/64, Aleppo, Syria).
pl. II. Wall-painting of some of the "Forty Martyrs of Sebastea"
Byzantine eastern Anatolia 963-9 AD
(*in situ* "Dovecote church," Çavuşin, Turkey).

pl. III. Wall-painting of "John Tzimiskes," Byzantine eastern Anatolia 963-9 AD
(*in situ* "Dovecote Church," Çavuşin, Turkey).

pl. IV. Wall-painting of "Melito/Melias," Byzantine eastern Anatolia 963-9 AD
(*in situ* "Dovecote church," Çavuşin, Turkey).

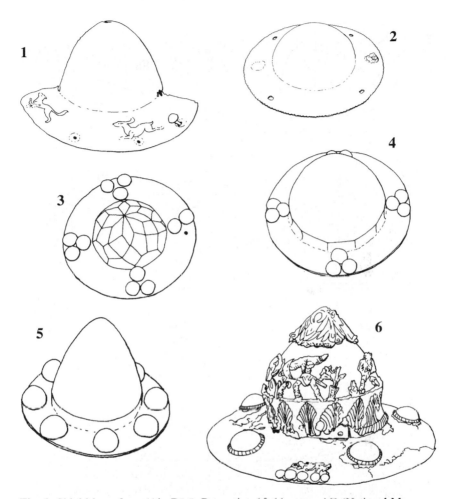

Fig. 1. Shield-boss from 'Ain Dārā, Byzantine 10-11 cents. AD (National Museum, inv. nr 1/64, Aleppo, Syria).
Fig. 2. Shield-boss from Dura Europos, Roman 3 cent. AD (Yale University Art Gallery, New Haven, USA).
Fig. 3. Shield-boss from western steppes, Hunnish 4-5 cents. AD (Hermitage Museum, St. Petersburg, Russia).
Fig. 4. Shield-boss from Crimea, Romano-Byzantine or Goth c. 400 AD (Hermitage Museum, St. Petersburg, Russia).
Fig. 5. Shield-boss from Crimea, Romano-Byzantine or Goth c. 400 AD (Hermitage Museum, St. Petersburg, Russia).
Fig. 6. Shield-boss from Nocera Umbra, Lombardic or Italo-Byzantine 7 cent. AD (Museo dell' Alto Medioevo, Rome, Italy).

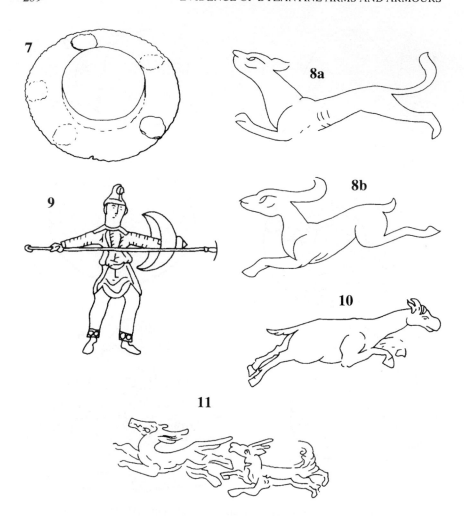

Fig. 7. Shield-boss from Castel Trosino, Lombardic late 7-early 8 cents. AD (Museo dell' Alto Medioevo, Rome, Italy).
Fig. 8 a-b. Shield-boss from 'Ain Dārā, Byzantine 10-11 cents. AD (National Museum, inv. nr. 1/64, Aleppo, Syria).
Fig. 9. Mosaic floor, Syro-Byzantine 531 AD (*in situ* Memorial of Moses church, Mount Nebo, Jordan).
Fig. 10. Wall painting, Umayyad c. 740 AD (*in situ* reception hall, Qusayr 'Amra, Jordan).
Fig. 11. Gold medallion from Mersin, Byzantine late 6 cent. AD (Hermitage Museum, St, Petersburg, Russia).

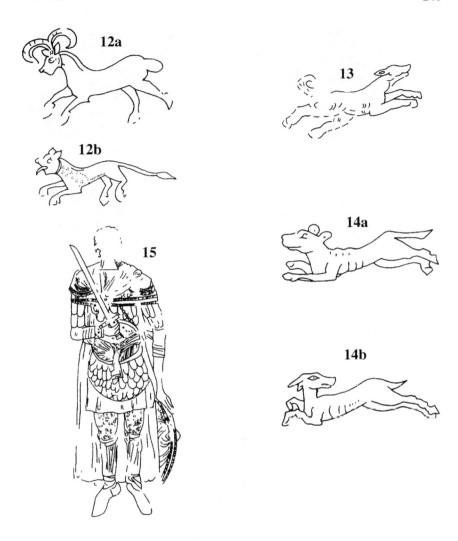

Fig. 12 a-b. Bronze dish from Daghestan, Byzantine 6-9 cents. AD (Hermitage Museum, St, Petersburg, Russia).
Fig. 13. Bronze plate from Daghestan, Byzantine 6-9 cents. AD (Hermitage Museum, St, Petersburg, Russia).
Fig. 14 a-b. Silver-gilt bowl, Byzantine 11-13 cents. AD (formerly in A. P. Bazilevsky collection, now in Hermitage Museum, St, Petersburg, Russia).
Fig. 15. Wall-painting of "Forty Martyrs of Sebastea," Byzantine eastern Anatolia 963-9 AD (*in situ* "Dovecote church," Çavuşin, Turkey).

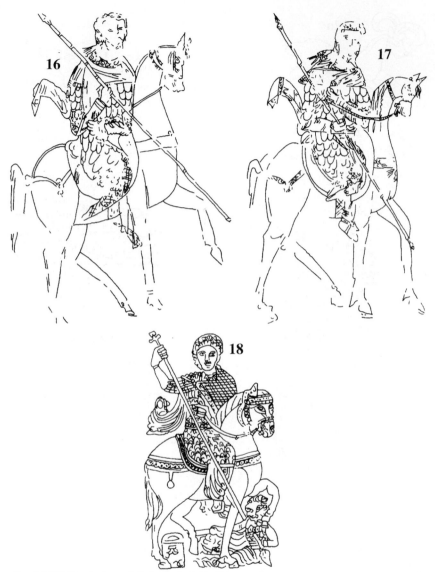

Fig. 16. Wall-painting of "John Tzimiskes," Byzantine eastern Anatolia 963-9 AD (*in situ* "Dovecote church," Çavuşin, Turkey).
Fig. 17. Wall-painting of "Melito/Melias," Byzantine eastern Anatolia 963-9 AD (*in situ* "Dovecote church," Çavuşin, Turkey).
Fig. 18. Carved wooden panel of a warrior-saint, Coptic 9 cent. AD (in situ church of Abū Sārga, Cairo, Egypt).

Fig. 19. "Guards at the gates of Gethsemane," Byzantine Psalter 9 cent. AD (Monastery of the Pantocrator, Ms. no. 61, f. 89r, Mount Athos, Greece).
Fig. 20. "Goliath," carved relief, Armenian early 10 cent. AD (*in situ* of Gagik, Aght'Amar, Lake Van, Turkey).
Fig. 21. Carved ivory box, Byzantine 11 cent. AD (Museo di Bargello, Florence, Italy).

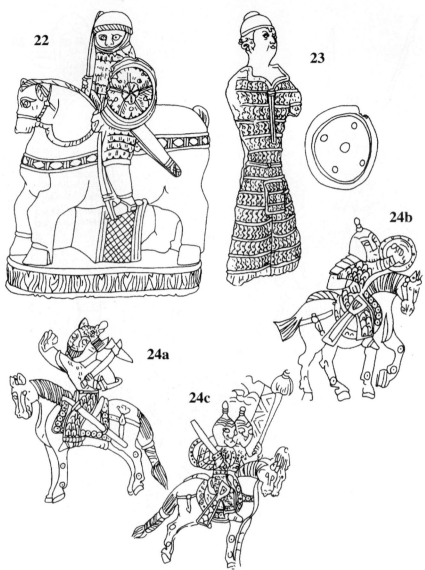

Fig. 22. Carved ivory box, chess knight from southern Italy, probably Byzantine or Siculo-Arab 11 cent. AD (Cabinet des Medailles, Bibliothèque Nationale, Paris, France).
Fig. 23. Stucco statuette from Kara Shar, eastern Turkestan 9 cent. AD (British Museum, London, England).
Fig. 24 a-c. Silver-gilt plate from Malo-Amkovaya near Perm, Sughdian 9-10 cents. AD (Hermitage Museum, St. Petersburg, Russia).

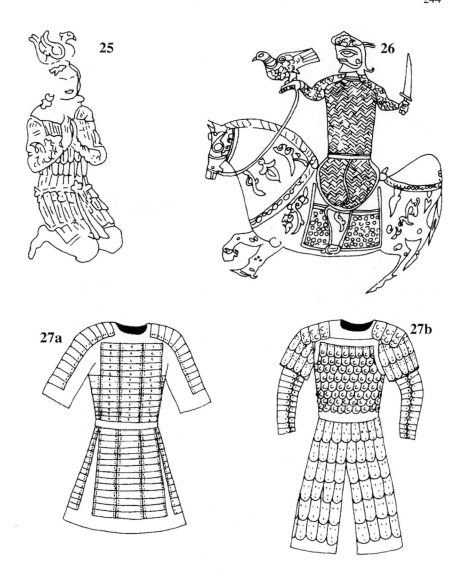

Fig. 25. Manichaean wall-painting of the ruling family of Idigutschai (Koço), Uygu 10-11 cents. AD (*in situ* Beszklik, Sinkiang, China).
Fig. 26. Slip-ware ceramic bowl from Nīshāpūr, eastern Islamic 10 cent. AD (Farough Collection, Tehran, Iran)
Fig. 27 a-b. Reconstructions of two armours from Kenkol, Kirgizia, Sughdian or Iranian nomad 1-5 cents. AD (after: I.K. Kozhomberdiev & Yu.S. Khudyakov).

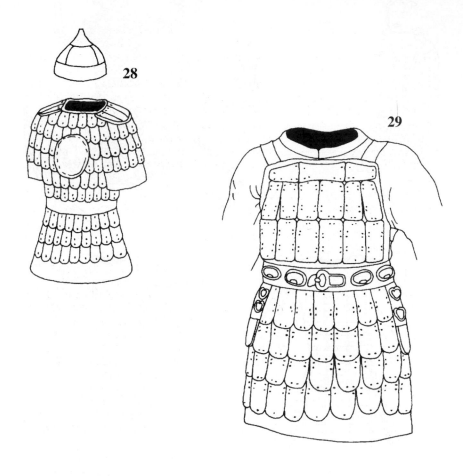

Fig. 28. Reconstruction of armour, Kirghiz, 9-10 cents. AD (after: Yu.S. Khudyakov).
Fig. 29. Reconstruction of a scale cuirass, Kimak 9-10 cents. AD (after Yu.S. Khudyakov).

THE IMPACT OF THE EUROPEAN COUCHED LANCE ON MUSLIM MILITARY TRADITION

It is now widely believed that the Frankish invaders of Syria, during the Crusades, owed their initial successes to their advanced military techniques.[1] While European superiority in arms and armour, with the notable exception of the cavalry-bow, has generally been acknowledged, one characteristic Frankish tactic has been highlighted above all others. This is the "couched" lance which gave the Frankish cavalry-charge its undeniably fearsome reputation. Such a tactic has been regarded not only as the greatest single development in lance-cavalry technique since the invention of the stirrup, but also as the logical outcome of the adoption of the stirrup. It has even been seen as a triumph of "Western technology" over the supposedly more conservative cultures of Byzantium and the Muslim World.

The purpose of this paper is to suggest that the reality was less clear-cut than such an analysis would suggest; that the couched lance was by no means universally accepted in Western Europe at the time of the First Crusade, that it was similarly not unknown outside the area, and that the couched technique itself ultimately proved to be a tactical dead-end.

First of all, it must be pointed out that the couched lance was only one of many ways by which a cavalryman could use this weapon in war. Nor can it be entirely separated from other techniques. Towards the end of the Middle Ages the European couched technique became so refined that a knightly cavalryman could hardly hope to use this weapon in any other way. In an earlier era, and in other parts of the world where such a degree of specialization was neither attempted nor achieved, cavalry could vary its lance-play in different combat situations. Hence it is necessary to differentiate between such techniques, despite the fact that many often merged one with another. Any such classification can only be a rough guide, perhaps doing no more than to aid an analysis of this complicated subject. It must also be borne in mind that contemporary illustrated sources cannot entirely be relied upon to provide exact representation of current military practice.

The horsemen in Plate III represent the basic attitudes assumed by cavalry in most medieval art work, though to some extent rationalized by my own limited riding experience. A1 and A2 illustrate the two extremes of over-arm position, although in fact most pictures do show one or other such extremes. Naturally Style A normally indicates that a weapon is being thrown. B, on the other hand, covers a multitude of downward thrusts, to left, right, or beyond the horse's head, to the front or rear of the horseman's body, using the right or left hand. C is more specific, but can be confusingly similar to E, which is the true couched lance. The only really important difference lies in the fact that riders C1 and C2 do not lock their lances between upper arm and trunk. Hence the lances of riders C are almost invariably held at the point of balance. The thumb on top of the shaft suggests, but does not confirm, a thrusting technique using the power of arm, shoulders, perhaps waist, and possibly also the horse's momentum. Knees, bent or straight, are likely to indicate either the traditional riding-seat of the culture in question, or the potential use of couched Style E. D is again more straightforward, clearly showing a thrusting technique using the power of arm, shoulder and perhaps waist. Style E is the couched lance. Usually this weapon is directed left of the horse's head but in many illustrations is clearly and deliberately shown being used to the right. F is intended to indicate both the potential and the limitations of this couched technique. Style G refers to all methods whereby the lance is held in both hands, either gripped firmly by both, or using one hand as a guide for the thrust rather as a snooker player guides his cue. The potential of this two-handed technique in making a sideways, cutting rather than thrusting, attack should become clearer later.

As this dissertation is primarily concerned with the military impact of one culture upon another, namely, that of the Frankish West upon Islam and to a lesser extent Byzantium via the Crusades, it would clearly be inadequate to view the development of lance-techniques solely chrono-logically. Such developments must also be seen geographically and, in an area of mass migration and cultural expansion, in relation to specific ethnic and cultural groups. During the Classical era of Islam, as in Crusader times and subsequent centuries, certain regions and peoples stand out as being of particular importance.

The Pre-Islamic Era

Islamic military techniques did not emerge in a vacuum. Unfortunately the Arabic poetry of the pre-Islamic era, or Jāhilīyah, is chronologically controversial. Even more serious is the dearth of pictorial evidence from Arabia. In fact we are reduced to noting, as in Plate IV, A–D, such tenuous parallels as that between a first century carving from Dura Europas, a sixth century Byzantine ivory, probably from Egypt, a twelfth century panel from the Capella Palatina ceiling in Palermo, and a fifteenth century miniature of Bedouin warfare from Iran. All show warriors on camel-back. The earliest is equipped with a lance and a small round shield. Bedouin traders on the carved ivory carry short spears and bows, while the warrior in Palermo has a small shield and what appears to be a long-handled mace. The fifteenth century warriors wield their long lances in the over-arm A1, or two-handed G, styles, but have no shields. All one can deduce from this sequence is some continuity of combat-techniques among the Bedouin, which in turn suggests that such techniques proved adequate for such camel-mounted warriors.

Written evidence is not entirely lacking. H. Lammens maintained that the throwing-javelin was not considered a proper weapon for an Arab.[2] He points out that it was a typical weapon of the Aḥābish, one of whom slew Ḥamza in this fashion at the battle of Uḥud,[3] and considers these warriors to have been mercenary or slave-infantry of South Arabian or Ethiopian origin. Given that most other sources state the Arabs were lance-fighters, one can assume that they used their spears for cutting or thrusting rather than throwing.

Before turning to the dominant pre-Islamic cultures of the Middle East, there is another nomadic people who should not be ignored—the Berbers. As cavalry in the armies of Rome, they were eventually superseded by heavier troops from the northern frontiers, but they later proved their worth to the Muslims. According to Herodatus, Berber infantry and cavalry both used the throwing-javelin, while the evidence of Ibn Bassām's *Al Dhakīra* suggests that this remained true under Islam.[4] Such a style of combat, relying as it did on dexterity, may have contributed to the lack of armour in the Maghreb, since such a lack cannot be attributed solely to climate. North Africa is no harsher than Northern Arabia, nor did it lack iron or wood for smelting.

Most writers agree[5] that in the early days of Islam the influence of Byzantine military doctrine was vital. Although I would suggest that the influence of Sassanian Iran was probably greater, there is no doubt that the ideal equipment listed by those unreliable pre-Islamic poets almost exactly paralleled contemporary East Roman issue.[6] Of course the well-documented Byzantine armies[7] were themselves influenced by military developments in the Middle East. Certainly Byzantine fashions in the use of cavalry spears changed more than once. With the employment of Goth Foederati to face Iran's heavy cavalry in the third century, a heavy thrusting lance became popular. According to Heliodorus (*Aethiopica, IX*, 15) such weapons were lashed to a horse's neck and supported by a rope around its croupe. J. F. Haldon sees the originators of this heavy-lance technique (Pl. IV, E–G), not as the Goths themselves, but as the Sarmatians, Parthians or Sassanians,[8] although unlike these troops, the Goths, according to Procopius, tended to wear little armour.

Following the Hunnish invasion of the 5th century and the Avar threat of the 6th, the lance declined in favour of the bow, the Byzantines evolving a composite archer-cum-lancer since they were apparently unable to train sufficient cavalry bowmen from within their own ranks.[9] Correspondingly there was a certain return to the javelin for those cavalry not trained in the bow. A lanyard twisted around its shaft gave a spin to this weapon, which seemed to improve accuracy.[10] This Style A is, however, rarely illustrated in the early period (Pl. V, A) compared to Style B, which appears on almost all cavalry tombstones.

Javelins seem to have been popular with the relatively heavily armoured, stirrup-using, Avars.[11] An apparent overall increase in the use of armour further strengthens the argument that body-protection developed in response to archery rather than close-combat. If the two-handed Style G was normal among those who did not throw javelins, then such a development would make sense, for a shield can hardly be used when both hands are thus occupied. Could, in fact, those highly regarded Optimates equipped with shields[12] have been javelin-throwers, while less regarded Foederati relied on heavy lances but no shields? The use of varied types of cavalry to support one another was described in detail by the Emperor Maurice in his *Strategikon*.[13] On the other hand there is still much debate on the importance of stirrups, both to lance-wielding cavalry and to horse-archers. Lynn White, Jr, insists that without them the lancer could make but a feeble thrust.[14] Meanwhile Haldon emphasises the fact that stirrups, and the Avar saddle with its greater support, enabled a horseman to wield his spear with one hand and so hold a larger shield in the other.[15]

Whereas such changes in the ranks of Byzantine cavalry are obvious, the situation in pre-Islamic Iran and Turkestan is less clear. Spear and bow seem similarly to have risen and fallen in favour,[16] this process being reflected in a story quoted by Al Tarṣūṣī in the twelfth century. According to this tradition archery fell into disfavour after Shapur I, but rose again with Bahram Gur.[17] This is certainly reflected in contemporary art, but although rulers and heroes later came to be represented as horse-archers, many ways of wielding a lance were also shown. At Taq-i-Bustan (c. 620) Khusrau II uses Style B, though to the left of his horse's head. On the earlier carvings at Naqsh-i-Rustam two figures in a frieze of Bahram II, and two in a frieze of Hormuzd II, use Style C2. They rest their lances on their left forearms, presumably to improve their accuracy. D2 appears on a well-known second- or third-century cataphract graffito from Dura Europos, and on a third century frieze of Prince Shapur at Firuzabad. Most important of all, however, are those sixth-seventh century frescoes from Panjikent on the borders of the Iranian and Turkish worlds in Turkestan. Here (Pl. V, B), Style G dominates among heavily armoured horsemen, all of whom use stirrups and a long-legged riding position, but carry no shields. As an exception, one fresco (Pl. V, c), shows a band of cavalry carrying small shields and possibly thrusting with one hand in Style D2.

Classical Islam

The Arabs who erupted from Arabia in the 7th century were short of horses. Those few they possessed were used sparingly, for example plying their lances on broken infantry.[18] Conquest, however, brought the Muslims wealth to equip more cavalry and grazing land to raise more mounts. The introduction by Marwān II (744–750) of Byzantine *Kurdūs* military formations perhaps accompanied other Byzantine fashions.[19] In the 12th century, Al Tarṣūṣī, for example, records that the long *qunṭarīya* (Gr. *kontarion*) lance, or beech or fir instead of reed and with its large "acorn-shaped" blade, was first used by the Byzantines' Arab allies in Syria.[20] In the late eighth century, Muslim cavalry possessed weapons that enabled them to dismount and meet an enemy charge as "pikemen".[21] By the ninth century two distinct types of horsemen served in the Caliphal armies, both being equipped with spears. Early in the 9th century Jāḥiz of Basra, in recording the claims of those Khurāsānis who helped the ᶜAbbāsids to power, listed an array of equipment that excluded the lance but then described them attacking their foes with such weapons.[22] Later he specifically refers to the lance's importance among Turks and Khāraji Arabs,[23] saying:

> "The lance of the Khāriji is long and penetrating, that of the Turk is short and hollow. The short hollow weapons are more deadly in effect and lighter to carry."[24]

A few years later Leo VI confirmed Turkish tactics by writing:

> "They throw their lance behind their shoulder and shoot with the bow.... When an occasion presents itself they take the lance again..."
> (Leo, *Tactica*, XVIII).

In the tenth century an Arab-Iranian style predominated in Syria, Ibn Hawqal describing the Banū Habīb deserting to the Byzantines as heavily armoured and equipped with swords and "lances of Hatt".[25] In Baghdad, meanwhile, a learned discussion on the word Rabā'ith[26] fortuitously informs us that spears with broad blades were still used by the Bedouin. Such a weapon would seem useful for both cut and thrust, perhaps being used in Style G if a line by Mutanabbī, "the lances struck the lances",[27] is to be taken literally.

Other evidence from somewhat later might indicate that the spear was more popular with Turks than with Iranians. Turkish heavy cavalry in the Delhi Sultanate carried both lance and short spear,[28] whereas the supposed Caucasian Albanians or Aghovani, mentioned as heavily armoured cavalry at Dorylaeum, "will not use any weapons except swords".[29]

In North Africa traditional light cavalry techniques seem to have survived largely unchallenged until the tenth century, although the Tūlūnids and Ikhshīdids of Egypt had introduced Turkish *ghulāms* presumably equipped in the current ᶜAbbāsid heavy cavalry style. Bedouin and Berbers formed the bulk of Fāṭimid cavalry; fifty thousand of the former fighting with spears as auxiliary cavalry according to Nāṣir-i-Khusrau.[30] M. Brett considers that by the early twelfth century these Arabs, late of Fāṭimid service, probably had considerable military capability though still using traditional *karr wa farr*, attack-and-retire, tactics.[31] In the Fāṭimid armies such cavalry supported a massed infantry advance, or were supported by that infantry during an enemy advance,[32] as in early Islam, presumably being armed with those Hatti lances and/or wooden "Khalandj javelins" which, according to Maqrizi, were stored in the arsenal of Caliph Mustanṣir.[33] It is also worth noting that infantry are more commonly portrayed in Fāṭimid illustrations than are cavalry, and that horsemen with swords or even maces—never bows—appear as frequently as do those bearing lances (Pl. V, D–H). Such lances often have broad blades. In 975 or 976 Fāṭimid experience of Alptekin's heavily armoured Turkish *ghulāms* (free, professional soldiers sometimes of slave origins) in Syria led to the adoption of more armour for men and horses,[34] a process that might also have been encouraged by the enrolment of some twenty thousand Byzantine prisoners of war in 997.[35]

Similarly, in Spain, cavalry grew heavier, though it is hard to say who was influencing whom. According to Al Tartūshī, in the late eleventh century, the tactical role of such cavalry was similar to that of Fāṭimid cavalry,[36] while an earlier extract from Al ᶜUmarī illuminated both the combat styles of the Andalusians and of the Berbers:

"The Spanish soldier is dressed in a coat of mail. If he is a person of power or consequence his horse is also covered with a coat of mail. He holds solidly in one hand a lance, long and thick, and in the other a shield in the same manner as do the Christians on whom he makes war. As for the Berber horseman, those who are noble or influential are among those alone who possess a coat of mail, and they fight without a [heavy] shield or a long, thick lance; but are armed with swords and lances with which they strike with a dexterity and sureness that is astonishing."[37]

11

After remarking on the long-legged riding position of the Andalusians, the author indicated that he considered the Berber style the more effective. If one allows that "baddies" are often portrayed as the hereditary foe in a frontier world such as Spain, there are plenty of Christian illustrations (Pl. VI, A–G) to confirm such a trend among the enemy; first towards a "Frankish" style of heavy cavalry, and then returning to lighter Berber techniques.

The Couched Style in Europe

Crusaders who marched east in 1097 were far different from those Franks who defeated the Muslims at Tours in 732. The Byzantine army similarly responded to the Muslim challenge. There were still many Gothograeci heavy cavalry, regarded by Haldon as literal and tactical descendants of late sixth century Gothic Optimates, in those forces overrun by Islam in the seventh century.[38] Following these disasters, Byzantine armies were converted from offensive to defensive formations. "Shadowing warfare" was evolved in which enemy invaders were forced to retire, though not necessarily destroyed.[39] This led Byzantine cavalry constantly to harry the Muslims rather than to close with them, and it inevitably affected their tactics and equipment. The weight of weapons and armour decreased. Mail was still worn but the lammellar cuirass shrunk to protect only the trunk,[40] and by the ninth century mounted archers had almost disappeared.[41]

When Byzantium returned to the offensive after 960, there was a revival in shock-cavalry trained for close combat.[42] Lances themselves reflected such changes. Under Maurice (582–602) the short spear was merely an alternative weapon for a mounted archer, but by the late ninth century the horseman's Kontarion was 4 metres long and with a 25 centimetres blade.[43] In the following centuries the Byzantines were famed for their long lances and for cavalry divided into heavy and light formations[44] (Pl. VI, I–J). That aggressive ruler, Nicephorus Phocas (963–969), was credited with making lance- and mace-armed cavalry Byzantium's decisive weapon. Both men and horses wore armour and were trained to charge in a blunted wedge formation.[45] There even seems to have been a revival of full-length armour by the eleventh century[46] (Pl. VII, A). Helmets with aventails covering the face, in addition to arm-, hand- and leg-protection, were worn. A re-adoption of the shield also indicates a development in lance-play. Very few Byzantine cavalry lancers carried shields in the sixth century, whereas almost all did so in the tenth. The same sources show that the large circular *thureoi* shields of the late ninth century had, by the late tenth, to some extent been replaced by kite-shaped shields just over 1 metre long.[47]

The role of heavy cavalry was to break enemy formations by a controlled charge. But as these troopers were unwieldy, their charge had to be decisive. Nicephorus envisaged a wedge formation twelve ranks deep with a blunted front rank of ten or twenty men. Lighter cavalry occupied the interior of this wedge. Interestingly enough the first four ranks consisted, not of lancers, but of men armed with sword or mace. Lancers occupied the wings from the fifth to the twelfth ranks.[48] The limitations of the lance as a true shock-weapon were here recognized. Collision-combat was left to sword and mace, while lancers on the flanks presumably hoped to catch the foe as he broke away from the Byzantine charge. Such careful tactics may explain Byzantine contempt for Frankish heavy cavalry, whom they regarded as the easiest of their foes,[49] although at the same time raising just such troops for their own army.

In Western Europe there seems to have been relatively little development of arms or tactics after the fall of the Roman Empire, and what changes there were appear to have followed developments in Byzantium. The kite-shaped cavalry shield of the 11th century could be an exception. Probably developed from an infantry shield, it might have originated in southern France.[50] This larger shield was worn rather than held, its weight being carried by the shoulder as well as the arm which meant that it could hardly be moved. It was, in fact, akin a piece of armour protecting the horseman's left side, but also limiting his movement in the saddle. As such it went well with a heavy, though not necessarily couched, lance. The newly adopted long-legged riding position similarly inhibited a rider's movement. French-style saddles with high cantle and pommel appear increasingly frequently in eleventh and twelfth century illustrations, for example in the numerous *Beatus* manuscripts of the Apocalypse from northern Spain.[51] Such saddles similarly restricted mobility, though making a horseman hard to unseat. Harness improvements of ultimate Central Asian origin, such as chest- and crupper-straps, also fixed the saddle more securely to the horse "fore and aft". Taken together the kite-shield, long-legged riding position, high cantle and pommel, chest and crupper straps, effectively enabled an armoured man to use his lance in Style E, as well as Styles C and D. Yet it limited body movement for Styles A or B and making Style G virtually impossible (Pl. VII, B–E). But taken to excess such trends could, as they later did, oblige him to use Style E and no other.

Although the couched-lance technique may not have been invented in Northern Europe, it was adopted there with greater enthusiasm than elsewhere for both social and military reasons. A fully armoured cavalry-man (Pl. VII, F–H), soon to become the "knight" of the High Middle Ages, was already more than a warrior. He was becoming part of an exclusive social caste whose code of conduct often governed his mode of combat. A knight should fight a knight, both being similarly equipped. Normally independent of any disciplined formation, they could thus attack one another in a style approved by caste and custom, seeking no "unfair" advantage and craving "honour" over simple victory. This might not yet have been the case in the eleventh century, but features of the tournament were already appearing. While William the Conqueror's horsemen on the *Bayeux Tapestry* could revert to Styles A and B (Pl. VIII, A–C) after failing to break the English shield-wall by a charge using Styles C, D and E (Pl. VIII, D–F) and reverting to these styles for the final pursuit, the almost contemporary author of the *Song of Roland* appeared to write his work as a "triumph" for the new Knight with his characteristic couched-lance.[52] This author's use of two distinct terms for wielding the lance[53] probably differentiates between Styles C, D and E. Certainly he regarded it as dis-honourable to throw one's weapon rather than closing with the foe.[54] Such knightly ideals of combat were, however, to remain mere ideals for another century, even among the knightly class themselves.

The Seljūks

The immediate cause of the Crusade was Byzantium's collapse before the invading Seljūks (Pl. IX, A), of which the battle of Manzikert in 1071 was the most notable episode. The battle of Doryleum in 1098 was similarly the most important event, in Anatolia, of the Christian reaction. Whereas the Muslim victory had been won by the Seljūk Sultan's professional army backed up by turcoman tribal contingents, the later Muslim defeat was largely suffered by such tribal warriors backed up by the personal ᶜAskar of a minor Seljūk prince.[55]

Although the combat techniques of the Turkish tribes were to have a profound effect on Muslim professional armies, these Central Asian styles were epitomized by the nomadic turcomans themselves. The manuscript that best describes such techniques was the romance of *Warqa wa Gulshāh*. Probably written in the mid-eleventh century,[56] the earliest existing copy of this tale, now in the Topkapi Library, is no earlier than the late twelfth century. Yet its illustrations are very useful. The story was written for a Turkish warrior-society and pays considerable attention to military details. Lance, sword, bow, mace and lassoo are mentioned as the cavalryman's weapons, while the story itself gives seven detailed accounts of lance-combats. On two occasions these weapons are "turned" or "twirled" before striking.[57] On another a lancer fences with a swordsman.[58] Two verses make it clear that warriors slackened or let go their reins before "advancing the points of their lances" or striking a blow.[59] Unarmoured arms and legs were prime targets in this fencing style of lance-play.[60] Nor were lances always thrust: "He struck him a cutting blow of the lance to make him loose the stirrups."[61] Such details suggest lance-play of Style G which is in fact frequently portrayed in the *Warqa wa Gulshāh* illuminations (Pl. IX, B–D). Finally there is a reference to a javelin being thrown from horseback,[62] recalling references to those Turks who similarly threw javelins at Doryleum.[63] Not many years later the young ᶜImād al Dīn Zangi himself reportedly hurled a lance at the gates of Tiberius, though surely only as a gesture of defiance or daring.[64]

Although the battle of Manzikert has often been analysed,[65] one feature of the whole Byzantine failure to halt the Seljūks has but rarely been pointed out. That was the Christian Empire's inability to revert to those guerrilla tactics that had proved so effective four centuries earlier.[66] Instead, the Byzantines increasingly emphasized those heavy cavalry techniques that they themselves had instigated and which, in a more extreme form, were now being used by the Franks both in the East and in Europe[67] (Pl. IX, E–G). This tendency was reinforced by initial Crusader successes, and by that large number of European mercenaries employed by Byzantium[68] in the twelfth century. Such a mingling of military styles of Anatolia (Pl. IX, H) was aided by the growth of a mixed Turkish-Greek population in Bithynia, by the conversion of many Anatolians to Islam, by a steady flow of Turkish refugees into still Byzantine territory, and by the recruitment of Greeks, Armenians, Kurds, Georgians[69] and Franks by the Seljūk rulers.

The Crusades

Even if it were true that the First Crusaders had the world's finest military equipment[70] we still know less about their combat styles than, for example, those of the Normans at Hastings. Whereas F. Lot thinks they threw their lances, Ross attributes this to the chroniclers' persistent use of archaic terms.[71] But Crusader combat-styles do soon become clearer. The Frankish charge with lances was a feared battle tactic, yet the Franks also learned to use such charges in a controlled manner. In this they followed both Byzantine precedent and military common sense. Unlike Nicephorus Phocas's wedge formation, however, the Franks relied primarily on the lance. Although Crusader cavalry probably did not fight in orderly squadrons like the Byzantines, such formations could perhaps have been fielded by such disciplined forces as the Military Orders. Cavalry charges were normally made, not by the mass of horsemen, but by selected units at selected targets,[72] and if, as at the siege of Damascus, the cavalry was prevented from making such charges, this itself was considered worthy of record by an eye-witness.[73]

Outside Damascus the Crusaders were inhibited by terrain. At Ramle in 1101 the ranks of Fāṭimid infantry were a wide open target. Yet the Franks still needed three charges to break their disciplined foes. Another famed charge was that launched by the Templers who "burst through the enemy squares"[74] when the latter emerged from Acre. But this latter infantry was not apparently supported by cavalry, and may still have been on the move when hit. A third charge was at Arsūf. Here the Crusaders attacked when the Muslims, perhaps weary and careless, had "purposely dismounted from their horses in order to take better aim at our men with their darts and arrows."[75]

By contrast a Frankish lancer was far less effective against a moving, mounted, target. Usāma ibn Munqidh, for example, describes a Frank who had momentum enough only to make one pass at his retreating foes.[76] Yet Usāma also indicates that above all he feared to turn his back on a Frankish lancer, though to face him directly could prove equally disastrous. In 1109 Usāma saw two warriors, both armed with lances, press home their attacks and slay each other on their first pass.[77] More human, perhaps, were the reactions of two similarly armed men who both swerved aside at the last moment.[78]

Why did Crusader cavalry lay such emphasis on the lance? A horse, however well trained, will rarely gallop right into an obstacle, human or otherwise, unless it can see a way around. But a lance enables a horseman to strike a target as he passes, and from a range of some feet. Except when couched it also enables him to thrust at a target while his horse is stationary. But couched, a lance can only be used against an impassable obstacle if the horse is trained to push. This high saddle, and the rigid riding position, plus the fact that the lance was held behind its point of balance to give greater reach in addition to being locked beneath the rider's upper arm, may, when taken all together, indicate that such a pushing technique holds the secret of early Frankish successes against ranks of infantry. Perhaps the Fāṭimids at Ramle were jostled rather than smashed into defeat! Heavy

15

European armour and large shields would then have been particularly useful, as infantry immediately behind the first rank were normally expected to cover their "jostled" comrades with arrows and javelins. The care with which Crusaders on the march maintained close order suggests that they were equally aware of the danger of cavalry, not riding down their infantry, but widening such gaps as might appear.[79]

When cavalry met cavalry the combat inevitably dissolved into a *mêlée*, if one side did not flee. Here the couched lance seemed to provide no advantage, yet men are constantly recorded as being unhorsed,[80] often by lance thrusts in circumstances where only a rider's arm could give power to his blow.[81] The high saddle and low stirrup associated with lance Style E also made it difficult for dismounted men to remount.[82] Yet it would be wrong to see only the couched-lanced Franks suffering in this way, for Bahā' al Dīn records the death of a Muslim during the siege of Acre who "had dismounted to pick up his lance, and was trying to remount his horse, which was very restive, when the Franks swooped down on him and killed him".[83] Nor were the Franks then limited to the couched-lance technique, for Usāma records them reversing their lances to jab down at an unhorsed man.[84] Perhaps the development of light cavalry, the Turcopoles or that section of them who were mounted,[85] resulted from limited Frankish success in the *mêlée*. Certainly Usāma records Frankish cavalry removing armour to achieve greater manoeuvrability.[86]

The development of European weapons and armour in the twelfth and thirteenth centuries is well documented. High saddles with supporting pommel and cantle became increasingly common, as did the heavier lance (Pl. X, A–E). François Buttin's claim that even before the thirteenth century heavy cavalry used only couched Style E may be an exaggeration,[87] but it still leaves open the possibility of less well-equipped cavalry being less rigid in their techniques (Pl. X, F–I).

Although medieval Europe produced no literature to compare with Islam's *Furūsiyya* manuals (see below), Jean de Meun's *L'Art de Chevalerie*, written in 1284, was an updated translation of an anonymous tenth century Byzantine *De Re Militari*. In it he still thought it relevant to discuss the thrown lance.[38] Extracting a lance from its victim could always cause a fractured wrist if done carelessly, and couched Style E made such extraction even more difficult. A sharpened lance may embed itself in a shield or transfix a foe, and if a horse is moving fast, the lance, if it does not shatter, must either be abandoned or reversed in passing and then withdrawn. Jean de Meun stated that "two fingers depth" was sufficient to slay,[89] and such minimal penetration also simplified extraction.

Meanwhile changes in the European lance-blade, which was becoming smaller and more pointed, were clearly designed to puncture armour rather than cause those wide wounds earlier recorded by Usāma as resulting from Frankish lance thrusts.[90] A broad blade could disable even if it did not strike a vital organ, but was less capable of piercing armour. This— the late 13th century—was an era in which rigid body-armours were reintroduced into Western Europe, and the adoption of the so-called "coat-of-plates" began a process that culminated in the totally encased horseman of the fifteenth century. This looks like the logical result of Europe's preoccupation with the couched, penetrating, lance, yet paradoxically, it has been suggested that this so-called "coat-of-plates" may even have been of Near Eastern origin.[91] Appearing late in the twelfth century the *cuirie*, probably of *cuir-bouilli* hardened leather plates,[92] was worn over a mail hauberk. It, and a poncho-style cuirass worn by that traditionally negro "Moorish" Saint, Maurice, in Magdeburg Cathedral (Pl. XI, I), are relatively similar in concept both to the leather or metal Muslim *djawshan* and to the comparable Byzantine *klibanion*.[93] Here (Pl. XI) we may have a case of parallel evolution, but it is, in my opinion, also significant that the names of two other forms of armour that appeared in Europe at this time, the *aketon* (c. 1300) and the *jazerant*, both have Muslim origins: *al quṭn* (Arabic, *cotton*) and *kazāghand* (Persian, *cloth-covered mail jerkin*).[94] Such early semi-rigid body-defences were not necessarily proof against a lance-thrust. Usāma again records that Abū Bakr Bishr died from a Frankish lance blow in the chest, despite the gilded *djawshan* that he wore.[95] Equally it is possible, indeed probable, that such armours to protect the trunk, rather than the limbs, were not intended primarily to stop a lance but to ward off arrows and bolts, since both the longbow and the crossbow were growing in importance at this time.

Islam during the Crusades

Clearly there were great changes in Muslim military techniques from 1100 to 1300, but traditional styles still predominated, though with increased emphasis on horse-archery in most areas. Crusader chronicles still mention Muslims throwing javelins from horseback[96] in the late twelfth century, yet only rarely is it possible to work out whether these troops were Turks, Kurds, local Arabs or Bedouin. During the siege of Damascus in 1148 the defenders threw javelins,[97] but these men were probably infantrymen of the local ʿaḥdāth or militia. Meanwhile Usāma's mention of Arab Bedouin javelins fails to indicate whether they were thrown by mounted men or infantry.[98]

Muslims were, however, clearly capable of unhorsing Crusader knights both in the *mêlée*[99] and when charging into a body of Frankish horsemen from the flank,[100] despite the fact that by this time the latter were almost certainly using lance Style E.

Occasionally a minor engagement is described in detail by both sides. Near Ramle on 17th June, 1192, a Frankish convoy was ambushed by Saladin's Bedouin who unseated, sometimes more than once, numerous knights, though rarely injuring them. Some Turks then joined in, and the Frankish report mentions javelins being thrown and more serious injuries being inflicted.[101] This engagement seems to reflect the differing combat styles of Turks and those Arabs used by Saladin in ambushes because of their speed and agility.[101] The latter preferred to use lances[102] which were traditionally of reed, as noted even by their foes.[103] Such reed-lances, longer than those of the Turks, could prove a hindrance in an emergency. Usāma recorded that Fāris ibn Zimān, a Bedouin warrior, apparently tripped his own horse while trying to turn and face a lance-armed foe,[104] Perhaps Fāris was hiding behind his horse's neck and attempting to strike from beneath its head, as advised by later Furūsiyya manuals.[105]

Heavier lances were introduced by the Muslims, though not apparently among the Bedouin. Who precisely used them is not always clear. One would hardly expect those "light cavalry", mentioned by Bahā' al Dīn and others,[106] to use them. Similarly the close-combat weapons of "heavy cavalry", where specified, tend to be sword or mace.[107] This seems to be borne out by figures depicted on Mamlūk inlaid metalwork where heavily armoured men rarely carry spears (Pl. XII, A–C). Usāma's solitary reference to a new heavy lance, 18 to 20 cubits long,[108] is hardly flattering as the owner was barely able to lift it. Especially heavy lances could be effective when wielded by exceptionally strong men. During the Crusaders' march from Acre to Arsūf, one of Saladin's Mamlūks, Aiaz the Tall, was killed in single combat between the two armies.[109] The anonymous chronicler of the Third Crusade recalled with awe that he "carried a lance heavier than two of ours, to which he gave the name Aias Estog".[110]

It would probably be wrong to see in such tales, references to those all-steel lances mentioned by Mayer,[111] since the latter were hollow and, paradoxically, rather light. Given the limited tube-manufacturing technology of the age, they were necessarily also short.

Usāma's memoirs provide the most detailed insight into Muslim lance-play prior to the writing of our surviving Furūsiyya manuals. His descriptions of combat show obvious parallels with European techniques. Normal equipment included shield and lance,[112] and the lancer preferred to receive his foe on his left, shielded side.[113] On the other hand, the fact that an over-enthusiastic thrust could make the youthful Usāma slip from his saddle,[114] and that a crosswind could easily catch his pennon and divert his aim,[115] suggest lance Styles C or D, not a couched weapon beneath his elbow.

With a greater concern for tactics and less for the "honour" of a jousting type of charge, Usāma attempted always to attack his mounted foe from the undefended side or rear.[116] He himself feared to turn his back on a lancer, although he was trained to thrust his lance to the rear and ride facing in that direction if need be[117] (Pl. XII, D–E). Usāma also records that horsemen without lances feared to engage men so armed.[118]

The training of a Muslim horse-archer in the twelfth century gave special attention to combatting a lancer, who should be engaged at a greater distance than a swordsman. If attacked by a lancer and a horse-archer, the former was to be disposed of first.[119] Most sources also suggest that a horse-archer now reverted to a sword or mace, rather than to a lance, when forced into close combat.[120]

Here again is the problem of which combat-technique did most to stimulate the wearing of heavier armour in the Middle East. Mayer indicates that mail, reinforced with laminate or lamellar, was increasingly used in the Middle East after the Mamlūks seized power in the latter half of the 13th century.[121] Gorelick uses both Rashīd al Dīn's history and numerous pictorial sources to argue that it was the Mongols—horse-archers above all—who forced such a change in Iran, Iraq and Syria.[122] Middle Eastern Muslims, far from learning to fight like the Crusaders,[123] adopted virtually nothing from their Frankish foes. They may well have paid greater attention to warfare, writing many military manuals and improving their tactics and armaments,[124] but technical developments were largely "home-grown", or learned from further East, not West.

This was, however, not at that time true of Muslim Spain, nor perhaps entirely of the Maghreb. During the twelfth century, heavily armoured European mercenaries, probably cavalry from Sicily (Pl. XI, F–H), served in the Zīrid armies of Tunisia.[125] In Spain, Catalan and French mercenaries were employed by the Almoravids,[126] and even in the late eleventh century the unknown Frankish author of the *Song of Roland* betrayed real knowledge of Muslim territories and peoples.[127] In Spain, European influence persisted at least until the end of the thirteenth century in equipment and lance-techniques. This is clearly shown both by illustrated sources (Pl. XIII, A–C) and in the writings of Ibn Ṣāʿid. Andalusians, he said, modelled their equipment on that of their foes, similarly fighting with shield and long lance in the charge, weighted down by shield, long thick lance and coat of mail; "Consequently their one aim is to stick solidly to the saddle and to form with the horse a veritable iron-clad whole".[128]

The Furūsiyya Manuals

During the Crusading era, the first surviving Furūsiyya manuals were written. They are of great importance, but must be used with care since their terminology is unclear and it is not certain that all the exercises described were in use at the time of writing. They are, however, deeply rooted in traditional Middle Eastern military styles. In fact, as A. D. H. Bivar has pointed out, Ayyūbid and Mamlūk Furūsiyya manuals still describe light and heavy cavalry comparable to those in early Byzantine military treatises.[129] This is equally apparent in the formations they suggest for cavalry and infantry; infantry preceding cavalry during an advance, infantry covering cavalry when on the defensive.[130] Yet Furūsiyya manuals, concerned as they were with specific military skills, are also firmly rooted in the reality of later medieval warfare, even obliging those involved in the "lance-game" to play in full armour while riding fully-armoured horses.[131]

Given that the best horse-archers of the area were tribal turcomans rather than professional soldiers, the emphasis given to lance-training in those works is not surprising. Ayalon, however, considers that this resulted from the ceremonial role such lance-exercises played at the end of the Annual Pilgrimage.[132] He also reports that such a preoccupation with manoeuvring the lance could, in a later century, lead to a neglect of horsemanship.[133] That aspect of lance-play which involved striking a target used a variety of the latter, both elevated and on the ground, those on the ground being similar to nineteenth century Indian Army "tent-pegging".[134] Other exercises such as the *birdjas* suggest a javelin thrown from the saddle, though this again is not clear.

Somewhat more straightforward are Furūsiyya references to the use of lances in real combat. Here it is interesting to compare two 14th century manuscripts from opposite ends of the Mediterranean: Al Anṣarī from the east and Ibn Hudhail from the west. Such sources can be surprising, as when Ibn Hudhail advises a horseman with a sword to keep a lancer on his unshielded right side, implying that the lancer would attempt to attack

PLATE III

Diagram showing the various ways in which the lance could be used
E1 and E2. Show the Couched Lance and details of the two methods of holding it
F. Shows the effective radius of the Couched styles E1 and E2

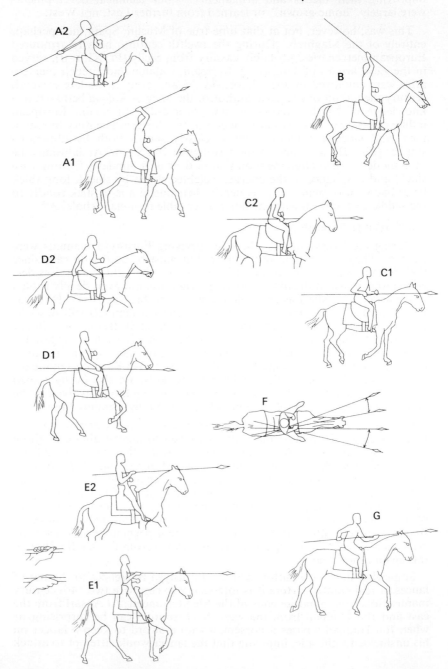

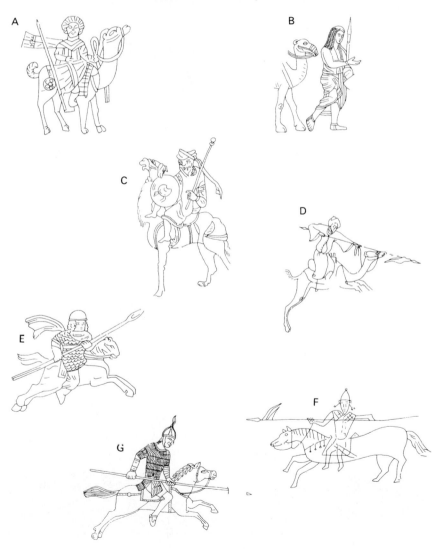

IV

PLATE IV

A. Frieze from Dura Europos, late 3rd century
Yale University Art Gallery, New Haven, Conn.

B. "Joseph sold to the desert traders", Throne of St. Maximianus
Byzantine ivory probably made in Egypt, *c.* 550, *Cathedral Museum, Ravenna*

C. Painted panel from Capella Palatina Ceiling, Palermo, Sicilian-Fāṭimid style, *c.* 1140

D. "Battle of the Rival Clans", from *Khamseh* of Nizāmī, Persian, 1442
British Library (MS. Add. 25900, f.121v)

E. Tombstone of Sarmatian *foedorati*, Roman, 5th century(?). *Provenance unknown*
(After a sketch by P. Nicolle, Esq.)

F. Graffito, Gothic, Sarmatian or proto-Bulgarian, 3rd-4th century
Provincial Archaeological Museum, Preslav, Bulgaria

G. "Isola Rizza Dish", Lombardic, late 6th or early 7th century
Castelvecchio Museum, Verona

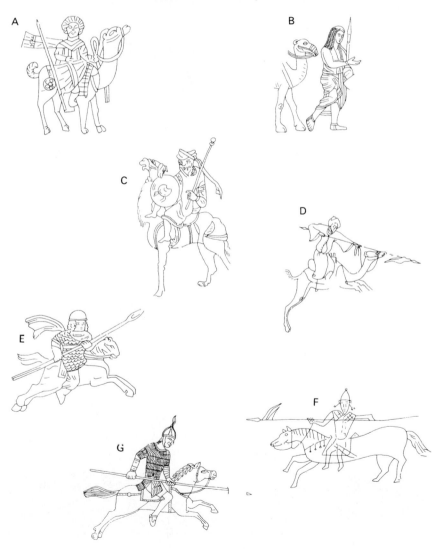

PLATE V

A. Frieze of St. George, Coptic, 8th century (?). *Coptic Museum, Cairo*

B. Fresco from Piandjikent, Turkestan, north and west walls of Reception Hall XXII/1, Soghdian, 7th-8th century. *Hermitage, Leningrad*

C. Fresco from Piandjikent, Turkestan, battle scene 3rd row Room VI/41, Soghdian, 7th-8th century. *Hermitage, Leningrad*

D. Painted papyrus, Egyptian, 10th century. *Bib. Nat., Vienna* (Rainer Coll. MS. 954)

E. Wooden panel from Fāṭimid Palace, Egyptian, 11th century. *Museum of Islamic Art, Cairo*

F. Painted paper from Fustāt, Egyptian, 11th-12th century. *Museum of Islamic Art, Cairo*

G and H. Painted panels from Capella Palatina Ceiling, Palermo
Sicilian-Fāṭimid style, c. 1140

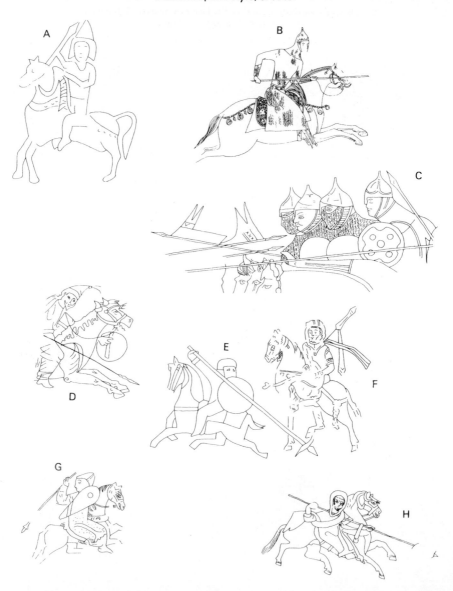

PLATE VI

- A. *"Beatus of Tavera"* (f. 126r.). Spanish, 975. *Cathedral Museum, Gerona*
- B. Fragment of painted plate from Madina al Zahra. Andalusian, 10th century
  Madina al Zahra Museum, Spain
- C. Ivory box made for 'Abd al Malik al Muzaffar, Andalusian, 1005
  Cathedral Treasury, Pamplona
- D. Ablution basin, Andalusian, early 11th century. *Archaeological Museum, Jativa*
- E. *Beatus*, Spanish, 11th-12th century. *Cathedral Museum, Gerona*
- F. *Beatus of Liebana*, Spanish, 12th century. *Pierpont Morgan Library, New York*
- G. *"Canto CXIII"*, *Cantigas of Alfonso X*, Spanish, late 13th century. Escorial Library, Spain
- H. Painted wooden panel, Spanish, *c.* 1300. *Palau del Marquès de Lliò, Barcelona*
- I. Two horsemen from *Skylitzes*, Byzantine, late 11th century
  Bib. Nac. Madrid (Cod. 5-3.N2)
- J. Followers of Job, *Studite Psalter*, Byzantine, 1066. *British Library* (MS. Add. 19352, f.74)

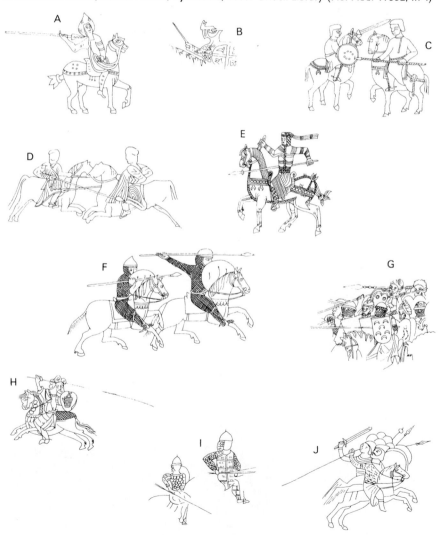

IV

PLATE VII

    A. Carving above West Door, Church of Nicorzminda, Georgia, U.S.S.R.
        Georgian, mid-11th century

        B. *De Bellis*, South Italian, 1028. *Library, Monte Cassino*

    C. "History of the Maccabees", *Atlantic Bible*, South French, 11th century
        Bib. Laurenziana, Florence (MS. Edili 126)

D. "Legend of King Arthur", Porta della Pescheria, Modena Cathedral, Lombard, 1099-1106

E. Carving over North Door, Church of San Nicola, Bari. South Italian, early 12th century

F. *Psalterium Aureum*, Carolingian, 841-872. *Library of the Chapter of St. Gall, Switzerland*

        G. Psalter, Carolingian, 9th century. *Bib. Munic., Amiens*

    H. Bible, North French, 11th century. *Bib. Munic., Arras* (MS. 559F.)

PLATE VIII

"Bayeaux Tapestry", Norman, *c.* 1077, *Bishop's Palace, Bayeaux*, showing **A**, lance-style A1; **B**, lance-style A2; **C**, lance-style B; **D**, lance-style D2; **E**, lance-style C1; **F**, lance-style C or E

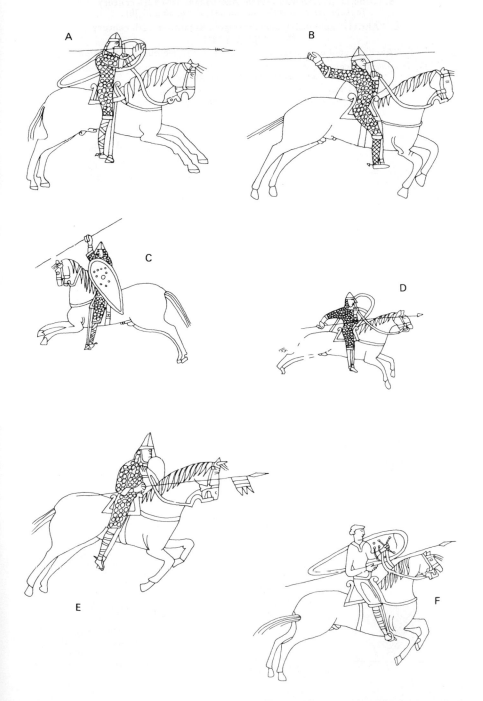

IV

PLATE IX

A. Seljūk Turks, *Skylitzes*, Byzantine, late 11th century
Bib. Nac. Madrid (Cod. 5-3.N2, f.234)

B, C and D. *Warka wa Gulshāh*, Azerbaijani, late 12th century
Topkapi, Istanbul (MS. Hazine 841, ff. 18, 35 and 38)

E. "Akritas" gold dish from Chernigov, Byzantine, 12th century
Hermitage, Leningrad

F. "Akritas" gold dish, Byzantine, 12th century. *Hermitage, Leningrad*

G. Fragment of ceramic dish, from Agora, Athens, Byzantine, 12th century
Archaeological Museum, Athens

H. "The Return of the Magi", *Four Gospels*, Armenian, 1262
Walters Art Gallery, Baltimore (MS.W.539, f.19r)

PLATE X

A. West Door, Church of San Zeno Maggiore, Verona. Lombard, c. 1139

B. "Defeat of the Danes", *Life of St. Edmund*, English, 1125-1150
Pierpont Morgan Library, New York (MS. 736)

C. *Libro de Privilegios*, Spanish, c. 1130
Archivo Catedralico de Santiago de Compostella, Spain ("Tumbo A")

D. Fresco, Templar Church, Cressac, French, 12th century

E. "Roland and Oliver", stained-glass window, Apse, Chartres Cathedral,
French, 12th century

F. "Army of Charlemagne", *Codex Calixtinus* (f.162v), French, 12th century
Archivo Catedralico de Santiago de Compostella, Spain

G. Catalan knight, painted wooden panel, Spanish, c. 1300
Palau del Marquès de Llió, Barcelona

H and I. Israelite warriors, *Maciejowski Bible* (ff.45v. and 12r), French, c. 1250
Pierpont Morgan Library, New York

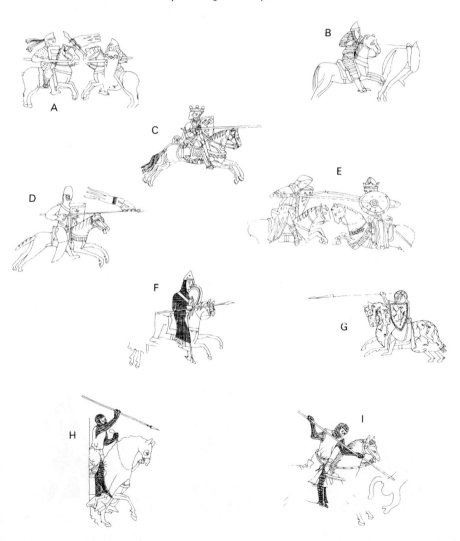

PLATE XI

A. Silver repousse dish, Khorasanian, 9th-10th century. *Hermitage, Leningrad*

B. *Warka wa Gulshāh*, Azerbaijani, late 12th century
Topkapi, Istanbul (MS. Hazine 841, f.3/6)

C. Battle scene on Minai-ware bowl, Persian, early 13th century
Freer Galle of Art, Washington (No. 43.3)

D. "Centurian a Crucifixion", *Gospels*, Syriac, 1216-20
British Library (MS. Add. 7170, f.151r)

E. Inlaid bronze bowl, Mamlūk, late 13th century
Victoria and Albert Museum (Acc. No. 740-1898)

F. "Arabs attacking Edessa", *Skylitzes*, Byzantine, late 11th century
Bib. Nac. Madrid (Cod. 5-3. N2, f.208)

G. "The Slaughter of the Priests and People of Nob", *Rome Casket*, carved ivory box,
Sicilian or South Italian, 12th century. *Palazzo di Venezia Museum, Rome*

H. Carved Capital, cloisters, Cathedral of Monreale, Palermo, Sicilian, 12th century

I. "St. Maurice", carved figure, German, late 13th century. *Cathedral Museum, Magdeburg*

PLATE XII

A. "Baptistry of St. Louis", Mamlūk inlaid bowl, c. 1300. *Louvre, Paris*

B. Inlaid brass tray, Mamlūk, late 13th century. *Museum of Islamic Art, Cairo*

C. Inlaid candlestick, Mamlūk, late 13th or early 14th century
Collection of Dr. Paolo Costa, London

D. Inlaid candlestick, Persian, 1225. *Museum of Fine Art, Boston* (No. 57.148)

E. Inlaid candlestick, Mamlūk, late 13th or early 14th century
Collection of Dr. Paolo Costa, London

F. "Henry VI's entry into Palermo", *Chronicle of Peter of Eboli*, Sicilian, c. 1197
Burgerbibliothek, Berne (MS. Cod. 120/II)

G. Carved capital, cloisters, Cathedral of Monreale, Palermo. Sicilian, 12th century

H. Painted panel from Capella Palatina Ceiling, Palermo. Sicilian-Fāṭimid style, c. 1140

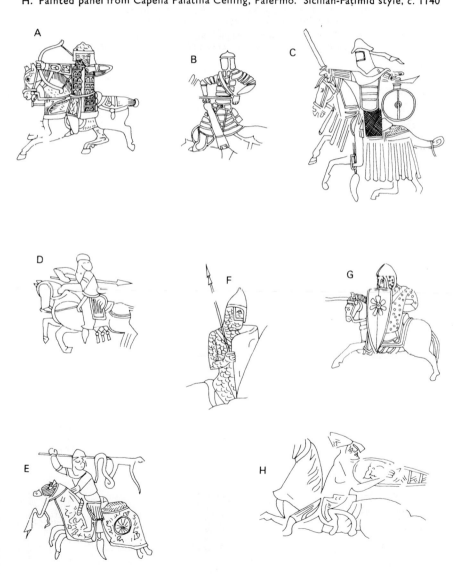

PLATE XIII

A. "Faragut slain by Roland", carved capital, Palace of the Dukes of Granada, Estella
Spanish, 12th century

B. "Canto XLVI", *Cantigas of Alfonso X*, Spanish, late 13th century
Escorial Library, Spain

C. "Canto XXVII, Bodyguard of Sultan", *Cantigas of Alfonso X*
Spanish, late 13th century. *Escorial Library*, Spain

D and E. *Nihāyat al Sul*, Mamlūk, 15th century. *British Library* (MS. Or. 3631)

F. *Kitāb Majmū' fī al Rumh wa Ghayrihi*, Mamlūk, 15th century
Revan Kosku Collection, Istanbul

G. *Ibn Akhī Khazām*, Mamlūk, 1470. *Bib. Nat. Paris* (MS. Arabe, 2824, f.69r)

H. Wall painting, Torre de las Damas, Alhambra, Granada. Andalusian, 14th century

I. Painted leather ceiling, Sala de los Reyes, Alhambra, Granada
Andalusian-Italian style, late 14th century

J. "Retablo de San Jorge", Valencian, c. 1420
Victoria and Albert Museum, London (Acc. No. 1217-1864)

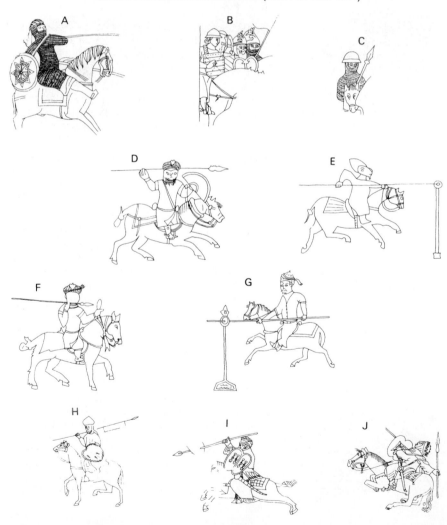

a swordsman from the shielded left.[135] The author also describes in detail how a lancer should protect himself by leaning into his shield to accept the weight of an enemy's thrust, holding his polished leather shield at an angle to provide a glancing surface and then pushing the enemy's weapon aside with this shield.[136] Wielding a shield in this fashion is very unlike typical European practice with heavy wooden shields, and is further emphasized by Ibn Hudhail's insistence on a shield that is not too heavy for the hand.[137] He also advises his reader to take the lightest possible lance "proportional to his size and strength". Lances, he said, were earlier of 10 cubits length but now it was permissible to use a shorter version, thick enough for the finger-tips to touch the palm of the hand when grasping it.[138] Clearly by Ibn Hudhail's time, in the later fourteenth century, the European fashion of heavy lances, rigid riding- and combat-techniques, had been abandoned in Andalusia.

Al Anṣarī's work also suggests that the heavy lance was of limited use in the Muslim east, not being used by lightly equipped "scouting parties" nor, apparently, by cavalry counter-attacking a foe who threatened their encampment. These latter troops used sword, mace or battle-axe.[139]

Among the few Furūsiyya manuals so far edited, that of Al Aqṣarā'ī seems to describe the various lance-play exercises in most detail. In such manuals Lance Styles B to G are all represented, sometimes also illustrated (Pl. XIII, D–G), and although Style A "like a javelin" is mentioned,[140] the weapon is not actually thrown.

Style B is rarely, though more explicitly, mentioned in connection with various riding-sequences.[141] Here the lance is held above the head, the rider looking from "beneath it" to strike his blow. He may also rest his lance horizontally on his shoulder, bracing the shaft against his cheek.[142]

To differentiate between Styles C and D in these manuscripts seems impossible, and both are probably indicated where the lancer holds the weapon in his "cupped" hand. A particular version of Styles C and D, possibly hinted at earlier by Usāma, is however analysed in detail. It instructs a rider to lean forward and thrust his lance from behind the protection of his horse's neck.[143]

Style E, the couched style, crops up as often as do Styles C and D, though only once is it categorized as a Rūmi fashion. This is, most interestingly, in a chapter entitled "The Syrian Attack", where various points are emphasized: the lance held to the rear of its point of balance, its being locked beneath the armpit, its blade kept left of the horse's head, the horse's head reined back, and the reins grasped firmly instead of relaxed as in most other Furūsiyya styles.[144] Elsewhere Al Aqṣarā'ī describes the couched lance being used more flexibly. This includes resting the shaft on the left forearm, sliding it forward through the hand so that it is no longer held at the point of balance, swinging it around behind the head or back to extract the blade from its target, even pulling it across one's chest in "Khurāsāni fashion" and then returning it to a couched position beneath the arm-pit.[145] These manoeuvers are far from current European couched lance styles. Ibn Hudhail similarly indicates that Maghrebi and Andalusian horsemen had abandoned the rigid European fashion, reversing their lances or even "making it like wings behind one's back" to extract a blade as one's horse moves past.[146] Europeans seemed to make no such provision for thus extracting their weapons.

The two-handed Style G is, as always in written or illustrated sources, the easiest to distinguish. It is still mentioned as often as the others in Al Aqṣarā'ī's work where it is usually characterized by one hand being "stretched forward".[147] Interestingly enough, to lift the lance in both hands is regarded as a "Bedouin" fashion.[148] Similarly to lie flat along the horse's neck and make one's attack in Style G with the lance close to the right-hand side of the horse's neck is a "mawallad" style suitable for horsemen bearing no shields. The choice of such terms as "Khurāsāni", "Bedouin" or "mawallad" for specific aspects of lance-technique may well indicate the origin, real or imagined, of such Muslim styles.

Later Lance Warfare

After the Franks' loss of their last hold in Syria in 1291, the military styles of Europe and the Muslim World went their divergent ways. This fact alone must show that the warriors of each camp were reacting to differing military imperatives. The increasingly heavy couched-lance cavalry of Europe met, or were thought to meet, the needs of medieval European warfare. By 1380–90, in fact, a lance-rest fixed to the one-piece breastplate first appeared in Europe on the monument of Walter von Hohenklinger in Zurich, and on a North Italian armour in the Trapp Armoury at Churburg, Alto Adige.[149] The lighter, more manoeuvrable and diversified cavalry of Islam certainly met Muslim military needs. Islam expanded on all fronts, except that of Andalusia, once the Mongols had been absorbed. To quote G. T. Scanlon:

> "The military supremacy of the Mamlūk and Ottoman societies was based on something more than mere numbers and hit-and-run tactics.... They maintained the tempo of success, initiated by Saladin, throughout the fourteenth and fifteenth centuries. It must have been based on superior patterns of logistics and armament and tactics, as their discipline canalized their zeal".[150]

It was not only ironic but surely significant that John VIII Palaeologus, last but one ruler of that Byzantine Empire which once so deeply influenced the military styles of Islam, was portrayed on the reverse side of Pisanallo's famous bronze medallion, dressed as a typical Islamic light-cavalry horse-archer.[151]

Similarly, it is worth noting that even in Spain, Christian horsemen were soon recorded as riding and fighting in the *jinete* Moorish light-cavalry style. The overarm lance, Style A, also reappears in Spanish art during the fourteenth and fifteenth centuries; for example on the Victoria and Albert Museum's superb "Retablo de San Jorge", Acc. No. 1217-1864).[152] When in the fourteenth century Ibn al Khaṭīb described recent changes in the arms and tactics of Granada, he might also have been describing a general trend throughout Iberia. "Long lances with double edges" and the heavy armour of earlier times had disappeared, to be replaced by "small cuirasses, light helmets, saddles of the Jinete type with short stirrups, leather shields and sharper (more pointed) lances"[153] (Pl. XIII, H–J). In later medieval illustrations of Muslim warriors, both Islamic such as the numerous and very fine illuminations from Iran, and European such as later versions of various Crusading Chronicles, lance Styles A1, A2, B and G overwhelmingly predominate, particularly the latter. In Northern Europe the couched style remains supreme in such works of art, but in the South a sprinkling of other styles appear.

All this suggests that Muslim warriors, far from falling over themselves to imitate supposedly more advanced European combat-styles, were generally influencing rather than being influenced. An answer as to why this was so might be found in the reality, rather than the romanticized myth, of cavalry warfare. This reality differed little from place to place or era to era. Equipment altered, as did tactics, but men and horses did not.

Combat with the Lance—the Reality

Only recently have historians used "psychological" techniques, developed during and after the Second World War, to probe the probable stresses faced by men and animals in pre-industrial warfare. Some historians are also now looking with a far more critical eye at certain episodes that reportedly occurred in medieval battles. J. D. P. Keegan, the military historian, recently asked many very pertinent questions.[154] For example, what is "cavalry shock", were infantry more afraid of horses or of the men on them, did cavalry fear archers more or less than they feared other cavalry, what happened when "charging" cavalry met disciplined infantry in ranks and at what speed did they come into contact? What effect did this impact have on any second rank of cavalry or on further ranks of infantry, what happened when two forces of cavalry on the move met head-on and how closely packed were such units when they collided, and how in fact did cavalry "pass through" other cavalry or indeed "ride down" infantry?

In discussing these issues, Keegan makes the vital point that, "we have to make a judgement about the difference between what happens in a battle and what happens in a violent accident".[155] Unfortunately medieval illustrations of battle often portray what looks like the split-second prior to a violent accident, rather than realistic combat. This is often true even where European knights are shown jousting with couched lances. In a real "joust" the horses pass by one another, after which they, with or without their riders, continue until they either stop or are stopped. Such a state of affairs could only be duplicated in battle if the two forces of cavalry were in single ranks, reasonably open order, and having agreed on the identity of their personal opponents beforehand—a most unlikely occurrence, even though it would have suited the ideal of chivalric warfare perfectly!

Although the European knight fought with both sword and lance, the latter weapon could prove a decisive one if such heavy cavalry were used both at the correct moment and in suitable terrain. Crusader heavy cavalry, if they caught their foes dismounted and in disarray, or in the flank or better still in the back, almost invariably drove their enemy before them. This is clear in all chronicles from whichever side they were written. Yet it seems equally clear that if the Muslims could dodge aside, outpace the heavy Franks, wind their horses, or even engage them in a disorganized static *mêlée*, then the Europeans enjoyed little or no advantage. As a lancer, rather than a swordsman, the Crusader cavalryman was indeed a powerful, but singularly inflexible, battlefield weapon, and this alone would account for the Muslim's relative lack of interest in copying Frankish styles in this field. Rather than seek to meet the Frank on his own highly limited terms, the Muslim made use of his own sophisticated tactical traditions to deny a Frankish lancer that tactical situation that he needed to make proper use of his solitary advantage.

Even developments inside Europe itself seem to support this view of the couched lance as something of a tactical dead-end. When faced with disciplined, or at least desperate, missile-armed infantry in close order, particularly those behind a simple series of sharpened stakes, the chivalry of France were halted again and again by the archers of England. The Burgundians later met a similar fate at the hands of Swiss pikemen. In all such instances the heavily armoured and inflexible cavalry were either unable to reach their foes, or had lost that momentum essential to the couched-lance technique by the time they did reach their objectives. Almost all military historians, from Oman to Keegan, agree on this interpretation of the downfall of the European knight in the 14th and 15th centuries. Only where such cavalry came upon disorganized infantry in open country, or lighter cavalry dispersed and for some reason unable to escape, did heavily armoured knights normally seem able to use their couched lances to full effect. Such circumstances were, of course, more akin to massacre than to combat, since other factors, perhaps other weapons in the hands of other troops, or simply tactical circumstances, had already reduced their foes to such a vulnerable condition.

The above critique of one of medieval Europe's most characteristic military institutions may be considered exaggerated, but it does seem to the author highly probable that one reason for the success of Muslim armies against European couched-lance cavalry, both in Syria and later in the Balkans, stemmed from their refusal to be thus reduced to vulnerability. It may also, in part, derive from the Muslims cavalryman's unwillingness to be lured down the tactical dead-end that was soon to render European cavalry almost incapable of fighting anybody except European cavalry.

BIBLIOGRAPHY

Primary Sources

ᶜUmar ibn Ibrāhīm al Awsī al Anṣarī, "Tafrij al Kurūb fī Tadbīr al Ḥurūb", trans. G. T. Scanlon, *A Muslim Manual of War*, Cairo, 1961.

Anon., "Gesta Francorum", trans. R. Hill, *The Deeds of the Franks and other Pilgrims to Jerusalem*, London, 1962.

Anon., "Itinerarium Peregrinorum", trans. and edit. K. Fenwick, *The Third Crusade*, London, 1958.

Anon., *The Song of Roland*, trans. D. L. Sayers, London, 1957.

Muḥammad ibn ᶜĪsā al Ḥanafi al Aqṣarā'ī, "Nihāyat al Su'l wa'l Umnīya fī Taᶜlim Aᶜmāl al Furūsiyya", edit. A. S. M. Lutful-Huq, *A Critical Edition of Nihayat al Sul*, Unpub. Ph.D. thesis, Univ. of London, 1956.

ᶜIzz al Dīn Ibn al Athīr, "Kāmil al Tawarīkh", trans. F. Gabrieli, in *Arab Historians of the Crusades*, London, 1969.

Ayyūqī, trans. A. S. Melikian-Chirvani, "Le Roman de Varqe et Golšāh", *Arts Asiatiques*, Vol. XXII, Paris, 1970.

Bahā' al Dīn Ibn Shaddād, "Al Nawādir al Sulṭānīyya wa'l Maḥāsin al Yūsufīyya", *Recueil des Historiens des Croisades. Hist. Orient.* Vol. III, Paris, 1884.
Bahā' al Dīn Ibn Shaddād, trans. C. W. Wilson, "What Befell Sultan Yusuf", *Palestine Pilgrims' Text Society*, Vol. XIII, London, 1897.
Ibn Hawqal, edit. J. H. Kramers, *Bibliotheca Geographorum Arabicorum*, Vol. II (2nd edition), Leyden, 1938.
Ibn Hawqal, trans. A. A. Vasiliev in *Byzance et les Arabes*, Vol. II, part 2, Brussels, 1950.
ʿAlī ibn ʿAbd al Raḥmān Ibn Hudhail, "Ḥilyat al Fursān wa Shiʿār al Shudjʿān", trans. L. Mercier, *La Parure des Cavaliers et l'Insigne des Preux*, Paris, 1922.
Jamāl al Dīn Ibn Wāṣil, "Mufarrij al Kurūb fī akhbār Bani Ayyūb", trans. F. Gabrieli, in *Arab Historians of the Crusades*, London, 1969.
ʿImād al Dīn al Iṣfahānī, "Al Fath al Qussī fi'l Fatḥ al Qudsī", trans. F. Gabrieli, in *Arab Historians of the Crusades*, London, 1969.
Ibn Ishāq, *The Life of Muhammad, Apostle of God*, trans. E. Rehatsek, edit. M. Edwardes, London, 1964.
ʿAmr ibn Baḥr abū ʿUthmān al Jāḥiẓ, *Fadā'il al Atrāk*, edit. ʿAbd al Salām Muḥammad Hārūn, Cairo and Baghdad, 1965.
ʿAmr ibn Bahr abu ʿUthman al Jahiz, trans. C. T. Harley Walker, "Jahiz of Basra to Al Fath ibn Khaqan on the Exploits of the Turks and of the Army of the Khalifate in General", *Journal of the Royal Asiatic Society*, London, 1915.
Leo VI, *Tactica*, trans. J. de Maizeroi, Paris, 1771.
Al Mutanabbī, "Al Mutanabbī, Recueil Publié à l'Occasion de son Millenaire", *Memoires de l'Institut Francais de Damas*, Beirut, 1936.
Al Mutannabbī, trans. A. A. Vasiliev, in *Byzance et les Arabes*, Vol. II, part 2, Brussels, 1950.
Abū Yaʿla Ḥamza Ibn al Qalānisī, "Dhail taʿrīkh Dimashq", trans. F. Gabrieli, in *Arab Historians of the Crusades*, London, 1969.
Muḥassin ibn ʿAlī al Tanūkhi, trans. D. S. Margoliouth, *The Table-Talk of a Mesopotamian Judge*, London, 1922.
Murḍā ibn ʿAlī ibn Murḍā al Tarṣūṣī, trans. A. Boudot-Lamotte, *Contribution à l'Etude de l'Archerie Musulmane*, Damascus, 1968.
Murḍā ibn ʿAlī ibn Murḍā al Tarṣūṣī, edit. and trans. C. Cahen, "Un Traité d'Armurerie Composé pour Saladin", *Bulletin d'études orientales de l'Institut Francais de Damas*, Vol. XII, Damascus, 1948.
Usama ibn Munqidh, *Kitab al I'tibar*, edit. H. Derenbourg, Paris, 1886.
Usama ibn Munqidh, "Kitab al Iʿtibar", trans. P. H. Hitti, *Memoires of an Arab-Syrian Gentleman*, Beirut, 1964.
William of Tyre, "Historia Rerum in Partibus Transmarinis Gestarum", *Recueil des Historiens des Croisades*, Vol. I, Historiens Occidental, Paris, 1844.

Secondary Sources

D. Ayalon, "Notes on the Furūsiyya Exercises and Games in the Mamlūk Sultanate", *Scripta Hierosolymitana*, Vol. IX, Jerusalem, 1961.
Bashir Ibrahim Bashir, *The Fāṭimid Caliphate, 386/996–487/1094*, unpub. Ph.D. thesis, Univ. of London, 1970.
A. D. H. Bivar, "Cavalry Equipment and Tactics on the Euphrates Frontier", *Dumbarton Oaks Papers*, No. 26, Washington, 1972.
C. Blair, *European Armour*, London, 1958.
M. Brett, "The Military Interest of the Battle of Ḥaydarān", *War, Technology and Society in the Middle East*, edit. V. J. Parry and M. E. Yapp, London, 1975.
F. Buttin, "La Lance et l'Arrêt de Cuirasse", *Archaeologia*, Vol. XCIX, London, 1965.
M. Canard, "La Procession du Nouval An chex les Fāṭimides", *Annales de l'Institut des Etudes Orientales*, Vol. X, Paris, 1952.
M. Canard, "L'Expansion Arabe: le Problème Militaire" (Settimane di Studio del Centro Italiano di Studi sull' Altro Medioevo XII, Spoleto, 1965), in M. Canard, *L'Expansion Arabo-Islamique et ses Répercussions*, London, 1974.
R. H. C. Davis, *The Normans and their Myth*, London, 1976.
S. Digby, *War-Horse and Elephant in the Delhi Sultanate, a Study of Military Supplies*, Oxford, 1971.

H. W. Glidden, "A Note on Early Arabian Military Organization", *Journal of the American Oriental Society*, Vol. LVI, New Haven, Conn., 1936.

M. V. Gorelick, "Oriental Armour of the Near and Middle East from the eighth to the fifteenth centuries as shown in works of art", *Islamic Arms and Armour*, edit. R. Elgood, London, 1979.

J. F. Haldon, *Aspects of Byzantine Military Administration: the Elite Corps, the Opsikion, and the Imperial Tagmata from the Sixth to the Ninth Century*, unpub. Ph.D. thesis, Univ. of Birmingham, 1975.

J. F. Haldon, "Some Aspects of Byzantine Military Technology from the Sixth to the Tenth Centuries", *Byzantine and Modern Greek Studies*, Vol. I, Oxford, 1975.

D. R. Hill, "The Role of the Camel and the Horse in the Early Arab Conquests", *War, Technology and Society in the Middle East*, edit. V. J. Parry and M. E. Yapp, London, 1975.

A. B. de Hoffmeyer, *Arms and Armour in Spain—a Short Survey*, Vol. I, Madrid, 1972.

J. D. Howard-Johnston, *Studies in the Organization of the Byzantine Army in the Tenth and Eleventh Centuries*, unpub. Ph.D. thesis, Univ. of Oxford, 1971.

J. D. P. Keegan, *The Face of Battle*, London, 1976.

H. Lammens, "Les Aḥābīs et l'Organization Militaire de la Mecque au Siècle de l'Hégire", *Journal Asiatique* (11th series), Vol. VIII, Paris, 1916.

E. Lèvi-Provençal, *Histoire de l'Espagne Musulmane*, Paris, 1950–67.

E. Lèvi-Provençal, *L'Espagne Musulmane au Xème Siècle*, Paris, 1932.

R. Levy, *The Social Structure of Islam*, Cambridge, 1957.

H. E. Mayer, *The Crusades*, Oxford, 1972.

L. A. Mayer, *Mamlūk Costume*, Geneva, 1956.

J. Prawer, *The Crusaders' Kingdom*, New York, 1972.

E. M. Quatremère, *Mémoires Géographiques et Historiques sur l'Egypte*, Paris, 1811.

H. Rabie, "The Training of the Mamlūk Fāris", *War, Technology and Society in the Middle East*, edit. V. J. Parry and M. E. Yapp, London, 1975.

D. J. A. Ross, "L'Originalité de 'Turoldus': le Maniement de la Lance", *Cahiers de Civilization Medievale*, Vol. VI, Poitiers, 1963.

S. Runciman, *A History of the Crusades*, London, 1971.

H. Russell Robinson, *Oriental Armour*, London, 1967.

M. A. Shaban, *Islamic History, AD600–750, a New Interpretation*, Cambridge, 1971.

R. C. Smail, *Crusading Warfare, 1097–1193*, Cambridge, 1956.

E. Sordo, *Moorish Spain*, London, 1963.

B. Thordeman, *Armour from the Battle of Wisby, 1361*, Uppsala, 1939.

S. Vryonis, Jr., "Byzantine and Turkish Societies and their Sources of Manpower", *War, Technology and Society in the Middle East*, edit. V. J. Parry and M. E. Yapp, London, 1975.

L. White, Jr., "The Crusades and the Technological Thrust of the West", *War, Technology and Society in the Middle East*, edit. V. J. Parry and M. E. Yapp, London, 1975.

NOTES

1. Lynn White, Jr., "The Crusades and the Technological Thrust of the West", *War, Technology and Society in the Middle East*, edit. V. J. Parry and M. E. Yapp, London, 1975. p. 98. (This anthology cited hereafter as *WTS*.)

2. H. Lammens, "Les Aḥābīs et l'Organization Militaire de la Mecque au Siècle de l'Hégire", *Journal Asiatiques* (11th series), Vol. VIII, 1916, pp. 443 and 475.

3. Ibn Ishāq, *The Life of Muhammad, Apostle of God*, trans. E. Rehatsek, edit. M. Edwardes, London, 1964, p. 108.

4. Beshir Ibrahim Beshir, *The Fatimid Caliphate, 386/996–487/1094*, unpub. Ph.D. thesis, Univ. of London, 1970, pp. 67–70.

5. See, for example, F. Lot, *L'Art Militaire et les Armeés au Moyén Age*, Paris, 1946, pp. 58–61.

6. Helmet, shield, lance, sword, bow, arrows, coat of mail and coif of mail. See M. Canard, "L'Expansion Arabe: le Problème Militaire" (Settimane di studio del Centro Italiano di studi sull'alto medioevo XII, Spoleto 1965), in M. Canard, *L'Expansion Arabo-Islamique et ses Répercussions*, London, 1975, pp. 46–7.

7. A. D. H. Bivar, "Cavalry Equipment and Tactics on the Euphrates Frontier", *Dumbarton Oaks Paper*, No. 26, Washington, 1972, and J. F. Haldon, "Some Aspects of Byzantine Military Technology from the Sixth to Tenth Centuries", Byzantine and Modern Greek Studies, Vol. I, Oxford, 1975. (The latter work cited hereafter as *BMGS*.)

8. *BMGS*, p. 12.

9. *Ibid.*

10. D. J. A. Ross, "L'Originalité de 'Turoldus': le maniement de la Lance", *Cahiers de Civilization Medievale*, Vol. VI, 1963, p. 129.

11. *BMGS*, p. 21.

12. J. F. Haldon, *Aspects of Byzantine Military Administration: the Elite Corps, the Opsikion, and the Imperial Tagmata from the 6th to the 9th century*, unpub. Ph.D. thesis, Univ. of Birmingham, 1975, p. 11, n. 19.

13. Bivar, *op. cit.*, pp. 288–90.

14. Lynn White, Jr., *loc. cit.*

15. *BMGS*, p. 22, n. 57.

16. Bivar, *op. cit.*, pp. 274–5.

17. Bivar, *op. cit.*, pp. 284–5.

18. D. R. Hill, "The Role of the Camel and the Horse in the Early Arab Conquests", *WTS*, p. 37.

19. H. W. Gliddon, "A Note on Early Arabian Military Organization", *Journal of the American Oriental Society*, Vol. LVI, 1936, pp. 88–91.

20. Al Tarṣūṣī, trans. C. Cahen, "Un Traité d'Armurerie Composé pour Saladin", *Bulletin d'Etudes Orientales de l'Institut Francais de Damas*, Vol. XII, 1947–8, pp. 103–63.

21. See *Battle of Zab*, Vol. III, p. 40, reproduced in *Annales quos scriptit Abu Djafar Mohammed ibn Djarir at-Tabari cum aliis edit M. J. de Goeje*, Lugduni Batevorum, 1879–1901.

22. Al Jāhiz, "Fadā'il al Atrāk", trans. C. T. Harley Walker, "Jāhiz of Baṣra to Al Fath ibn Khāqān on the Exploits of the Turks and the Army of the Khalifate in General", *Journal of the Royal Asiatic Society*, October 1915, p. 646.

23. Al Jāhiz, *op. cit.*, p. 666.

24. Al Jāhiz, *op. cit.*, p. 671.

25. Ibn Ḥawqal, edit. J. H. Kramers, *Bibliotheca Geographorum Arabicorum*, Vol. II (2nd edition), Leyden, 1938, pp. 211–12.

26. Al Tanūkhī, trans. D. S. Margoliouth, *The Table-Talk of a Mesopotamian Judge*, London, 1922, p. 58.

27. Al Mutanabbī, "Al Mutanabbī, Recueil Publié à l'Occasion de son Millenaire", *Memoires de l'Institut Francais de Damas*, Beirut, 1936, pp. 106–11.

28. S. Digby, *War-Horse and Elephant in the Delhi Sultanate, a Study of Military Supplies*, Oxford, 1971, pp. 15–6.

29. Anon., "Gesta Francorum", trans. R. Hill, *The Deeds of the Franks and other Pilgrims to Jerusalem*, London, 1962.

30. Beshir Ibraham Beshir, *The Fatimid Caliphate, 386/966–487/1094*, unpub. Ph.D. thesis, Univ. of London, 1970.

31. M. Brett, "The Military Interest of the Battle of Haydaran", *WTS*, p. 88.

32. Beshir, *op. cit.*, pp. 76–9.

33. E. M. Quatremère, *Memoires Géographiques et Historique sur l'Egypte*, Vol. II, Paris, 1811, p. 378.

34. Beshir, *op. cit.*, pp. 69–71.

35. Beshir, *op. cit.*, pp. 51–2.

36. E. Lévi-Provençal, *Histoire de l'Espagne Musulmane*, Vol. III, Paris, 1967, p. 100.

37. E. Lévi-Provençal, *L'Espagne Musulmane au Xème Siècle*, Paris, 1932, pp. 144–6.

38. Haldon, *Aspects of Byzantine Military Administration*, pp. 153 and 181.

39. J. D. Howard-Johnston, *Studies in the Organization of the Byzantine Army in the 10th and 11th centuries*, unpub. Ph.D. thesis, Univ. of Oxford, 1971, pp. 228–9.

40. *BMGS*, pp. 25–7.

41. Howard-Johnston, *op. cit.*, p. 288.

42. Howard-Johnston, *op. cit.*, pp. 282–3.
43. Howard-Johnston, *op. cit.*, pp. 289–90, and *BMGS*, pp. 32–3.
44. Howard-Johnston, *loc. cit.*
45. Howard-Johnston, *op. cit.*, p. 286.
46. *BMGS*, p. 36, n. 125.
47. *BMGS*, pp. 18, 21 and 33–4.
48. Howard-Johnston, *op. cit.*, pp. 275 and 293–4.
49. Howard-Johnston, *op. cit.*, p. 224.
50. Lynn White, Jr., *op. cit.*, pp. 99–100, and A. B. de Hoffmeyer, "Military Equipment in the Byzantine Manuscript of Skylitzes in the Biblioteca Nacional in Madrid", *Gladius*, Vol. X, 1966, pp. 84–5.
51. See, for example, Ada Bruhn de Hoffmeyer, *Arms and Armour in Spain*, Vol. I, Madrid, 1972, pp. 115–43.
52. Ross, *op. cit.*, p. 136.
53. Francois Buttin, "La Lance et l'Arrêt de Cuirasse", *Archaeologia*, Vol. XCIX, 1965, p. 80.
54. Ross, *op. cit.*, pp. 136–7.
55. S. Runciman, *A History of the Crusades*, Vol. I, London, 1971, pp. 62–3 and 185–6.
56. Ayyūqī, trans. A. S. Melikian-Chirvani, "Le Roman de Varqe et Golšāh", *Arts Asiatiques*, Vol. XXII, 1970, p. 6.
57. Ayyūqī, *op. cit.*, verses 365 and 407.
58. Ayyūqī, *op. cit.*, verse 440.
59. Ayyūqī, *op. cit.*, verses 446 and 522.
60. Ayyūqī, *op. cit.*, verses 540–1 and 543–4.
61. Ayyūqī, *op. cit.*, verse 447.
62. Ayyūqī, *op. cit.*, verse 1153.
63. Anon., *The Deeds of the Franks* (See note 26 above).
64. Ibn al Athīr, trans. F. Gabrieli, in *Arab Historians of the Crusades*, London, 1969, p. 55.
65. See, for example, C. Cahen, "La Campagne de Mantzikert d'après les sources Mussulmanes", *Byzantion*, Vol. IX, 1934, pp. 613–42, and J. Laurent, *Byzance et les Turks Seldjoucides jusqu'en 1081*, Nancy, 1913, p. 43 and n. 10.
66. Howard-Johnston, *op. cit.*, p. 236.
67. Lynn White, Jr., *op. cit.*, p. 100.
68. *BMGS*, pp. 40–1.
69. S. Vryonis, Jr., "Byzantine and Turkish Societies and Their Sources of Manpower", *WTS*, pp. 133–4 and 141.
70. Lynn White, Jr., *op. cit.*, p. 98.
71. Ross, *op. cit.*, p. 130.
72. R. C. Smail, *Crusading Warfare, 1097–1193*, Cambridge, 1956, p. 210.
73. Ibn al Qalānisi, trans. F. Gabrieli, *op. cit.*, p. 58.
74. Anon., "Itinerarium Peregrinorum", trans. K. Fenwick, *The Third Crusade*, London, 1958, p. 26.
75. *Ibid.*, p. 92.
76. Usāma ibn Munqidh, "Kitāb al Iᶜtibār", trans. P. H. Hitti, *Memoires of an Arab-Syrian Gentleman*, Beirut, 1964, pp. 96–7.
77. Usāma, *op. cit.*, pp. 125–6.
78. Usāma, *op. cit.*, p. 151.
79. Smail, *op. cit.*, p. 189.
80. Anon., *The Third Crusade*, pp. 131–2 (see note 66 above).
81. Usāma, *op. cit.*, p. 87.
82. Ross, *op. cit.*, p. 131.
83. Bahā' al Dīn, "Al Nawadir al Sultaniyya", trans. C. W. Wilson, in *Palestine Pilgrims' Text Society*, Vol. XIII, London, 1897, p. 338.
84. Usāma, *op. cit.*, p. 88.

85. Smail, *op. cit.*, pp. 111–12.
86. Usāma, *op. cit.*, p. 68.
87. Buttin, *op. cit.*, p. 90.
88. Buttin, *op. cit.*, p. 79.
89. Buttin, *op. cit.*, p. 80.
90. Usāma, *op. cit.*, p. 76.
91. B. Thordeman, *Armour from the Battle of Wisby, 1361*, Uppsala, 1939, pp. 288 and 292.
92. Claude Blair, *European Armour*, London, 1958, p. 38.
93. *BMGS*, p. 27.
94. See D. Nicolle, *Early Medieval Islamic Arms and Armour*, Madrid, 1976, pp. 66–70, and Blair, *op. cit.*, p. 33.
95. Usāma, *op. cit.*, p. 25.
96. Anon., *The Third Crusade*, pp. 22, 131–2 and 151.
97. Ibn al Qalānisi, trans. F. Gabrieli, *op. cit.*, p. 58.
98. Usāma, *op. cit.*, p. 79.
99. Usāma, *op. cit.*, p. 86.
100. Bahā' al Dīn, *op. cit.*, pp. 229–31.
101. Anon., *The Third Crusade*, pp. 131–2 (see note 66 above), and Bahā' al Dīn, *op. cit.*, p. 342.
102. Bahā' al Dīn, *op. cit.*, p. 161.
103. William of Tyre, "Historia Rerum in Partibus Transmarinis Gestarum", *Recueil des Historiens des Croisades*, Vol. I, Paris, 1844, p. 925.
104. Anon., *The Third Crusade*, p. 93 (see note 66 above).
105. Usāma, *op. cit.*, p. 66.
      Al Aqsarā'ī, "Nihāyat al Su'l wa'l Umnīya fī Taꜥlim Aꜥmāl al Furūsiyya", edit. A. S. M. Lutful-huq, *A Critical Edition of Nihayat al Sul*, unpub. Ph.D. thesis, Univ. of London, 1956, p. 196.
106. Bahā' al Dīn, *op. cit.*, pp. 133 and 313.
107. Bahā' al Dīn, *op. cit.*, p. 160 and Jamāl al Dīn Ibn Wasil, "Muffarrij al Kurūb fī akhbār Bani Ayyūb", trans. F. Gabrieli, in *Arab Historians of the Crusades*, London, 1969, pp. 290–1.
108. Usāma, *op. cit.*, p. 131.
109. Bahā' al Dīn, *op. cit.*, pp. 284–5.
110. Anon., *The Third Crusade*, p. 84 (see note 66 above).
111. L. A. Mayer, *Mamluk Costume*, Geneva, 1956, p. 46.
112. Usāma, *op. cit.*, p. 114.
113. Usāma, *op. cit.*, p. 78.
114. Usāma, *op. cit.*, pp. 68–70.
115. Usāma, *op. cit.*, p. 132.
116. Usāma, *op. cit.*, pp. 90 and 151.
117. Usāma, *op. cit.*, pp. 87 and 90.
118. Usāma, *op. cit.*, p. 92.
119. Al Tarsūsī, trans. A. Boudot-Lamotte, *Contribution à l'Etude de l'Archerie Musulmane*, Damascus, 1968, p. 144.
120. *Ibid.*, and Smail, *op. cit.*, p. 82, n. 4.
121. Mayer, *op. cit.*, pp. 37–8.
122. M. V. Gorelick, "Oriental Armour of the Near and Middle East as shown in works of art", *Islamic Arms and Armour*, edit. R. Elgood, London, 1979, pp. 36–40.
123. Lynn White, Jr., *op. cit.*, pp. 100–1.
124. Al Ansārī, "Tafrīj al Kurūb fī Tadbīr al Hurūb", trans. G. T. Scanlon, *A Muslim Manual of War*, Cairo, 1961, pp. 4–5.
125. Brett, *op. cit.*, pp. 82–3.
126. Lévi-Provençal, *Histoire d'Espagna*, p. 74.
127. Anon., *The Song of Roland*, trans. D. L. Sayers, London, 1957, p. 9.
128. Lévi-Provençal, *L'Espagne Musulmane*, p. 146.

129. Bivar, *op. cit.*, p. 290.
130. Al Anṣarī, *op. cit.*, pp. 105 and 107.
131. D. Ayalon, "Notes on the Furūsiyya Exercises and Games in the Mamlūk Sultanate", *Scripta Hierosolymitana*, Vol. IX, Jerusalem, 1961, p. 48.
132. Ayalon, *op. cit.*, pp. 47–8.
133. Ayalon, *op. cit.*, p. 53.
134. H. Rabie, "The Training of the Mamlūk Fāris", *WTS*, p. 156.
135. Ibn Hudhail, "Ḥilyat al Fursān", trans. L. Mercier, *La Parure des Cavaliers et l'Insigne des Preux*, Paris, 1922, pp. 238–9.
136. Ibn Hudhail, *op. cit.*, pp. 269–71.
137. *Ibid.*
138. Ibn Hudhail, *op. cit.*, pp. 246–50.
139. Al Anṣarī, *op. cit.*, pp. 80 and 108.
140. Al Aqṣarā'ī, *op. cit.*, p. 191.
141. Al Aqṣarā'ī, *op. cit.*, pp. 182 and 184.
142. Al Aqṣarā'ī, *op. cit.*, p. 185.
143. Al Aqṣarā'ī, *op. cit.*, p. 196.
144. Al Aqṣarā'ī, *op. cit.*, p. 197.
145. Al Aqṣarā'ī, *op. cit.*, pp. 192–3.
146. Ibn Hudhail, *op. cit.*, pp. 246–50.
147. Al Aqṣarā'ī, *op. cit.*, p. 186.
148. Al Aqṣarā'ī, *op. cit.*, p. 187.
149. Vesey Norman, *Arms and Armour*, London, 1964, figs. 32 and 50.
150. Al Anṣarī, *op. cit.*, p. 21.
151. G. A. dell'Acqua, *L'Opera Completa dell'Pisanello*, Milan, 1972, p. 39.
152. C. M. Kauffman, "The Altar-piece of St. George from Valencia", *Victoria and Albert Museum Yearbook 2*, London, 1970, figs. 3–4.
153. E. Sordo, *Moorish Spain*, London, 1963, p. 136.
154. J. D. P. Keegan, *The Face of Battle*, London, 1976, pp. 87, 94–6, 154–8 and 153–5.
155. *Ibid.*, pp. 94–5.

V

ARMES ET ARMURES DANS LES ÉPOPÉES DES CROISADES

I. Terminologie

Les épopées des croisades contiennent de nombreux termes concernant les armes et les armures. Elles incluent d'une part presque tous les termes auxquels on peut s'attendre dans les sources françaises de la fin du 12e siècle, d'autre part certains mots rares ou qui paraissent inconnus. Pour commencer, j'aimerais énumérer les termes que l'on trouve le plus fréquemment dans les épopées des croisades. Ce sont, quant à l'épée et à ses différentes parties: *espee*[1] pour l'arme entière, *branc*[2], peut-être *alemiele*[3] et *glavie*[4] pour la lame, et *poins*[5] pour la poignée. *Segnal*[6] pourrait se référer aux quillons. De telles épées étaient invariablement suspendues à la *ceinture*[7]. Les termes pour les poignards sont plus discutables et pourraient inclure *mesericorde*[8], *coutiaus*[9] et *cotel*[10]. Le poignard *mesericorde* est cependant normalement considéré comme une arme de la fin du 13e siècle et du 14e.

Les haches et les massues sont assez fréquentes dans les épopées. Parfois le *haces*[11] est indiqué comme étant de forme «Danoise» ce qui pourrait signifier une arme d'infanterie utilisable avec les deux mains, alors qu'ailleurs le *haces* est clairement décrit comme étant maniable à deux mains. La *guisarme*[12] est maintenant largement considérée comme une hache d'infanterie à long manche; elle est présente dans les épopées. La *mace*[13] est indiquée une fois comme étant en fer, alors qu'à la fin du 12e siècle les têtes de telles armes auraient dû être en un métal plus ordinaire. Le *martel*[14] est aussi évoqué une fois et il est clairement désigné comme une arme. Ce mot pourrait se référer à une massue islamique à tête de marteau non-symétrique, le *gurz*, attendu que ce terme a été utilisé par la mère de Corboran.

1 Abbréviations: (pour les indications bibliographiques voir, dans l'*Appendice* de ces *Actes*, Table I).
   A   *La Chanson d'Antioche* (éd. S. Duparc-Quioc)
   A (P) *La Chanson d'Antioche* (éd. P. Paris)
   B   *La Naissance du Chevalier au Cygne,* version *Béatrix*
   Ch   *Les Chétifs*
   Cig   *Le Chevalier au Cygne*
   E   *La Naissance du Chevalier au Cygne,* version *Elioxe*
   B – 1068, 1333, 2182, 2245; Ch – 199, 651, 654, 762, 789, 817, 982, 1019, 1049, 1110, 1262, 1311, 1851, 2011, 3896, 3980; Cig – 2387; E – 1151.
2 B – 1533; Ch – 188, 762, 1052, 1157, 3896.
3 B – 1333.
4 E – 1027, 1037.
5 Ch – 651, 1050, 1262; Cig – 2378.
6 Ch – 1049.
7 B – 2182; Ch – 762, 789 et *passim*.
8 Ch – 790, 819, 1114.
9 B – 1393.
10 Ch – 200, 419, 424, 791, 1240, 1318.
11 B – 2094; Ch – App. VI 24, 82, 99, App. XII 128; E – 857.
12 Ch – App. VI 26; E – 857.
13 Ch – 816, 1464, App. XII 128.
14 Ch – 440.

Les termes qui se réfèrent aux armes à bâton sont nombreux et variés. Ils concernent la *lance*[15] et l'*espiel*[16] pour l'arme entière, *pic*[17] et *piaus*[18] pour un autre type de lance et de pique, *agie*[19], *museral*[20], *dart*[21] et *gavrelos*[22] pour diverses javelines. Le *faussar*[23] pourrait être une sorte d'arme d'infanterie à poignée courte, à longue lame et à un seul tranchant qui est devenu peut-être le postérieur *falchion*, alors que ce dernier était sans aucun doute un type spécialisé d'épée plutôt qu'une arme à bâton. La *glave*[24] se réfère à une lame, *baston*[25] et *anste*[26] à la poignée d'une arme, *pignons*[27] aux lame ou empennage d'une javeline légère, et *vanière*[28], *gonfanons*[29], *ensegne*[30] et *ataces*[31] à divers types d'accessoires décoratifs en tissu. Le terme *verge*[32] constitue un problème, mais il pourrait peut-être s'agir d'une première version de la tardive arme d'infanterie française appelée *vooge*. Les termes concernant le tir à l'arc sont plus simples. Ces termes incluent *ars*[33], *arc manie*[34], *arc de cor*[35] et *arc turcois*[36] qui concernent divers types d'arcs à main, *saietes*[37] et *flece*[38] pour les flèches, *coivre*[39], *carcais*[40] et vraisemblablement *reliere*[41] pour les carquois, *arbalestre*[42] pour l'arbalète, *quariaus*[43] et peut-être *materas*[44] pour l'arbalète à carreau.

Les armes de siège jouent un rôle peu important dans les épopées des croisades, mais incluent des *engins*[45] non-spécifiés et aussi les échelles *escieles*[46], les catapultes *perieres*[47] et *mangouniaus*[48] et peut-être même les contre-poids (en fonction) *trebucier*[49]. Le *boufois*[50] était une tour de siège en bois parfois mobile, alors que l'*orguel*[51] pourrait se référer

15 B − 1067, 1331−2, 1472, 2032, 3027; Ch − 739, 794, 1395, 1468, 4086; E − 785, 3165, 3168.
16 B − 2447; Ch − 620, 736, 3982, App. VI 24; E − 3398.
17 B − 2093; Ch − 816.
18 B − 2093; Ch − App. XII 809.
19 Ch − 3610.
20 Ch − 3610.
21 Ch − 90, 260, 737, 814, 1463, 2012, 3567, 3609, 3612, App. I 17, App. XII 66, 316.
22 Ch − 1463.
23 Ch − App. VI 25, App. XII 66, 367.
24 E − 785.
25 B − 1381; Ch − 462, App. VII 88, 282.
26 Ch − 1006; Cig − 2374.
27 B − 1400; Ch − App. I 22, App. XII 312, 455.
28 B − 1400.
29 Ch − 1312.
30 Ch − 1396; Cig − 2373, 2696−7.
31 E − 3085.
32 Ch − 462.
33 Ch − 356, 737, 810, 4084; E − 858, 1027.
34 E − 2154.
35 Ch − 3588, 3595; A(P) − VI 33v903, VII 44v1080.
36 Ch − 1852, App. XII 65.
37 Ch − 737, 815, 3567, 3609, 3733, 4045, 4085; E − 2156.
38 Ch − 813; E − 1067.
39 Ch − 810.
40 Ch − 4084.
41 Ch − App. XII 67.
42 Ch − 1390, App. XII 67; E − 845, 858, 1057.
43 Ch − 1852, 4045, App. XII 67; E − 858, 1066.
44 Ch − 3610.
45 E − 917, 919.
46 B − 2095.
47 B − 1955, 1998; E − 1053.
48 B − 1955, 1998.
49 E − 1078.
50 E − 922.
51 E − 922.

à une machine de siège non identifiée. Le *Feu Gregois*[52] est mentionné et est, une seule fois, transporté dans les *cofiniaus d'arain*[53]. Le terme de loin le plus commun pour le bouclier est *escu*[54] bien que *targe*[55] et *targe de cuir*[56] soient aussi mentionnées. *Roile*[57] est, bien sûr, un bouclier rond utilisé par les Infidèles. *Boucle*[58] se réfère à la bosse de métal, *quiral*[59] probablement à la couverture en cuir d'un bouclier de bois, *quige*[60] à une sangle de soutien portée autour des épaules, *enarmes*[61] à des sangles portées autour du bras et du poing. *Pisons de longes*[62] pourrait se référer à des houppes décoratives semblables à celles alors populaires en Espagne, tandis que *conniscances*[63] se réfère à des motifs héraldiques peints sur le bouclier.

Les casques sont certainement les points les plus intéressants de l'épopée des croisades. Là, nous trouvons quelques termes nouveaux et qui pourront être très utiles. *Elme*[64] est le mot commun pour casque avec *elme de quir boli*[65], casque en cuir dur constituant un type plus spécifique. Le capuchon de mailles qui se rattache à la cotte de mailles couvrant le corps est appelé *coife*[66]. La partie inférieure de cette coiffe qui se lace sous le menton est la *ventaille*[67]. Le terme *capelier*[68] pourrait se référer à un bonnet rembourré pour appuyer le heaume; quant aux *cerveliere*[69], ce pourrait être ou la même chose ou un petit casque porté sous la coiffe de mailles. Le *flanboiant*[70] est dans la plupart des cas un accessoire décoratif en tissu pour le casque, peut-être une antique version du *volet* et du *lambrequin*. D'autres termes se réfèrent à des parties spécifiques du casque. Ceux-ci incluent *crois*[71] pour l'armature principale d'un *Spangenhelm* à segments, *cercle*[72] pour sa bordure inférieure, *maistre*[73] pour ses segments. *Henepier*[74] pourrait se référer à la partie supérieure de tels casques. Ce terme pourrait aussi évoquer la totalité du bol du casque s'il était porté avec un masque. *Nasel*[75] se réfère à une protection pour le nez dans un casque de forme conique, bien que certains nasaux larges semblent souvent faire partie des masques. D'autres termes se réfèrent aux différentes parties du Grand Heaume ou plutôt à ses versions antérieures. Cela me paraît être le cas de *candelabre*[76] pour la partie supérieure plate ou plus

52 Ch – 738, 742, App. XII 68.
53 Ch – App. XII 68.
54 B – 1030, 1046, 1067, 1392, 1531, 2031, 2993, 3036; Ch – 189, 620, 739, 792, 809, 1019, 1052,
   1395, 2440, 3612, 3895, App. XII 729; Cig   2372, 2696 – 7; E – 783, 3144.
55 B – 2033, 3036; Ch – 1005, 1007, 1020, 2012, 4081; E – 771.
56 Ch – App. XII 380.
57 Ch – 3566, App. XII 452.
58 B – 1533, 2034, 3037; Ch – 1020, 1057, 4082.
59 Ch – 1057.
60 B – 1076; Ch – 1057, App. XII 459, 730.
61 Ch – 983, 1395, App. XII 149; Cig – 855; E – 783.
62 E – 3153.
63 E – 3148.
64 B – *passim;* Ch – *passim;* Cig – *passim;* E – *passim.*
65 Ch – 808.
66 B – 1073; Ch – 1055, 1070, 1095; E – 784, 1063, 1068, 1150.
67 Ch – 1156, 2108, 4076; Cig – 671, 888.
68 Ch – App. VII 284.
69 E – 1068.
70 E – 3135–6.
71 Ch – 1017.
72 Ch – 1018, 2438, 4077.
73 Cig – 680.
74 Cig – 2763.
75 Cig – 872, 883; E – 3138.
76 Cig – 681; E – 3137.

probablement pour la bordure rivetée de la partie supérieure plate de tels casques, *fenestral*[77] pour le masque et *mentonal*[78] pour la partie inférieure de telle protection pour la face mais aussi peut-être pour la jugulaire. Les termes *uelliere*[79] et, avec plus d'incertitude, *esma*[80] se réfèrent aux fentes pour les yeux mais pourraient aussi signifier la totalité du masque.

Les termes pour l'armure posent peu de problèmes quant à leur interprétation. *Armeure*[81] se réfère à l'armure en général alors que le mot commun pour la maille de haubert est *auberc*[82]. *Brogne*[83] et moins souvent *cotiele*[84] apparaissent aussi. Les anneaux de la cotte de mailles sont appelés *malles*[85], alors que le *gambeson*[86] se réfère au vêtement ouaté porté au-dessous du haubert. Ceci était probablement une idée musulmane ou byzantine relativement nouvelle en Europe occidentale, puisque les types antérieurs de protection rembourrée étaient probablement de feutre. La *cote armeoire*[87] était probablement un surcot. *Jaserans*[88] et d'autres variations de ce terme se réfèrent à une veste en cotte de mailles couverte d'une étoffe piquée et rembourrée d'orgine islamique dont le nom perse était *kazhagand*. L'épopée des croisades est une des premières sources européennes à donner ce terme. La *Chanson de Roland* est la première et ensuite il y a un trou de presque un siècle avant que ce terme réapparaisse. *Clavain*[89] pourrait se référer à une courte armure qui couvrait la poitrine, armure de facture lamellée ou écaillée et également d'origine islamique, dont le nom perse était *jawshan*. Cependant, ce terme pourrait aussi se référer à un ancien type de cuirasse de cuir semi-rigide, souvent appelée *cuirie* qui était portée avec un haubert. Cette mystérieuse partie de l'armure a pu être inspirée par le *jawshan* musulman. On pourrait aussi, mais c'est moins probable, y voir un camail écaillé pour la protection du cou. Le type de protection pour les membres, de loin le plus commun, était une cotte de mailles pour les jambes, appelée *causes*[90]. Le mot *quisse*[91] pourrait désigner, outre la cuisse elle-même, une protection pour cette partie du corps, mais cela est douteux; le terme *genellieres*[92] pourrait se référer à un certain type de protection du genou. Les mitaines en cotte de mailles faisant partie d'un haubert à manches longues sont appelées *manicle de fer*[93].

Les épopées des croisades sont aussi utiles pour ce qui concerne le harnais du cheval, mais mon propos regarde uniquement la barde du cheval. Il pourrait y avoir dans ces manuscrits des références concernant la barde du cheval, mais aucune n'est claire. *Poitral*[94] se réfère à la large lanière pour le poitrail plutôt qu'à une partie de l'armure qui aurait plus tard été appelée *peytral*. La *couverture*[95] pourrait signifier une housse décorative ou un

77 Cig – 882.
78 Cig – 883.
79 Cig – 2402–3; E – 1064.
80 Ch – App. VII 284.
81 B – 1954, 2449; E – 3142.
82 B – *passim;* Ch – *passim;* E – *passim.*
83 Ch – App. XII 379; Cig – 2372.
84 B – 1279.
85 B – 1377, 2035; Ch – 787, 807, 4075; E – 1070.
86 E – 790.
87 B – 3038.
88 A – 1026; B – 2449, 3038, 2087; Ch – 199, 1469, 3229; E – 3118.
89 Ch – 785, 805, 1463, 3498, 3566, 3895.
90 B – 1038, 1070, 1380, 2179, 2242; Ch – 785, 805; App. XII 726; E – 784.
91 Ch – 955.
92 E – 790.
93 Ch – 1110.
94 B – 1246; Ch – 773, 3987.
95 B – 1291, 1293.

caparaçon non-protecteur. De même les *afeutremens*[96] se réfèrent probablement au feutre placé au-dessous de la housse, bien que ceci puisse aussi signifier un caparaçon plus lourd qui portait des protections.

D'autres instruments utilisés pour le contrôle des foulées incluent le *baston,* un bâton ou la poignée d'une arme, le *corgie*[97], lanière ou fouet, et le *aquillon*[98], aiguillon.

II. Le développement des armes et des armures pendant le 12e siècle

Bien qu'évidemment je n'aie pas le temps d'offrir une description détaillée des armes et des armures du 12e siècle européen, j'aimerais bien, néanmoins, noter quelques points. A cette époque, on était toujours dans la période dite de la cotte de mailles, mais il serait faux de croire que l'equipement militaire n'avait pas changé de la moitié du 11e siècle au début du 13e. L'adoption de la lance en arrêt, qui était fermement retenue entre la partie supérieure du bras et la poitrine, a été fondamentale, ainsi que celle de la haute selle de guerre avec sa lanière pour le poitrail qui amortissait les chocs et permettait la mise en position droite des jambes du cavalier. L'utilisation accrue du tir à l'arc et particulièrement de l'arbalète par l'infanterie, a aussi été une caractéristique importante des guerres du 12e siècle. Ces points ont été des facteurs importants dans le développement des armures défensives.

Pour résumer l'histoire des développements du 12e siècle, on pourrait dire que, bien que la cotte de mailles haubert ait été le type dominant des armures, elle s'est allongée jusqu'à inclure des manches longues, parfois avec des mitaines en mailles et des pans qui arrivaient jusqu'aux genoux du cavalier. Les vêtements rembourrés étaient alors plus communément portés sous la cotte de mailles, bien qu'en réalité il soit possible qu'ils aient toujours été portés. Les boucliers ont vu leur forme et leur taille varier, mais le vieux bouclier en forme de cerf-volant fut probablement le plus commun jusqu'aux environs de 1200. Les épées étaient alors plus minces et plus éffilées, mais dans quelques regions de l'Europe du sud, sous influence arabe, un type d'épée large et à peine effilée restait en usage. La disparition des oreilles horizontales du dessous de la lame de la lance a coïncidé avec l'adoption de la lance en arrêt. Vers 1200 aussi le Grand Heaume à sommet plat est apparu et les phases de son développement commencent vers 1175 dans la lame funéraire de Nicolas III de Rumigny; on peut facilement en suivre le développement dans la sculpture de l'époque. Une telle protection était, originellement, une réponse au risque de coups horizontaux à la tête et au cou, portés pour la plupart par la lance en arrêt, les flèches ou les arbalètes. Les casques à sommet plat étaient évidemment bien moins efficaces contre un coup porté vers le bas par une épée ou une masse. Certaines formes de protection corporelle semi-rigide étaient très probablement connues vers 1200, mais elles étaient normalement invisibles sous le haubert et le surcot, du moins den Europe occidentale. Certains témoignages écrits suggèrent aussi que les petites plaques de l'armure pour les points d'articulation des membres avaient été adoptées plus tôt que les sources picturales le laisseraient suggérer.

Ce serait aussi une bonne idée de jeter un regard rapide sur la situation du Moyen-Orient: les Etats croisés et leurs voisins. Il est maintenant établi que les musulmans n'étaient pas toujours aussi légèrement équipés qu'on le pensait. La cotte de mailles haubert et le casque conique étaient communs en Egypte Fatimide et en Syrie, où la lance et l'epée étaient aussi les armes dominantes de la cavalerie. Le tir à l'arc était important, mais était

96 B − 2184; Ch − 1637, 1647.
97 Ch − 463.
98 Ch − 463.

normalement utilisé par l'infanterie. Les arbalètes étaient utilisées, mais surtout dans les combats navals. Chez les Turcs, les Seldjoukides et leurs successeurs, les styles d'armures de l'Iran oriental et de l'Asie centrale étaient dominants. Ceux-ci incluent la cotte de mailles rembourrée et couverte d'une étoffe *kazhagand,* la cuirasse *jawshan* lamellée et dans une moindre mesure un camail en mailles à part. Celui-ci était fixé au rebord du casque et ne faisait pas partie du haubert. L'armure du cheval lamellée ou peut-être faite de mailles couvertes de tissu, mais plus communément de feutre ou d'étoffe piquée était depuis longtemps plus commune qu'en Europe. La plupart de ces styles, iraniens et turcs, reflètent l'importance de l'arc dans les guerres d'Asie. Certaines de ces modes, particulièrement le *kazhagand* et peut-être aussi le *jawshan* lamellé et le camail de mailles à part, ont influencé les styles dans les Etats croisés. Par conséquent, ils auraient aussi eu une influence sur l'Europe occidentale. Le masque rigide, qui bientôt evolué jusqu'à devenir le Grand Heaume, pourrait cependant avoir été une évolution particulière à l'Europe ou avoir été partiellement le résultat d'une influence byzantine. De Byzance et de l'Europe orientale, la tradition européenne a emprunté des styles militaires ou le tir à l'arc jouait un rôle très important.

III. Illustrations comparatives

Je voudrais maintenant illustrer mon propos par plusieurs photographies ou dessins de ces objets qui apparaissent dans les épopées des croisades.

1. La première série d'illustrations provient naturellement de France. Je commence avec cette arme portée par Joseph dans la «Fuite en Egypte» sur un bas-relief de la cathédrale d'Autun, daté de 1120 à 1130. Je crois que ce doit être un *faussar.* (Chapiteau, *in situ* Cathédrale, Autun)

2. Les suivantes sont des bas-reliefs de Vézelay, d'environ 1130. Notez la masse qui est portée par un personnage qui doit être musulman. Ainsi que ces armes à bâton munies de crochets portées par des Italiens et le grand arc de ce chasseur lydien. (Tympanum, *in situ* Cathédrale, Vézelay)

3. Ceci est une gravure en relief de Goliath datée d'environ 1145 sur la façade de St. Gilles du Gard. Notez l'armure à écailles très réaliste et les énarmes, c'est-à-dire les lanières de soutien pour le bouclier. (Façade, *in situ* St. Gilles du Gard)

4. Ici, deux figures contrastantes sur un chapiteau de 1155, à Clermont-Ferrand. Notez un *ventaille* qui est desserré et un autre, serré, qui couvre la bouche. («Générosité et Avarice», *in situ* Notre-Dame-du-Port, Clermont-Ferrand)

5. Un autre chapiteau, cette fois-ci à Mozat, d'environ 1160, celui-ci montre lui aussi un *ventaille* desserré. («Résurrection», *in situ* Mozat, Puy-de-Dôme)

6. Voilà un pion d'échecs du 12e siècle, provenant du sud de la France, qui montre un type de casque similaire à celui de Clermont-Ferrand. Mais ici l'armature à forme croisée et le rebord, ou *cercle,* sont clairement visibles. (Pièce d'échecs en ivoire, Midi 12e siècle, Bargello, Florence)

7. Ici, plutôt que d'art il s'agit d'archéologie. Il s'agit de deux épées françaises qui ont survécu, elles datent probablement de 1150 à 1175. (Gauche: épée française, lame avec l'inscription GICELINMEFECIT, collection privée; droite: épée française, coll. P.-R. Royer)

8. Un coffre de mariage peint, originaire de Bretagne, d'environ 1150 à 1170, montre deux boucliers d'infanterie peu connus et illustre la variété des styles à cette époque. («Tristan et Morhaut», Trésor de la Cathédrale, Vannes)

9. Une enluminure de la fin du 12e siècle, le *Psautier de La Charité,* montre un bouclier plus normal et une large *guige* qui le supporte. («Goliath», région de la Loire, Ms. Harl. 2895, f. 51b, British Library, London)

10. Parmi des vitraux les plus anciens de la cathédrale de Chartres, il y a le vitrail «Roncevalles». Il comprend des représentations claires de casques avec des masques. Maix ceux-ci ne semblent pas couvrir le menton. Cela représente un stade très ancien dans le développement du Grand Heaume. (c. 1218, *in situ* Cathédrale, Chartres)

11. Là, des casques semblables, mais à sommet plat, apparaissent sur un autre vitrail illustrant le meurtre de Becket. (ca. 1210, *in situ* Cathédrale, Chartres)

12. Les vitraux en forme de médaillon de Chartres sont un peu plus tardifs. Tous deux montrent des versions du Grand Heaume plus ou moins anciennes. («Croisés», ca. 1220 *in situ* Cathédrale, Chartres)

13. Une pierre gravée en relief, qui est maintenant dans l'église St. Nazaire à Carcassonne date, probablement, du début du 13e siècle. A part une splendide représentation d'un mangonneau actionné par plusieurs hommes, elle montre aussi une variété intéressante d'épées effilées et larges. («Siège de Carcassonne», *in situ* St. Nazaire, Carcassonne)

14. Ici encore, des bas-reliefs du sud de la France du début du 13e siècle. Ceux-ci proviennent de la façade de St. Trophime à Arles. Ils montrent quelques-unes des plus anciennes illustrations d'une coiffe en mailles à part. (*in situ*, façade St. Trophime, Arles)

15. Les bas-reliefs du début du 13e siècle situés le long du côté oriental du cloître de St. Trophime montrent aussi un casque maintenu par une jugulaire. Ceci est une figure étonnament rare. Ici aussi, il y a sans doute un haubert de facture écaillée. (Gauche: pilier sculpté; droite: chapiteau sculpté, *in situ* Cloître de St. Trophime, Arles)

16. La fameuse «Maciejowski Bible» est, bien sûr, plus tardive que les épopées des croisades. Mais elle renferme des illustrations très claires du *quisse* rembourré et de ces armes d'infanterie à poignée courte que j'ai appelées *faussar*. (Gauche: «Israélites repoussés devant Aï»; droite: «Délivrance de Lot», région de Paris c. 1250, ff. 10r et 3v, Pierpont Morgan Library, New York)

17. Maintenant quelques objets tirés de sources allemandes. Celles-ci diffèrent des sources françaises sur divers points, mais montrent les mêmes tendances générales. Cette figure de bronze doré sur un chandelier d'environ 1140 est fidèlement copiée sur un modèle d'origine byzantine. Il semble peu évident qu'une telle armure à écaille ait été portée en Allemagne. (De l'Abbaye de St. Nicolas, Gross-Comburg, Landesbildstelle Stuttgart)

18. Sur cet *Enéide* de la seconde moitié du 12e siècle apparaît une variété de formes transitoires de casques, dont certains semblent être des Grands Heaumes. (Ms. Germ. 20282, Deutsche Staatsbib., Berlin)

19. L'*Hortus Deliciarum,* d'environ 1180, désormais détruit, malheureusement, montrait une forme haute de *Spangenhelm,* qui était caractéristique de l'Allemagne. Il montrait aussi des banderolles de lance très variées et quelques mailles *causes* d'un type qui ne protégeait que le devant des jambes. (détruit en 1870)

20. L'*Ingeborg Psalter* d'environ 1195 montre un *ventaille* de mailles lacé sur le côté de la coiffe et aussi une coiffe jetée en arrière sur les épaules. («Massacre des Innocents», Ms. 1695, f. 18v, Musée Condé)

21. Ce *Jungfrauenspiegel* d'environ 1200 montre aussi une forme ancienne du Grand Heaume avec une ou deux fentes pour les yeux, ainsi que le *guige* d'un bouclier. (Kestner Museum, Hannover)

22. Ici encore nous avons une épée qui a survécu, mais cette fois-ci elle est d'origine germanique. Cette épée date d'environ 1200. (Wallace Collection, London)

23. Des formes transitoires plus anciennes du Grand Heaume apparaissent sur le tombeau en argent de Charlemagne, datant du tout début 13e siècle. (Trésor de la Cathédrale, Aix-la-Chapelle)

24. Des formes plus développées apparaissent moins d'une génération plus tard, sur le coffre de l'Abbé Nantelme à St. Maurice en Suisse. (Abbaye de St. Maurice, Suisse)

25. Cette tête gravée de la Cathédrale de Bamberg est intéressante pour plusieurs raisons. Probablement datée de 1230, non seulement elle montre une rare lanière pour le menton, mais elle offre aussi une explication technique et constructive d'une forme diffuse de casques dont les profils étaient concaves et non convexes. («St. Maurice», Museum des Historischen Vereins, Bamberg)

26. Les sources britanniques offrent aussi des témoignages intéressants. Ici, vous voyez une rare *hace* de guerre du 12e siècle, de l'Aberdeenshire, illustrant le développement plus tardif de la fameuse hache danoise. (Inv. 727, National Museum of Antiquities, Edinburgh)

27. Deux têtes de lance provenant du sud de l'Angleterre illustrent quelques changements intervenus depuis le 12e siècle. Celle de gauche date du milieu du 12e siècle et est simplement une version plus substantielle et plus imposante des types plus anciens, alors que celle de droite montre une large et grossière tête de lance de la fin du 12e siècle ou du début du 13e siècle conçue pour percer les armures et les boucliers les plus résistants. (Gauche: inv. L.32, Bury. St. Edmunds Museum; droite: inv. 11.406, Guildhall Museum, London)

28. Ici, quelques vitraux de Cantorbéry, de la fin du 12e siècle, montrent un guerrier dont l'équipement est presque semblable à ceux représentés sur la tapisserie de Bayeux un siècle plus tôt. (*in situ* Canterbury Cathedral)

29. Un manuscrit datant de la même période montre le même type de haubert à manches courtes, mais cette fois-ci porté avec un type ancien de Grand Heaume avec une seule fente pour les yeux. (*Bestiaire,* Ms. Harl. 4.751 f.8, British Library, London)

30. Un autre manuscrit, de 1200 environ, montre des casques à sommet plat mais cette fois sans masque, dans un cas même sans *nasel*. (*Life of St. Guthlac,* Ms. Harl. Roll Y.6, British Library, London)

31. Ces grossières mais très importantes peintures murales de la fin du 12e ou du début du 13e siècle montrent aussi bien des casques à sommet plat que des casques de forme conique assemblés avec des masques. (*in situ* All Saints Church, Claverley)

32. Un type étrange de casque comparable pouvait autrefois être vu sur l'effigie de l'Eglise des Templiers à Londres. Il semblait y avoir une armature sur la face du combattant mais pas véritablement de masque (Geoffrey, Earl of Essex, *in situ* endommagé, Temple Church, London)

33. Un type semblable de protection semble être repérable sur la peinture du meurtre de Becket datant du début du 13e siècle. Peut-être qu'un masque pouvait être assemblé sur une telle armature, il s'agirait alors probablement du *mentonal* des épopées des croisades. (Ms. Harl. 5.102 f.32, British Library, London)

34. Ces deux statues datées de la même époque étaient originairement à Hereford. Leur intérêt est dans la protection des épaules, qui étaient probablement rembourrées. (Victoria and Albert Museum, London)

35. Cette effigie gravée de Sir Robert de Vere, que certains datent de 1221, est particulièrement importante parce qu'elle montre non seulement des *quisses* rembourrées mais aussi un exemple ancien de protection blindée pour les genoux. (*in situ,* St. Mary`s Church, Hatfield Broad Oak)

36. En revanche, ces statues de guerriers placées sur le fronton de la cathédrale de Wells, d'environ 1230 à 1240, portent un équipement déjà vieillot à l'époque. Celui-ci comprend un Grand Heaume avec une seule fente pour les yeux. A ce propos, je pense que le terme *candelabre* pourrait se référer au bord riveté du Grand Heaume. Cette seconde figure porte une sorte de capuche rembourrée qui probablement se portait au-dessous du Grand Heaume à sommet plat, et en plus un certain type de protection pour le cou qui pourrait être un *clavain*. (*in situ* façade ouest, Cathedrale, Wells)

37. Un autre exemple de capuche rembourrée semblable à celle que l'on a vue sur une autre effigie dans l'Eglise des Templiers à Londres. (Effigie, début du 13e siècle, *in situ* endommagé, Temple Church, London)

38. Cette effigie anglaise du 13ᵉ siècle porte un Grand Heaume plus ordinaire. Le terme *crois* s'applique dans ce cas aussi bien au sommet que sur le front. (*in situ* l'église, Whitworth)

39. Une effigie légèrement plus tardive située dans l'Eglise des Templiers comporte un autre exemple d'une forme très antérieure de protection du genou, composée de plaques de cuir dur. («Robert de Ros», 1200–1250, *in situ* endommagé, Temple Church, London)

40. Ce fameux dessin d'un croisé agenouillé fait par Matthew Paris environ entre 1225 et 1250, comporte plusieurs traits déjà mentionnés mais d'une manière encore plus claire. (*Westminster Psalter* 1225–1250, Ms. Roy. 2.A.XXII, British Library, London)

41. Une autre illustration d'un manuscrit fait par Matthew Paris ou l'un de ses assistants aux environs de 1245 montre une délicate représentation d'un caparaçon. La décoration supplémentaire autour de la tête suggère qu'un chanfron était porté au-dessous du caparaçon. («Bataille de Stamford Bridge», *Chronica Majora* c. 1245, Ms. Ee. III, 59, f. 32v, Cambridge University Library)

42. Avant d'abandonner les sources britanniques, j'aimerais vous montrer cet exemple de masse ailée du 13ᵉ siècle que l'on trouve à Londres. (Macue, Anglais, London Museum)

43. Les sources italiennes peuvent jeter une lumière supplémentaire sur les faits que nous étudions. Nous voyons ici, datant du tout début du 12ᵉ siècle, un encadrement de porte de la région d'Apulie où est clair l'influence byzantine. Cette influence transparaît notamment dans la forme d'une cuirasse écaillée ou lamellée qui était portée au-dessus du haubert. (Probablement «Croisés devant Jérusalem», début du 12ᵉ siecle, *in situ* porte nord, église de San Nicola, Bari)

44. En revanche, ce relief ciselé de Vérone est typique de l'Europe occidentale à l'exception des représentations plus récentes des masques qu'il comporte. A cette époque, de telles protections étaient presque toujours ajoutées aux heaumes coniques par ailleurs normaux. Le heaume à sommet plat devait, en fait, faire maintenant son entrée. («Roland et Faragut», c. 1138, *in situ* façade, San Zeno, Verona)

45. Sur un chandelier romain en pierre ciselée, datant des environs de 1170, on trouve, parmi une grande variété de heaumes et d'armes une jugulaire d'un type rare, un poignard plus rare encore, une forme de *Spangenhelm* cadrée et des écus avec des bandes renforcées probablement en métal. Il peut y avoir également un *gambeson* rembourré sous le haubert. On voit une arme à bâton courbée d'un genre que nous avons vu précédemment à Vezelay et déjà associé aux Italiens. (Chandelier sculpté par Nicola d'Angelo et Pietro Vasselletto, ca. 1170, San Paolo fuori le Mura, Roma)

46. Une peinture murale peu connue de la fin du 12ᵉ siècle, située à Spolète comporte une représentation très claire d'un heaume conique avec un masque, et d'un haubert avec seulement une mitaine pour la main qui tient l'épée et des chausses en mailles. («Assassinat de Becket», murales, fin du 12ᵉ siècle, *in situ* Santi Giovanni e Paolo, Spoleto)

47. Une peinture murale également peu connue du début du 13ᵉ siècle située à Aquilée montre un exemple tardif d'un écu en forme de cerf-volant ainsi qu'une forme de heaume très particulière à l'Italie avec une protection le long de la nuque. Le heaume peut aussi être lacé derrière la tête comme il est dit dans les épopées des croisades, ce qui peut expliquer par ailleurs le manque presque universel de jugulaire. (*in situ* crypte, Cathédrale, Aquileia)

48. Ce psautier du nord-est de l'Italie ou peut-être de Thuringe, est de la première moitié du 13ᵉ siècle. Il comporte de claires illustrations de *quisses* rembourrées et ce que je crois être, par son aspect anguleux, la représentation d'un arc primitif au profil plat. (*Psalterium B. Elizabeth*, Ms. CXXXVII, ff. 1v et 139v, Museo Arch. Nazionale, Cividale dei Friuli)

49. La dernière illustration d'origine italienne est une plaque en ivoire du début du 13ᵉ siècle que l'on peut voir à Ravenne, elle semble décrire le large *nasal* du heaume, peut-être un

cerveliere porté sous une coiffe de mailles. (Plaque d'ivoire du *Trône de Frédéric de Hohenstauffen*, Museo Nazionale, Ravenna)

50. Avant de conclure, je voudrais faire référence à deux sources siciliennes et à une provenant des Etats croisés eux-mêmes. La première date de la fin du 12ᵉ siècle, il s'agit des chapiteaux du cloître de Monreale. L'équipement illustré ici est par bien des aspects différent de celui vu plus au nord et il fait apparaître le haut degré de l'influence byzantine et islamique dans une région culturelle frontalière. Ces chapiteaux particuliers décrivent le heaume conique avec masque et cuirasses écaillées ou lamellées d'inspiration évidemment byzantine et islamique, aussi bien que d'autres aspects exceptionnels. (*in situ* Cloître, Cathédrale, Monreale)

51. La *Chronique de Pierre d'Eboli* date probablement des premières années du 13ᵉ siècle. Elle comporte des détails que vous avez vus auparavant, notamment des heaumes avec de larges protège-nez. On y trouve une des premières illustrations européennes d'un caparaçon, ainsi qu'un mangonneau à force-d'hommes. L'arc composé de lames pré-seldjoukides, d'une forme essentiellement byzantine et arabe, et l'arbalète sans étrier apparaissent assez fréquemment. De gauche à droite et de haut en bas: «Siège de Salerno», «paysan en combat avec Diopuldo», «Garde d'Henri», «Richard d'Acerra capturé à Capoue», «Bohémiens devant Naples», «Siciliens», *Liber ad honorem augusti* de Pierre d'Eboli, Cod. 120, ff. 116a, 130a, 137a, 15a, 131a, Bürgerbib., Bern)

52. Finalement il y a ces deux sceaux du tout début du 13ᵉ siècle, de l'empire latin de Constantinople. Le premier montre un heaume avec un masque et peut-être une mitaine séparée pour le bras qui tient l'épée, alors que le second montre sans doute un autre exemple d'un cadre de heaume autour du menton que je crois être le *mentonal*. (Le haut: Sceau de Henri I de Constantinople, Cabinet des Médailles, Bib. Nat., Paris. Le bas: sceau de Baudouin I de Constantinople, 1204/5, perdu, Schlumberger Sigillographie)

10

11

12

13

14

16

25

26

27

29

28

34

30

32

33

31

35

36

37

38

32

39

42

40

43

41

45

44

34

51

VI

Arms and Armor Illustrated in the Art of the Latin East

The purpose of this paper is to try to discover whether the visual arts of the Latin East contain evidence of differences between the military equipment of the Crusader States and that of Western Europe. The most important visual sources are, of course, manuscripts produced at Acre in the second half of the thirteenth century, though other sources such as carvings in ivory or stone, Eastern Christian or Syriac manuscripts, and various forms of visual art from Frankish Cyprus and Greece may also be useful.

The men who established the Latin States in Syria and Palestine would have relied primarily on European forms of equipment, mostly manufactured in the West. Yet even at this early date some Eastern Mediterranean influences could be expected. Not only were local troops employed, particularly Armenians who often fought for the Crusader states,[1] but documentary sources also make it quite clear that weapons and armor changed hands following battles between Christians and Muslims.[2] This is not the place to discuss the degree of similarity between crusader, Fāṭimid, Armenian, Arab, Kurdish or even Saldjūq Turkish equipment[3] since it is the difference between these military traditions that is more important in the present context.

One complicating factor could, however, be that Western European arms and armor were by no means uniform in the twelfth and thirteenth centuries. Although there had, perhaps, been a greater degree of uniformity in European military technology and military fashion during the eleventh and twelfth centuries than at any other time, there remained clear differences between, for example, northern French styles of the late eleventh century and of the twelfth

---

1 Raymond C. Smail, *Crusading Warfare, 1097-1193* (Cambridge, 1956), p. 47; Hans E. Mayer, *The Crusades*, trans. John Gillingham (2nd ed., Oxford, 1988), pp. 92, 157.

2 Among the many references to military equipment changing hands following a Christian or Muslim victory are those in Fulcher of Chartres' account of the battle of Ascalon in *A History of the Expedition to Jerusalem*, trans. Rita Ryan, ed. H.S. Fink (Knoxville, 1969) pp. 127-128, and in Usāmah ibn Munqidh's *Kitāb al I'tibār*, ed. Philip H. Hitti (Princeton, 1930), p. 149.

3 Usāmah ibn Munqidh, pp. 51-52; David Nicolle, *The Military Technology of Classical Islam* (unpubl. Ph.D. thesis, Edinburgh University, 1982), pp. 193-194, 219, 381.

328

and those of Norman Italy.[4] Norman Italy and Sicily were, of course, already under considerable Byzantine and Maghribi Islamic influence.[5] Late thirteenth and early fourteenth century Italian arms and armor, not only from the Mezzogiorno and Sicily but also from central and northern Italy, also differed to a marked degree from the military equipment of France or Germany.[6] In fact the military technology and fashions, as well as the military organization and tactics, of thirteenth-century Italy may have a special significance where the arms of the later Crusader States are concerned. The historical reasons for this include trade as well as political and cultural contacts.[7]

The role of Byzantium was, course, also important. The Byzantine influence on some of the arts of the Latin East is clearly visible, but how much military or technological impact Byzantium had on the Crusader States is less clear. It might have been considerable but a realistic judgment would require much more study of the arms, armor and general military history of later Byzantium. This remains a relatively neglected subject, particularly regarding the fourteenth and fifteenth centuries, but one whose importance is gradually being appreciated by Byzantinists.[7*] Twelfth-century Comnenid Byzantium adopted a great deal from Western Europe,[8] while Palaeologue Byzantium of the later thirteenth and the fourteenth centuries may have been under even stronger Turkish influence.[9]

For convenience in this article, all works of art produced by Latins in the Middle East, or executed in a basically Western European style, will be referred to as "Crusader Art." Illustrations of armed and armored men abound in such sources but here I shall focus on examples portraying unusual equipment, particularly that which might have resulted from local or regional influence. Before doing so, however, it is important to stress the fact that in general such

---

4 David Nicolle, *The Normans* (London, 1987), pp. 4-8, 28-46.
5 David Nicolle, "The Monreale Capitals and the Military Equipment of Later Norman Sicily," *Gladius* 15 (1980), 87-103; Id., "The Cappella Palatina Ceiling and the Muslim Military Heritage of Norman Sicily," *Gladius* 16 (1983), pp. 45-145.
6 Lionello G. Boccia and Eduardo T. Coelho, *L'arte dell'armatura in Italia* (Milan, 1967); Lionello G. Boccia, "L'armamento in Toscana dal Millecento al Trecento," and "L'armamento quattrocentesco nell'iconografia toscana," in *Civiltà delle arti minori Toscana. Atti del I Convegn. Arezzo, 11-15 maggio 1971* (Florence, 1973), pp. 193-212.
7 Good bibliographies on this subject may be found in various articles in *Crusades*, ed. Setton, including: Helene Wieruszowski, "The Norman Kingdom of Sicily and the Crusades," 2:3-44; Elizabeth Chapin Furber, "The Kingdom of Cyprus, 1191-1291," 2:599-629; Jean Longnon, "The Frankish States in Greece," 2:235-276; Peter Topping, "The Morea, 1311-1364," 3:104-140.
7* Since the presentation of this paper, an excellent study of Byzantine arms and armor has been published, written by Taxiarchis Kollias, *Byzantinische Waffen* (Vienna, 1988).
8 Rudi P. Lindner, "An Impact of the West on Comnenian Anatolia," in *XVI. Internationaler Byzantinistenkongress. Akten* (Vienna, 1982), from prepublication photocopy.
9 Deno J. Geanakoplos, "Greco-Latin Relations on the Eve of the Byzantine Restoration: The Battle of Pelagonia-1259," *Dumbarton Oaks Papers* 7 (1953), 101-141; Id., *Emperor Michael Paleologus and the West, 1258-1282* (Cambridge, Mass., 1959); Michael J. Angold, *The Administration of the Nicean Empire, 1204-61* (unpubl. D. Phil. thesis, Oxford University 1967-68), passim.

Crusader Art depicted arms and armor identical to those seen in Western Europe. Hence it is only a minority of items which will be investigated here.

Most of the unusual or non-Western elements dating from the twelfth century reflect Byzantine or Armenian artistic influence. This, however, was a highly stylized, traditional and iconographic influence which stemmed from a Byzantine or Armenian art which may not itself have reflected military equipment in current use by Byzantine or Armenian warriors. Still less might it reflect weaponry used in the Latin States of the Middle East. Such purely iconographic influences probably include the apparent splinted or lamellar upper-arm defenses and skirts worn by the figure of Joshua in a twelfth-century Syriac Gospel (fig. 19A) which might have been made in the Principality of Antioch (Cambridge University Library, MS 01.02). Comparable defenses had also appeared somewhat earlier on the ivory bookcover of Queen Melisende's Psalter now in the British Museum (fig. 15A-B). Splinted or lamellar arm and groin protections are portrayed throughout the thousand-year history of Byzantine art. They were almost certainly based upon ancient Greek and Roman items of equipment, in particular the shoulder-covering *pteruges* which had served in part as unit identification marks since the days of Alexander the Great.[10] Such pseudo-Classical armor may conceivably have been worn by Palace troops on ceremonial occasions but is most unlikely to have been issued as genuine protective equipment by the twelfth and thirteenth centuries, still less so in the fourteenth and fifteenth. To further complicate this matter a third figure on Queen Melisende's ivory book cover, one who represents *Fortitude* (fig. 15B), wears similar upper-arm and groin defenses as part of a full-length armor. The most logical interpretation of *Fortitude's* armor would see it as a long lamellar cuirass, perhaps of hardened leather, similar to those worn by some Muslim warriors and perhaps also by provincial Byzantine or Armenian troops. Then there is the question of why such an "Oriental" form of armor has been given to one of the Virtues while Goliath (fig. 15C) and *Avarice* (fig. 15A) wear armor which is at least partially of mail and which would thus seem closer to crusader equipment. Perhaps the fact that Queen Melisende was herself the daughter of an Armenian princess and granddaughter of the Armenian ruler Gabriel of Malatya may hold a clue. Melisende also did much to foster good relations between Latins and Armenians.[11]

Such pseudo-Classical and Byzantine-inspired iconographic styles can still be seen in one *Histoire Universelle* (fig. 32B, B & C) of c. 1286 from the scriptorium in Acre (Ms. Add. 15268, British Library, London). This manuscript will be discussed again as it also includes figures who might have been influenced by the current reality of thirteenth-century Byzantine arms and armor rather than simply by Byzantine artistic convention. Concerning the problem of what Byzantine warriors really wore, it is worth studying a small early thirteenth

10 Nick Sekunda, *The Armies of Alexander the Great* (London, 1984).
11 Runciman, *Crusades*, 2:232.

century carved marble tympanum from Larnaca (fig. 20A-B). This was made at a time when the island of Cyprus was already under Latin rule (Victoria and Albert Museum, London, inv. A2-1982). The mail hauberks, coifs, and chausses worn by Pilate's soldiers and by guards at the Holy Sepulcher are typically Western. Yet the absence of surcoats over such mail armor would have been unusual in, for example, early thirteenth century France. It appears, however, to be common in Byzantine art of the later twelfth, the thirteenth and the early fourteenth centuries. Other equally detailed but rather later Cypriot sources such as the *Icon of The Virgin Mary* (fig. 38) and the *Icon of St. Nicholas* from the church of St. Nicholas tis Steyis in Kakopetria (fig. 39) (both in the Byzantine Museum of the Archbishop Macarios III Foundation, Nicosia) show purely Western warriors with mail hauberks, surcoats and, in one case, a Great Helm. A series of earlier and better-known carvings from Nazareth (Church of the Annunciation Museum, Nazareth) seems to reflect Mediterranean European prototypes both in the style of carving and in the military equipment portrayed (fig. 14A-C). One feature is, however, extremely interesting and would have been unusual in an European context. This is the very broad and spade-like arrowhead used by a demon who draws a recurved composite bow (fig. 14C). Such arrowheads had long been used by Muslim archers who employed them in hunting and also against unarmored foes or those protected only by quilted "soft" armors. A great many have been found in Central Asian Turkish archeological sites, in the region where such arrowheads may have first evolved. Such a device may well have seemed diabolical to unaccustomed Westerners.

Of those manuscripts illuminated in the Latin East, one of the earliest is an *Histoire Universelle* dating some where between 1250 and 1287 (fig. 33A-K) which might have come from the Principality of Antioch (Vatican Library, MS. Pal. Lat. 1963). Though damaged, most of the miniatures in this manuscript portray relatively light equipment comparable to that used in Italy or Spain. Given climatic conditions in the Latin East, similarities with southern Europe are understandable. A lack of surcoats, which is particularly noticeable on some of the illuminations in this manuscript, was also characteristic of some parts of the Iberian Peninsula and central and southern Italy as well as Byzantium. Perhaps the most interesting illumination illustrates the siege of Antioch by warriors of the First Crusade. This includes some well preserved "Saracen" defenders (fig. 33A-D) who indicate a good knowledge of Islamic equipment on the part of the artist. Among the attacking crusaders is a knight who rides a horse with an unusual form of *caparison* or horse-armor (fig. 33L). This picture is very damaged but a close inspection of the original drawing shows the *caparison* to have consisted of a single piece of material with a small cutout below the saddle. Normal European *caparisons* of this period consisted of two separate sheets tucked beneath the saddle's pommel and cantle. The most obvious parallels with this particular horse-covering are similarly constructed one-piece *caparisons* or horse-armors on two very fine examples of thirteenth-century Islamic metalwork. The best known is the famous Freer Gallery "Canteen" (Freer Gallery of Art, Washington, inv. 41.10) which, though purely Islamic in style and provenance, includes Christian scenes or subjects. This does not, however, mean that the many mounted warriors who also decorate its surface represent crusaders. They are totally Islamic in their equipment, costume, and harness. Half of the horses wear a variety of *caparisons* or armors while the remainder are uncovered. Far less well known is a magnificent inlaid candlestick-base which is probably from the late Ayyūbid period (private collection of Dr. Paolo Costa, Rome).[12] Both come from the Djazīrah region of northeastern Syria, northern Iraq or southeastern Turkey. Such forms of *caparison*, all of which probably illustrate heavy felt horse-armors known as *tidjfāf* in Arabic and *bargustuwān* in Farsi, similarly appear in the famous late twelfth- or early thirteenth-century *Warqa wa Gulshāh* manuscript from northwestern Iran (Topkapi Library, Istanbul, MS. Haz. 841). Furthermore an identical *caparison* is illustrated on a less well known early thirteenth century broken ceramic (fig. 47) which may have been made by a Syrian potter in the Principality of Antioch (Hatay Museum, Antakya, Turkey). This particular ceramic could, however, illustrate a Western warrior as he is dressed in a full mail hauberk and mail *chausses* rendered in a Byzantine manner.

Another unusual manuscript from the Latin East is the *Arsenal Bible* (Bibliothèque de l'Arsénal, Paris, MS. 5211) whose miniatures are illuminated in a very Byzantine style (fig. 35A-E). This is a more than normally realistic Byzantine style which could shed considerable light on the military equipment of the Comnenid Empire. The cavalry, though armored, are relatively lightly equipped and have more in common with the serjeants of Western Europe than with the knights. Their brimmed war-hats, or *chapels de fer*, and separate gauntlets both represent styles of equipment which would become common in Western Europe at a later date. There are, in fact, a few interesting instances where military equipment appears first in the art of the Latin East and only later in the West. Another example might be found in an illustration of the "Story of Troy" from an *Histoire Universelle* in Dijon (Bibliothèque municipale, MS. 562, f. 89v). Here a guardsman carries a dagger, perhaps an early form of *basilard*, on his right hip (fig. 36K). Such substantial daggers do not appear in European art until the close of the thirteenth century and were not common until the early fourteenth. Even then they seem first to have become popular in Italy, particularly in the Angevin south and in Tuscany.[13] It is, of course, worth noting that these two regions not only had much in common with each other but were

---

12   This candlestick-base was displayed in the "Nomad and City" exhibition at the Museum of Mankind (London, 1976). It has never been fully published, although drawings of the military figures were included in my unpublished Ph.D. thesis, *The Military Technology of Classical Islam,* fig. 300.

13   Shirley Bridges and John W. Perkins, "Some Fourteenth Century Neapolitan Military Effigies," *Papers of the British School at Rome* 24 (1956), 158-173; Claude Blair, "The Word 'Baselard'," *Journal of the Arms and Armour Society* 11.4 (1984), 193-206.

332

also in close cultural, political, and economic contact with Latin Greece, Byzantium and the Islamic lands of the Eastern Mediterranean. Furthermore it is a well-documented fact that many Muslim military elites had long considered it normal to carry both a sword and a _khanjar_ or other form of substantial dagger.[14]

The most widespread item of unusual equipment to be seen in manuscripts from crusader Acre is, however, the round or oval shield. While such shields may have been commonly used by Western European infantry, particularly in Italy and the Iberian Peninsula, they were not a normal item of what might be called "knightly" equipment. It is, therefore, remarkable to see how often they are placed in the hands of heavily armored Christian knights and other élite or "virtuous" warriors in the Acre manuscripts. Some are small enough to be regarded as bucklers (figs. 28J, 30C & 32C) but many others are slightly larger oval-shaped shields (fig. 30A, 31C & 32G). This time it could be misleading simply to see Islamic influence in an apparent preference for round or oval shields at a time when the Byzantines had largely adopted the long kite-shaped shield of the Westerners.[15] Instead the military situation of the late thirteenth century Eastern Mediterranean should be considered. The Crusader States were in final retreat with defensive siege warfare as their prime military consideration. This generally entailed fighting on foot in confined conditions. Here round or oval shields, held in the fist or strapped only to the forearm, would probably have been easier to manage than would larger kite-shaped heavy cavalry shields which were strapped to the upper- and forearm as well as being held tight against the body.

The Acre manuscripts also include other peculiar features, though these latter are generally associated with Muslims or "infidel" warriors. In addition to remarkably accurate drawings of Islamic sabres (fig. 31A), winged maces (fig. 29F), quivers (fig. 32K), Mamlūk headgear (fig. 29D & F) and Islamic styles of horse-harness, some other peculiar objects are apparently being thrown by hand (fig. 28A & B). Could these be crude representations of Mamlūk _qārūrah, qunbalah_, or other kinds of fire-grenade? The _Histoire Universelle_ now in the British Library (MS. Add. 15268) has already been described as having many Byzantine features. These include, in addition to brimmed war-hats (fig. 32C & H) similar to those in the _Arsenal Bible_, some apparently segmented or splinted neck defenses (figs. 32A, C & H). This type of armor would be worn by most warrior saints in fourteenth-century Byzantine and Balkan art and is similar to a rare form of scale or splinted neck protection occasionally seen with _bascinet_ helmets in early fourteenth century Western European art. The possibility that

14 Nicolle, _Military Technology_ (note 3 above), pp. 40-42.
15 Quite where the long cavalry shield popularly known as a "Norman shield" first originated is still a matter of considerable debate. Dr. Ada Bruhn de Hoffmeyer has argued that it was first developed in 10th- or 11th-century Byzantium: "Military Equipment in the Byzantine Manuscript of Scylitzes in Biblioteca Nacional in Madrid," _Gladius_ 5 (1966), 8-152.

the *bascinet* itself reflected Eastern Mediterranean influence is an interesting but as yet unresolved question. In addition this particular *Histoire Universelle* illustrates a body armor which could provide an Eastern Mediterranean prototype for the later Western European coat-of-plates (fig. 32B). On the other hand the illustration could be interpreted as a form of Islamic *kazāghand*, a mail jerkin or hauberk covered in decorated fabric and with a padded or quilted lining,[16] as might another illustration in the same manuscript (fig. 32G). Such a form of armor was certainly adopted in the West, probably via the crusades or from men who had served in Byzantine Anatolia. It entered European military terminology as the *auberc jaserant* and in various other linguistic variations.[17] Numerous Islamic terms or forms of military equipment are mentioned in literary sources which either reflected the ethos of Holy War against Islam, such as *The Song of Roland*, or which may originally have been written in the Latin East, such as certain sections of the Old French Crusade Cycle including *Beatrix, Elioxe* and *Les Chétifs*. In addition to the *auberc jaserant* [18] there are coifs in "Turkish" fashion,[19] these perhaps being fabric-covered, large *afeutremens* beneath saddles,[20] which might refer to felt horse-armor; various forms of mace [21] long before such weapons became popular in Europe; a multitude of javelins, some with clearly Arabic names [22] long after such weapons had been largely abandoned in most parts of Western Europe, plus composite bows of Turkish form;[23] Persian or Turkish rather than Arabic names for war-drums;[24] and tin containers for Greek Fire.[25]

Next come two very interesting engraved tomb-slabs of the Lusignan family (fig. 23A-B) from the former Cathedral in Famagusta (soon to be in the Limasol Historical Museum, Cyprus). They might date from the late thirteenth or early fourteenth centuries and one shows a sword hung from a baldric in a manner until then only seen in Byzantine, Western Islamic or Andalusian sources, and in Iranian illustrations of specifically Arab warriors. Potentially more important, however, are the plated greaves worn by this same Lusignan figure. Here a more accurate dating would be useful, for such leg defenses were only just coming into use in the West. They may first have appeared in southern and central Italy and

16   Assadullah S. Melikian-Chirvani, "The Westward Journey of the Kazhagand," *The Journal of the Arms and Armour Society* 11 (1983), 8-15.
17   Melikian-Chirvani, "Westward Journey," pp. 23-28.
18   Thomas A. Jenkins, ed., *La Chanson de Roland* (London, 1924), line 1647; Geoffrey M. Myers, ed., *The Old French Crusade Cycle*, 5: *Les Chétifs* (Alabama, 1981), pp. 7, 35, 74-75; Jan A. Nelson, ed., *The Old French Crusade Cycle* 1: *La Naissance du Chevalier au Cygne; Beatrix* (Alabama, 1977), pp. 184, 197-198; Emanuel J. Mickel, ed., *The Old French Crusade Cycle*, 2: *La Naissance du Chevalier au Cygne; Elioxe* (Alabama, 1977), p. 69.
19   *Beatrix*, pp. 153-154.
20   *Beatrix*, p. 178; *Chétifs*, p. 24.
21   *Chétifs*, pp. 12, 20-21, 35.
22   *Chètifs*, pp. 4, 8, 20-21, 35, 47, 84; *Chanson de Roland*, lines 2075 and 2156.
23   *Chètifs*, pp. 44, 82, 83, 120.
24   *Chanson de Roland*, lines 852 and 3137.
25   *Chétifs*, p. 120.

334

were almost certainly made of *cuir-bouilli* hardened leather.[26] While an Italian influence on Frankish Crusader Cyprus seems likely, the whole question of whether early Italian forms of hardened leather armor were an indigenous development or resulted from outside influence remains unresolved.[27] If the latter did lie behind Italian *cuir-bouilli* armor then the Latin States in Greece, and perhaps also Cyprus, are possible sources for such influence. If the arms of Latin Greece and Cyprus were different from those of, for example, Italy then the question arises of how such styles evolved and whether they were an internal development or reflected influence from elsewhere in the Eastern Mediterranean. The Anatolian Turks, North African Arabs and, to a lesser degree, the Mamlūks of Egypt and Syria made considerable use of leather armor. This would, however, normally have been used in hardened leather lamellar rather than consisting of large sheets of *cuir-bouilli* as in Italy and perhaps also here in Cyprus.

Too little is known about the arms and armor of Byzantium and the Balkans of the late thirteenth and the fourteenth century to judge the possible degree of Byzantine or Balkan influence on Latin Greece and Cyprus. A wall painting of St. George from the fourteenth-century Principality of Achaia does, however, pose some interesting questions (*in situ* Church of St. George, Geraki Castle, Greece). He is illustrated in late Byzantine style and on his leg is a slender riding boot, though this could also conceivably represent a flexible greave of thick leather (fig. 46). Such a boot is unlike that normally associated with the eleventh- to thirteenth-century Turks though it has clear parallels in fourteenth-and fifteenth-century Georgia and Iran. Perhaps it reflected the riding equipment of those Alans who fought for early fourteenth century Byzantium in large numbers.[28] Finally there is an unidentified form of decorated flap or sleeve covering part of his left arm which might just represent a hardened leather *rerebrace* such as those seen in early and mid-fourteenth century southern Italian sources.[29]

The evidence of both Christian and Islamic Middle Eastern art has sometimes been thought to reflect, either directly or indirectly, Western European military influence via the Crusades. A prime example of this is a well-known manuscript fragment from Fāṭimid Fustat (British Museum, Dept. of Oriental Antiquities, inv. 1938-3-14-01). In the lower right-hand corner a warrior equipped in purely

---

26 In addition to the effigies in Naples listed by Bridges and Perkins (note 13 above), similar southern Italian effigies are to be found in Salerno and Lucera Cathedrals. The most important central and northern Italian sources showing such *cuir-bouilli* armor are: the tomb of Guillaume Balnis, 1282 (Convent of the Annunziata, Florence); wall paintings in the "Dante Hall," c. 1288-92 (Town Hall, San Gimignano); effigy of Lorenzo di Niccolo Acciaiuoli, c. 1352 (Certosa di Valdema, Florence); and wall paintings, c. 1330-35 (Church of Sant'Abbondio, Como).

27 Lionello G. Boccia and Eduardo T. Coelho, "L'armamento di cuoio e ferro nel Trecento italiano," *L'Illustrazione italiana* 1.2 (1972), 24-27.

28 David Nicolle, *Hungary and the Fall of Eastern Europe* (London, 1988).

29 Bridges and Perkins (note 13 above), pp. 158-173.

European style is falling from his horse. His arms, armor and horse-harness are so accurately portrayed that the Egyptian artist must surely have seen twelfth-century crusader warriors or have had access to first-hand drawings of them. Furthermore one can assume that the Muslim warriors, who are perhaps emerging from the city of Ascalon, are even more truthfully represented. Meanwhile the helmet of the supposed crusader has the angled-forward crown or profile commonly seen in twelfth-century Western illustrations of warriors. The form subsequently appeared in Christian manuscripts from Syria of the late twelfth and the thirteenth centuries, including the Syriac Gospel already mentioned (fig. 19A), and other parts of the Djazīrah.[30] Such illustrations can be taken as evidence of Western military influence. On the other hand helmets with comparable outlines had already appeared in Middle Eastern art of the pre-crusading era. Examples include eleventh-century carved wooden panels from the Fāṭimid Palace in Cairo (Museum of Islamic Art, Cairo) as well as various somewhat doubtfully dated Byzantine sources such as the *Smyrna Octateuch* (Vatican Library, Cod. Gr. 746) and Cappadocian wall paintings in the Pürenli Seki Kilisesi (*in situ* Peristrema valley near Irhala, Turkey).

Where does this leave the question of who influenced whom in terms of military technology during the course of the crusades? It has been widely assumed that the crusaders and their successors in the twelfth- and thirteenth-century Latin States were technologically in advance of their Muslim and even Byzantine foes,[31] though perhaps inferior in terms of tactics and military organization. The old concept of the heroic crusaders finally succumbing only to vastly superior numbers of their fanatical foes is now defunct in most academic circles. Perhaps it is time to add to the "revisionist" view of crusader history by suggesting that in general military-technological terms the crusaders were not in advance of their Eastern Mediterranean foes. They might, in fact, have been inferior in certain significant respects. The precise history of the angled-forward conical helmet in which the front part of the helm was almost certainly thicker than the sides and rear, the fabric-covered and padded mail *kuzāghand* body armor, the use of hardened leather *cuir-bouilli* armor, perhaps the *bascinet* helmet with its extended protection for the sides and rear of the head, the coat-of-plates, large war daggers, and various other items of military equipment should be studied in detail. All—rather than merely some as is now clearly the case—might prove to have been inspired to some degree by Byzantine or Islamic styles.

30 "Syriac Gospels," 1216-20 (MS. Add. 7170, British Library, London); "Syriac Gospels," early-mid 13 cent. (MS. Syr. 559, Vatican Library); "Syriac Gospel," 1226 (Derzafaren Monastery, Midyat, Turkey).
31 Lynn White, jr., "The Crusades and the Technological Thrust of the West," in *War, Technology and Society in the Middle East*, ed. Vernon J. Parry and Malcolm E. Yapp (London, 1975), pp. 97-112.

Crusader illustrations of arms and armor in the Latin East

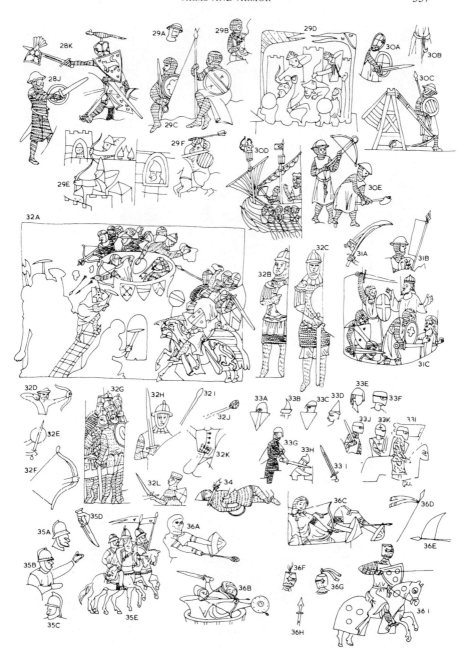

338

1   Coin of Baldwin II, Count of Edessa, 1100-1118 (BN, Cabinet des Médailles).
2   Coin of Baldwin II, Count of Edessa, 1100-1118 (BN, Cabinet des Médailles).
3   Coin of Raymond of Poitiers, Prince of Antioch, 1136-1149 (BN, Cabinet des Médailles).
4   Coin of Baldwin I, Count of Edessa, 1098-1100 (BN, Cabinet des Médailles).
5   Coin of Richard, Lord of Marash, Principality of Antioch, early 12 cent. (BN, Cabinet des Médailles).
6   Coin of Baldwin II, Count of Edessa, 1100-1118 (BN, Cabinet des Médailles).
7   Seal of Geoffrey of Bouillon, Jerusalem, 1099-1100 (after Prawer, *Histoire*).
8   Seal of a Count of Tripoli, 12 cent. (after Schlumberger, *Sigillographie de l'Orient Latin*).
9   Seal of a Viscount of Nablus, 12 cent. (after Schlumberger, *Sigillographie*).
10   Seal of a Prince of Galilee, 12 cent. (after Schlumberger, *Sigillographie*).
11   Seal of the Templars, 12 cent. (after Schlumberger, *Sigillographie*).
12   Seal of a Lord of Marash, Principality of Antioch, 12 cent. (BN, Cabinet des Médailles).
13   Carved relief, Palestine, 12 cent. (Museum of the Greek Orthodox Patriarchate, Jerusalem).
14   "Weapons of Demons." Carved capitals from Nazareth, late 12 cent. (Church of the Annunciation Museum, Nazareth).
15   A—"Pride;" B—"Fortitude;" C—"Goliath." (Ivory book cover from *Queen Melisende's Psalter*, MS. Egerton 1139, British Museum, London).
16   A-H—f.7v: "Weapons at Betrayal;" I—f.10r. "Guards at Holy Sepulcher;" J—f.18v: "Sagittarius;" K—f.23v: Decorated initial. *Queen Melisende's Psalter.*
17   "Centurion at the Crucifixion." Icon from the Crusader States, 12 cent. (St. Catherine's Monastery, Sinai)
18   Paintings of saints on columns, 12 cent. (*in situ* Basilica of the Nativity, Bethlehem).
19   A—f.63v: "Joshua;" B—f.199r: "Guard of Cyrus;" C—f.208v: "Army of Judas Maccabeus." Syriac Gospel, Principality of Antioch (?), late 12 cent. (University Library; Cambridge; MS. 01.02).
20   A—"Road to Calvary;" B—"Guards at the Holy Sepulcher." Carved marble tympanum from Larnaca, Cyprus, 1200-1250 (Victoria & Albert Museum, London, inv. A2-1982).
21   Coins of Bohemund IV, Prince of Antioch, 1201-1233 (BN, Cabinet des Médailles).
22   Coin of Raymond-Roupen, claimant to the Principality of Antioch, 1216-1219 (BN, Cabinet des Médailles).
23   Engraved monumental slabs of the Lusignan family, probably, from Aya Sofia Mosque (former Cathedral), Famagusta, late 13-early 14 cents. (soon to be in the Limasol Historical Museum, Cyprus).
24   Seal of Baldwin I, Latin Emperor of Constantinople, 1204-1205 (now lost, after Schlumberger, *Sigillographie*).
25   Seal of Henry I, Latin Emperor of Constantinople, early 13 cent. (BN, Cabinet des Médailles).
26   Seal of John II of Ibelin, Lord of Beirut, 1261 (Archivio di Stato, Venice).
27   A—f.166r: "Siege of Damascus;" B—129r: "Attack on Shayzar;" C-D—f.45r: "Muslim defenders, siege of Ma'arat;" E—f.45r: "Crusader attacking Ma'arat;" F—f.103r: "Siege of Tyre;" G—f.10v: "First Crusade;" H—f.18v: "Siege of Antioch;" I-K—f.36: "Capture of Antioch;" L—f.10v: "First Crusade;" M—f.27r: "Siege of Antioch;" N-O—f.36v: "Capture of Antioch." *History of Outremer*, Kingdom of Acre, c.1280 (M.E. Saltykov-Shchedrin State Public Library, Leningrad, MS. fr. fol. v. IV.5).
28   A-C—"Weapons of Muslim warriors;" D—f.91v: "Oedipus;" E—f.133v: "Death of Hector;" F—f.205v: "Holofernes;" G-H—"Helmets of Crusaders;" I—f.207v: "Soldier of Holofernes;" J—f.235r: "Soldier of Alexander;" K—f.96r: "Polyneices fights Tydeus." *Histoire Universelle*, Kingdom of Acre, c.1287 (BN, MS. fr. 20125).
29   A—f.64: "Crusaders massacre people of Antioch;" B—f.307v: "Crusaders before Jerusalem;" C—f.182v: "Crusaders before Shayzar;" D—"Siege of Tyre;" E—"Muslim defenders, siege of Damietta;" F—"Siege of Antioch." *History of Outremer*, Kingdom of Acre, 1286 (BN, MS. fr. 9084).

30   A—f.61: "Crusaders massacre people of Antioch;" B— 162v: "Crusader crossbowman;"
      C—f.42r: "Siege of Antioch;" D—f.63: "Crusaders attack Acre;" E—f.33: "Crusaders
      attack Nicea." *History of Outremer*, Kingdom of Acre, 1290-91 (Biblioteca Laurenziana,
      Florence, MS. Plu. LXI.10).
31   A—f.153v: "Weapons of defenders of Shayzar;" B—f.16r: "Standard bearer of Geoffrey
      of Bouillon;" C—f.48v: "Crusaders massacre people of Antioch." *History of Outremer*,
      Kingdom of Acre, 1287 (Bibliothèque municipale, Boulogne, MS. 142).
32   A—f.101b: "Scythians besiege their foes;" B-C—f.16r: "Soldiers of Nimrud;" D-
      E—f.1v: Border of frontispiece; F—f.123r: "Bow of Amazon;" G—f.71r: "Soldiers of
      Nimrud;" H—f.105v: Trojan or Greek warrior; I—f.48r: "Club of Joseph's brother;"
      J—f.104: "Mace of Goliath;" K—f.208r: "Warrior of Alexander;" L—f.136v:
      "Athenian in sea-fight." *Histoire Universelle*, Kingdom of Acre, c.1286 (BL, MS. Add.
      15268).
33   A-D—"Muslim defenders of Antioch;" E-F—f.31v: "Crusader warriors;" G-H—f.49r:
      "Crusaders massacre people of Antioch;" I—f.188r; J-L—f.40r: "Crusaders besiege
      Antioch." *Histoire Universelle*, Principality of Antioch (?), 1250-1287 (Vatican Library,
      MS. Pal. Lat. 1963).
34   "Goliath," *Book of Psalms*, Crusader States, 1275-1291 (Biblioteca capitolare, Padua,
      c.12, f.27b).
35   A-C—"Pharoah's Army;" D—f.81r: "Sacrifice of Jephtha's daughter;" E—"Army of
      Holofernes." *Arsenal Bible*, Kingdom of Acre, 1275-1291 (Bibliothèque de l'Arsénal,
      Paris, MS. 5211).
36   A—f.190: "Army of King Poros of India;" B-C—f.172v: "Army of King Poros of
      India;" D—f.86v: "Spear of Amazon;" E—f.86v: "Spear of Alexander;" F-G—f.70r:
      "Greeks;" H—f.51: "Spear of guard of Joseph in Egypt;" I—f.70r: "Greek;" J—f.51:
      "Soldier of Joseph in Egypt;" K—f.89v: "Greek or Trojan." *Histoire Universelle*,
      Kingdom of Acre, late 13 cent. (Bibliothèque municipale, Dijon, MS. 562).
37   A-C—"Soldiers in scenes of the Passion;" D—"St. George." *Icon of St. George*,
      Frankish (?) Greece, 13 cent. (Byzantine Museum, Athens, inv. 89).
38   "Donor figure," *Icon of the Virgin Mary*, Kingdom of Cyprus, c.1300. (Byzantine
      Museum, Archbishop Macarios III Foundation, Nicosia).
39   "Soldiers in story of Dominican or Carmelite Order." *Icon of St. Nicholas* from Church of
      St. Nicholas tis Steyis, Kingdom of Cyprus, late 13 cent. (Byzantine Museum, Archbishop
      Macarios III Foundation, Nicosia).
40   *Icon of St. Sergius*, Crusader States, late 13 cent. (Monastery of St. Catherine, Sinai).
41   Icons, Crusader States (?), 13 cent. (Monastery of St. Catherine, Sinai).
42   Fragment of Aldrevandini-style enamelled glass, Crusader States, Cyprus or Venice late
      13-early 14 cents. (Museum of London, inv. 134-190-1982).
43   Incised stone slab from Kastiliotis, Kingdom of Cyprus, 14 cent. (Historical Museum,
      Nicosia).
44   "St. George," wall painting, Kingdom of Cyprus, 14 cent. (*in situ* Church of Panagia
      Phorbiotissa Asinou, Cyprus).
45   Seal of Guy de la Tour, titular king of Thessaloniki 1314 (BN, Cabinet des Médailles).
46   "St. George," wall painting, Principality of Achaia, 14 cent. (*in situ* Church of St. George,
      Geraki, Greece).
47   Fragment of a sgraffito-ware ceramic dish from Al Mina, Principality of Antioch (?), early
      13 cent. (Hatay Museum, Antakya, Turkey).
48   A-B—"Sword of warrior Saint;" C—"Wooden club;" D—"Sword belt." Wall
      paintings, Venetian Crete, early 14 cent. (*in situ* Church of Panaghia Kera, Kritsa, Crete).
49   Funerary carving from Famagusta, Kingdom of Cyprus, mid-14 cent. (present
      whereabouts unknown, from a photograph in the possession of Mrs. T. Stylianou).

WOUNDS, MILITARY SURGERY AND THE REALITY OF CRUSADING WARFARE; THE EVIDENCE OF USĀMAH'S MEMOIRES

It is generally accepted fact that the soldiers of the medieval Middle East, be they Byzantines or Muslims, were supported by far more effective medical services than were the invading Western European Crusaders. Such support reflected the advanced medical science and everyday medical practice of Byzantine and Islamic civilizations. It also reflected a medical heritage built upon the Ancient Greeks, to which the medical knowledge of Persia, India and even China had been added. Yet few detailed studies have been made of this aspect of military history. The brutal and often horrific realities of medieval warfare have all too often been overlooked, even by military or medical historians, and one of the few exceptions was a detailed study of the skeletons found in grave-pits from the mid-14th century battle of Visby in Sweden[1].

Such archaeological evidence is, of course, by far the most reliable indication of what the realities of medieval warfare meant for those involved. But the written sources can also shed an interesting light. Here the student of the Crusades is fortunate in having the detailed memoires of a warrior, poet and courtier who was directly involved in several of the 12th century's most important campaigns. Furthermore this man had an accute eye for detail, a remarkably sharp memory and a keen interest in the sufferings that resulted from even the most minor skirmish. His named was Usāmah Ibn Munqidh. Almost every book on the Crusades quotes from his extraordinary memoires, the *Kitāb al I'tibār* or *Book of Reflection*[2]. Usāmah dictated this around 1184 AD at the

---

1. B. E. Ingelmark, "The Skeletons", in B. Thordeman, P. Nörlund & B. E. Ingelmark, *Armour from the Battle of Wisby 1361*, vol. I (Stockholm 1939), pp. 149-209.

2. Usāmah Ibn Munqidh, trans. P. K. Hitti, *Memoires of an Arab-Syrian Gentleman, or an Arab Knight in the Crusades* (New York 1927; reprinted Beirut 1964). Many Arabic editions of Usāmah's memoires have been published and currently one of the easiest to obtain is edited by Hassan Zain; *Kitāb al I'tibār* (Beirut 1988).

age of eighty-nine or ninety, four years before his death. By then he had retired from the turbulence of 12th century Syrian politics and his hand had become, as he himself said, *"too feeble to carry a pen after it had been strong enough to break a lance in a lion's breast"*[3]. Yet the *Kitāb al I'tibār* is still full of those colourful details which can so often return to an old man's memory.

Among them are entire chapters dedicated to notable blows with various weapons, stories of recovery after appalling wounds and of death from apparently minor hurts. Usāmah recounts the courage, endurance and suffering of horses as well as of men and this abundance of sometimes gruesome detail sheds considerable light on the realities of medieval warfare. Of course Usāmah is not only the source of such information. In general the historian of medieval European warfare has to rely on contemporary accounts, the most useful of which were written by participants though not necessarily by soldiers, and the careful of such evidence can paint a convincing picture of medieval combat[4]. Middle Eastern chronicles contain comparable information while the martial poetry of Christian and Muslim societies reflects both the nature of medieval warfare and the attitudes of those involved. Long before the illiterate armies of medieval European wrote or read military training manuals, Arab, Persian and Turkish soldiers had a highly developed tradition of *Furūsīyah* "military horsemanship" and the associated books that were read by junior officers as well as by military leaders. Then there is an abundant artistic record provided by manuscript illuminations, carvings, ceramics, decorated metalwork and so on, which portray battle in all its savagery.

Most surprising of all is how these varied sources of information agree. But few can compete with the *Kitāb al I'tibār* when it comes to the bloody details, for Usāmah Ibn Munqidh pulled no punches. He also seems to have been surprised by his own survival, though as a pious Muslim he attributed this to Divine Will; *"the hour of one's death is not brought nearer by exposing oneself to danger nor delayed by being over cautious"*[5].

Extracts from Usāmah's Memoires[6]: Note: the term *Frank* meant Crusader

---

3. P. K. Hitti, *op. cit., Memoires of an Arab-Syrian Gentleman, or an Arab Knight in the Crusades*, p. 194.

4. In stark contrast to the unconvincing descripions of most 19th and early 20th century historians, some modern scholars have reinterpreted the sources to bring out the true horror of a medieval battle. Perhaps the best is John Keegan in his *The Face of Battle* (1976, reprinted 1988), chap. 2 "Agincourt, 25 October 1415", pp. 69-100.

5. P. K. Hitti, *op. cit., Memoires of an Arab-Syrian Gentleman, or an Arab Knight in the Crusades*, p. 194.

6. Prof. Hitti's excellent translation contains several errors where military terminolo-

or anyone of western European Catholic Christian origins; the term *Ismāʿīlī* refered to a member of an extreme Shi'a Islamic sect also known as *Ḥashāshīn* (the "Assassins" of Western European sources) who waged a guerrilla war against the orthodox Sunni Muslim authorities in Syria; the term *Bāṭinīya* was another word for *Ismāʿīlī*. It is also worth noting that most 12th century Muslim professional armies and castle garrisons included one or more *Jarrāḥūn* surgeons trained to treat wounds in a remarkably modern manner. Footnotes refer to Hitti's traslation and to Zain's edition.

HEAD WOUNDS

My uncle, ʿIzz al Dawlah, may Allah's mercy rest upon his soul, received on that day (battle between two Muslim armies, 25 July, 1104) *a number of wounds, one of which was inflicted by a lance in the lower eyelid near the inner corner of the eye. The lance pierced through the eyelid to the outer corner. The whole eyelid fell down and remained suspended with its skin at the outer corner of the eye. And the eye kept all the time moving, being unable to settle in any definite position* (perhaps due to shock to the ocular muscles[7])... *The surgeon sewed the eye and treated it and it returned to its former position, so much so that the stabbed eye could not be distinguished from the other one* (Hitti pp. 83-4; Zain p. 58).

(Battle against Crusaders from Kafarṭāb) *One of them* (Crusader foes) *stepped towards Jumʿah al Numayri and struck him on his head, which was covered with a Qalansuwah* (type of tall hat). *The blow cut through the Qalan-suwah and wounded Jumʿah's forehead from which blood flowed until it was all drained, leaving his forehead open like the mouth of a fish. I came upon Jumʿah while we were yet in the throws of our conflict with the Franks and said to him, "Abū Maḥmūd, why don't you bandage your wound?" He replied, "This is no time for putting on bandages and dressing wounds". Now, Jumʿah had most of the time a strip of black cloth round his face on account of the soreness and enlarged veins which had afflicted his eyes for a long time. When he received that wound... the disease in his eyes vanished. He had no more opthalmia nor felt pain* (there appears to be no valid medical connection between the wound and the subsequent cure) (Hitti pp. 87-8; Zain p. 61).

(Numayr al ʿAllārūzi, a Muslim infantry soldier armed only with a dagger, attacks Crusader troops holed up in a cave) *Numayr now turned to the man*

---

gy, arms and armour are concerned. Some of the quotations in this article have, therefore, been corrected by Dr. D. C. Nicolle.

7. I would like to thank Dr. J. Middleton of Loughborough for this and subsequent medical comments on the wounds described by Usāmah Ibn Munqidh.

with a sword, intent upon attacking him. But the Frank immediately struck him with the sword on the side of his face and cut through his eyebrow, eyelid, cheek, nose and upper lip, making the whole side of his face hang down upon his chest. Numayr went out of the cave to his companions who bandaged his wound and brought him back during a cold rainy night. There his face was stitched up and his cut was treated until he was healed and returned to his former condition, with the exception of his eye which was lost for good (Hitti pp. 106-7; Zain p. 77).

One of our comrades, named Hammām al Ḥājj ("the Pilgrim") had an *encounter with one of the Ismāʿīs when they attacked the Castle of Shayzar* (Usāmah's home) *in a portico of my uncle's house, may Allah's mercy rest upon his soul. The Ismāʿī had in his hand a dagger while al Ḥājj held a sword. The Bāṭinite rushed on him with the knife but Hammām struck him with the sword above his eyes. The blow broke his skull and his brains fell out and were scattered over the ground. Hammām, laying his sword from his hand, vomited all that he had in his stomach on account of the sickening he felt at the sight of those brains* (Hitti p. 146; Zain p. 108).

The second morning as I was standing at Bandar Qanīn, a village near Shayzar, I saw three persons advancing, two of whom looked like human beings but the middle man had a face different from the face of human beings. When they came near us, behold! the middle man had had his face struck by the sword of a Frank in the middle of his nose and cut as far back as the ear-lobes. One half of his face was so loose that it hung over his chest. Between the two halves was an opening almost the width of a hand-span. With all that, he was walking between two men. In this condition he entered Shayzar. The surgeon sewed his face and treated it. The sides of the cut stuck together, the man recovered and returned to his previous condition and finally died a natural death on his own bed. He used to deal in beasts of burden and was nicknamed Ibn Ghāzi al Mashṭūb. His nickname Al Mashṭūb ("the gashed one") *he acquired as a result of that cut* (a plausible story though perhaps exaggerated) (Hitti p. 193; Zain p. 146).

(Battle between two Muslim armies, around 1137) *We had a soldier named Rāfiʿ al Kilābi* (an Arab), *a renowned cavalryman. We were engaged in a fight with the Banu Qarāja who had massed Turcomans* (famous as horse-archers) *and others against us... This Rāfiʿ was amongst those guarding the rear. He was wearing a Kazāghand* (mail-lined jerkin) *and a helmet without an aventail. He looked back in order to see whether he had a chance to stop and attack his pursuers. As he turned a flat-ended arrow* (chisel-ended arrow normally used for hunting) *hit him and cut his throat* (lit. "cut in the manner used to slaughter animals"), *thus slaying him. He fell dead on the spot* (presumably the arrow severed the jugular vein) (Hitti p. 74; Zain p. 50).

CHEST WOUNDS

(Usāmah's first battle, against Crusaders from Afāmiyah on 14 August 1119) *All of a sudden I saw him* (a Crusader knight) *spur his horse and as the horse began to wave its tail I knew that it was already exhausted. So I rushed on the horseman and struck him with my lance, which pierced him through and projected about a cubit* (50 cms) *in front of him... Moving backwards a little I pulled out my lance fully assuming that I had killed him...* (a few days later) *A messenger came to summon me before my uncle at a time in which it was not his custom to call me. So I hurried to him and saw that a Frank was in there. My uncle said to me, "Here is a knight who had come from Afāmiyah to see the horseman who struck Philip the knight, for the Franks have all been astounded on account of that blow which pierced two layers of links in the knight's mail hauberk and yet did not kill him". "How", said I, "could he have survived?" The Frankish knight replied, "The thrust fell upon the skin of his waist". "Fate is an impregnable stronghold", I exclaimed, but I never thought that the knight would survive that blow* (Hitti pp. 68-70; Zain p. 46).

I once witnessed, in an encounter between us and the Franks, one of our horsemen named Badi Ibn Talīl al Qushayri, who was one of our brave men, receive in his chest a lance thrust from a Frankish knight while clothed only in two cloth garments. The lance cut his breast-bone and came out of his side. He turned back right away but we never thought he would make his home alive. But as Allah, worthy of admiration is He, had predestined, he survived and his wound was healed. But for one year after that he could not sit up if he was lying on his back unless someone held his shoulders and helped him. At last his suffering entirely disappeared and he reverted to his old ways of living and of riding (Hitti p. 70; Zain p. 47).

One of the terrible blows I saw was struck by a Frankish horseman... to one of our cavalrymen named Sābah Ibn Qunayb of the Kilābi tribe (an Arab) *which cut three of his ribs on the left side (and three ribs from his right side;* missing from Hitti trans.) *while the edge of the Harbah* (broad-bladed javelin or staff weapon) *hit his elbow, cutting it in two just as a butcher cuts a joint. He died on the spot* (Hitti p. 76; Zain p. 52).

He (Usāmah's father, during a battle against fellow Muslims on 25 July 1104) *put on his Jawshan* (lamellar cuirass) *but the attendant in his haste neglected to fix the fastening on its side. A Khisht* (javelin) *hit him right in the place which the attendant had failed to cover up, just above his left breast, and issued above his right breast* (victim survived) (Hitti p. 80; Zain p. 79).

He (Iftikhār al Dawlah, governor of a castle in the mountains west of Shayzar) *told us his story* (of how he was attacked by four men with daggers)...

Then he said, "The back of my shoulder is itching in a place I can't reach", and he called one of his attendants to see what had bitten him. The attendant looked and behold, there was a cut in which was lodged the point of a dagger which had broken in his back and which he had not known about... The strength of this man was such that he could hold a mule at the ankle and give the animal a beating without it being able to free its foot from his hand. He could hold a horseshoe nail between his fingers and drive it into a board of oak. His appetite for food was commensurate with his physical strength - nay, it was even greater! (Hitti p. 148; Zain p. 109).

ABDOMEN WOUNDS

One of our troops, a Kurd named Mayyāḥ, smote a Frankish knight with a lance which drove one ring of his mail hauberk into his abdomen and killed him (probably also ruptured a major artery such as the aorta) (Hitti p. 76; Zain p. 52).

When I was in upper Mesopotamia in the army of the atabek (ʿImād al Dīn Zanki) a friend of mine invited me into his home. I went there accompanied by a groom named Ghunaym who was afflicted with dropsy and whose neck had become thin and whose abdomen had become inflated... Ghunaym took his mule into the stable, together with the grooms of the other persons invited. Among us was a young Turk who got drunk, went out to the stable, drew his dagger and rushed on the servants. They all escaped and ran out of the building except Ghunaym who, because of his weakness and sickness, had put a saddle under his head and lain down... Then the drunken man stabbed him with the dagger under his naval and cut in his abdomen a wound about four fingers (8 cms.) deep... The surgeon made frequent visits to my servant until he was better, could walk and do his work, but the wound would not close up completely. For two months it continued to excrete something like scabs and yellow water (probably ascites) then the cut at last closed up, the abdomen of the man resumed its normal condition and he returned to perfect health. So that wound was the cause of his regaining his health (dropsy is a retention of fluid due to heart failure; these symptoms sound more like the fluid resulting from an abdominal cancer and there is no valid connection between the wounding and the subsequent cure) (Hitti pp. 88-9; Zain p. 62).

ARM WOUNDS

On that same day (25 July 1104) my father, may Allah's mercy rest upon his soul, struck a cavalryman with his lance, making his own horse shy a little to one side, bent his arm while holding the lance and withdraw the lance from the victim.

Relating this story to me he said, "I felt something burning my forearm. I though it was caused by the heat from my Jawshan (lamellar cuirass) *but my lance fell from my hand. I turned by arm to see and all of a sudden realized that I had been pierced with a lance in my hand which was weakened because some of the nerves were cut". I was with him... when Zayd the surgeon was dressing his wound... My father said, "Zayd, take this pebble from the wound". The surgeon did not reply. He said again, "Don't you see this pebble? Won't you remove it from the wound?" Annoyed by his insistance, the surgeon said, "Where is the pebble? This is the end of a nerve* (possibly the ulnar nerve serving the forearm and hand) *that has been cut". In reality it was white as though it were one of the pebbles of the Euphrates* (Hitti pp. 80-1; Zain p. 55).

On that day (when the Ismāᶜlīs attacked Shayzar in 1109 or 1114) *I had an encounter with an Ismāᶜlī who had a dagger in his hand while I had my sword. He rushed on me with the dagger and I hit him in the middle of his forearm as he held the grip of the dagger in his hand with the blade close to his forearm. My blow cut off about four finger-lengths of the blade and cut his forearm in two in the middle. The mark of the edge of the dagger was left on the edge of my sword... The trace is there to this day* (Hitti p. 146; Zain p. 108).

(Muslim attack on Crusader-held castle of Afāmiyah) *Shihāb al Dīn* (ruler of Hamāh)... *was hit by an arrow from the castle which struck the bone of his forearm but it did not penetrate in the side of that bone as much as the length of a grain of barley. His messenger then came to me saying on his behalf, "Don't leave your position until you have rallied all our men who are scattered over the town, for I am wounded and I feel as if the wound were in my heart. I am going back..." Late in the afternoon I arrived in Shayzar and found Shihāb al Dīn in the home of my father trying to take the bandage off his wound and treat it. But my uncle prevented him, saying, "By Allah, you shall not take the bandage off your wound except in your own home". ...Accordingly Shihāb al Dīn mounted his horse at sunset and started for Hamāh* (about 25 kms away). *There he spent the second day and the next day, after which his arm turned black and he lost consciousness. Then he died* (almost certainly a case of gangrene) (Hitti pp. 75-6; Zain p. 51).

LEG WOUNDS

(Crusaders from the Principality of Antioch raid Shayzar around 1122) *Early the second morning I rode out in case the Franks did anything and behold, the same old man was sitting on a stone in my way with blood coagualted on his leg and foot. I said to him, "Happy recovery to you! What have you done?" "I took from them", he replied, "a horse, a shield and a lance. But as I was making my way out from among their troops, a footman pursued me and thrust his Quntāriyah* (a long spear) *through my thigh. But I still escaped with the horse, shield and lance". He spoke thus, belittling the thrust in him as though it were in somebody else. This man, named al Zammarrakal, is one of the devils of brigands* (Hitti pp. 71-2; Zain p. 48).

My eyes fell upon Jumʿah al Numayri... with half a Quntāriyah (long lance) *shaft thrust into him. It had struck the felt of the saddle where the lance came out through the saddle-cloth into his thigh, piercing to its rear. And the lance had broken in his thigh. I was alarmed at the sight but he said, "Fear not. I am safe". Then holding the point of the lance he drew it out of himself, while he and his horse were quite safe* (Hitti p. 86; Zain p. 60).

(Battle between Muslims and Crusaders in 1115) *I then saw one of our comrades in arms named Muhammad Ibn Sarāya, who was a young man hard and strong, charged by a Frankish knight... who struck Muhammad with a lance in his thigh. The lance pierced through the thigh. The Frank started to pull the lance back in order to take it out while Muhammad pulled the other way in order to keep it, thus making the lance go back and forth through his thigh until the thigh was gouged out. The lance was finally retained by him (Muhammad) after his thigh was irreparably damaged and he died two days later...* (probably from blood loss or infection) (Hitti p. 120; Zain p. 87).

(Muslim siege of the Muslim-held castle of Al Sawr in Kurdistan in 1133 or 1134) *It happened that a Nishābah* (heavy type of arrow) *from a Jarkh* (large form of crossbow) *hit one of the troops from Khūrāsān as he was kneeling and cut the "ball" of his knee joint in two. The man fell instantly dead* (possibly severed a major artery and bled to death) (Hitti p. 186; Zain p. 140).

WOUNDS TO HORSES

One of our companions named Hārithah al Numayri, a relative of Jumʿah, received in the chest of his mare a sideways blow of a lance. The lance pierced the mare which struggled until the lance fell out. Then the whole skin of its chest peeled down and remained suspended on the animal's forelegs (Hitti p. 75; Zain p. 51).

Among our troops was a Kurd named Kāmil al Mashtūb who was a repository of valour, religion and benevolence... He possessed an all black horse as big as a camel. A fight took place between him and a Frankish knight. The Frank dealt a blow to the horse beside the throatlatch (neck-strap of bridle). *The violence of the blow made the horse's neck turn to one side so that the lance came out through the lower part of its neck and hit Kāmil al Mashtūb's thigh, piercing it. But neither the horse nor the horseman budged on account of that blow. I often saw the scar of that wound in his thigh... No wound could have been bigger. The horse also survived and Kāmil later rode it in another battle in which he fought a Frankish knight who thrust his lance into the horse's breast bone and made the whole bone cave in. Again the horse did not budge, and it survived this second blow. Even after it healed up, one could close one's hand and stick it into the horse's chest... and still have room for it* (Hitti pp. 126-7; Zain pp. 92-3).

Tirād Ibn Wahīb rode one of his horses from the best breed and of great value. In the course of the battle the horse was hit by a lance in its side and its entrails came out. Tirād bound the saddle-strap (additional long strap used to tie up baggage) *around the wound in case the horse should step on its own entrails and tear them. Then he continued to fight until the battle was over, after which he entered al Raqqah* (a nearby town) *with his horse, which promptly died* (Hitti p. 128; Zain p. 94).

A horse was wounded under me as we engaged in combat at Ḥimṣ. The thrust of a lance cut its heart assunder (clearly an exageration, probably wounded in one lung) *and a number of arrows hit its body. But nevertheless it carried me out of the battle with its two nostrils pouring blood like the mouths of two water-skins, and yet I felt nothing unusual in its conduct. After I reached my companions, it died* (Hitti p. 127; Zain p. 93).

The evidence of Usāmah's memoires suggests several things. Firstly, men —or at least the fortunate few— seemed able to recover from appalling injuries if these did not destroy a vital organ. Gangrene and other forms of infection are rarely mentioned, perhaps because those who lived long enough to serve as soldiers had already built up considerable resistance to infection. The simple but healthy diet of the men involved, particularly those on the Muslim side, is also likely to have helped as the 12th century was not, in general, a time of famine or dearth in the Middle East.

Yet over and above these natural factors the remarkable skill of Middle Eastern "field surgeons", the *Jarrāḥūn,* is vividly portrayed in Usāmah's writing. These men were not the highly educated elite of the Islamic medical world; not those philosopher-doctors and experimental scientists whose names are still found in books on the history of medicine. They were everyday practitioners whose frequent success stands in stark contrast to the crude efforts of their Western European collegues. The occasionally barbaric methods of the latter were also described by Usāmah. In the following case Usāmah's uncle sent his own Christian Syrian physician to treat several sick people in a Crusader-held Lebanese castle near Afqah. The physician, named Thābit, returned to describe how a Western doctor had treated a knight with an abscess on his leg:

Then he said to the knight, "Which would you prefer, living with one leg or dying with two?" The latter replied, "Living with one leg". The physician

42

said, "Bring me a strong knight and a sharp axe". A knight came with the axe, and I was standing by. Then the physician laid the leg of the patient on a block of wood and bade the knight strike his leg with the axe and chop it off at one blow. Accordingly he struck it —while I was looking on— one blow, but the leg was not severed. He dealt another blow, upon which the marrow of the leg flowed out and the patient died on the spot... Thereupon I asked them whether my services were needed any longer, and when they replied in the negative I returned home having learned of their medicine what I knew not before (Hitti p. 162; Zain p. 122).

SUMMARY

Usāmah's Memoires are a mine of information on many aspects of 12th century Crusading warfare in the Middle East. This article provides a detailed analysis of wounds, both fatal and non-fatal, inflicted upon men and horses as described by Usāmah. It also attempts to draw some conclusions about the weapons used, the armour worn, and the physical resilience of the men involved.

Fig. 1. The popular image of medieval Islamic armies consisting only of horsesmen is contradicted by both written and pictorial evidence. Here on a mid to late 13th century inlaid bronze basin, probably from Syria, a foot soldier with a shield and dagger takes on a armoured horseman armed with a long sabre (Victoria & Albert Museum, inv. 740-1898, London).

Fig. 2. Few Islamic sources show the horrors of war as grafically as the *Warqa wa Gulshāh* manuscript. Its numerous painted illuminations illustrate a Persian love-epic of the 12th century though the manuscript itself was probably made for the Turkish warrior aristocracy of eastern Anatolia in the 13th or early 14th centuries. The *Warqa wa Gulshāh* manuscript also illustrates an appalling variety of violent deaths, as well as the weapons involved, and echoes Usāmah Ibn Munqidh's recollections with remarkable consistency. Here the rival tribes of Banu Shayba and Banu Zabba fight it out with horse-archery, long cavalry swords, on foot and on horseback. Of particular interest is the rider in the top righthand corner who falls with two arrows in his unarmoured thigh (*Warqa wa Gulshāh,* Ms. Haz. 841, f. 10/12a, Topkapi Lib., Istanbul).

Fig. 3. Another battle-scene in the *Warqa wa Gulshāh* manuscript shows a combat between the armies of Baḥrayn and Aden. In addition to a horseman being dragged down by a lassoo around his neck (top centre), a man on foot has been transfixed by an arrow right through his lamellar chest-protection (bottom centre) while a third has been hit in his unprotected throat by another arrow (top left) (*Warqa wa Gulshāh*, Ms. Haz. 841, f. 40/38b, Topkapi Lib., Istanbul).

Fig. 4. The *Warqa wa Gulshāh* poem and its accompanying illustrations lay considerable influence on individual combat between "champions", including the story's heroine Gul shāh. Here this warlike lady slays the villain with a lance thrust beneath his lamellar cuirass. The victim is armed with a spear and shield, and it is worth noting that 12th to 14th century Islamic cavalry training manuals, as well as Usāmah's memoires, make it clear that sword-armed horsemen were advised not to close with a spear-armed foe (*Warqa wa Gulshāh*, Ms. Haz. 841, f. 24/23b, Topkapi Lib., Istanbul).

Fig. 5. As well as portraying human bodies in various states of dismemberment in battle, the *Warqa wa Gulshāh* manuscript also shows the effect of medieval weapons upon horses, often as a means of illustrating the strength of various combatants. Here the heroine wrestles with an enemy named during the final stage of an otherwise equal contest. The injuries suffered by the horses illustrates those described in the verses but again mirrors some comments by Usāmah (*Warqa wa Gulshāh*, Ms. Haz. 841, f. 26/25b, Topkapi Lib., Istanbul).

Fig. 6. Again echoing gruesome details in Usāmah's memoires, this illustration from the *Warqa wa Gulshāh* shows a victim cut *"from head to saddle"*. Like many Western European artists of this period, the man who made this picture emphasized the horror of his scene by adding human entrails. With the return of supposed "realism" to Western art following the Renaissance such portrayals of the real impact of war upon the human body disappeared until Goya's *Horrors of War* early in the 19th century. Even today 20th century artists tend to show war's butchery in a symbolic rather than realistic manner (*Warqa wa Gulshāh*, Ms. Haz. 841, f. 11/13a, Topkapi Lib., Istanbul).

Fig. 7. From the 11th century, images of war in medieval Western European art tended to be dominated by the chivalric ideals of the knightly aristocracy. But there were exceptions, and the manuscript illuminations of Spain's Mozarab (Arabized Christian) communities provide a good example. While the cavalry charge nobly forward along the lower register of a portrayal of the siege of Jerusalem, made in Catalonia around 1100 AD, foot soldiers fight in the upper register. One of the latter has been struck a fearful blow in the thigh by a javelin or thrown spear (*Beatus Commentaries on the Apocalypse*, Biblioteca Naz., Turin).

Fig. 8. The *Great Canterbury Psalter*, made in England during the late 12th century, shows fully mailed warriors with helmets and the enormous shields used by Usāmah's Crusader foes in Syria. Here, in a battle probably between Israelites and Philistines, one man falls with a sword through his chest despite wearing a mail hauberk. Elsewhere the damage is inflicted upon unprotected faces and the upper edges of shields (*Great Canterbury Psalter*, Bibliothèque Nat., Ms. Lat. 8846, f. 2v, Paris).

VIII

^cAin al Ḥabīs. The cave de Sueth

(Map/reference = Jordan 1/50,000 Sheet 3155 II, Series K 737 ed. 2. — Palestine Grid
reference = 229237)

THE SITE

^cAin al Ḥabīs, which is normally translated as Spring of the Hermit's
retreat, is an extraordinary archaeological site in both historical and geographical
terms. Wādī Ḥabīs is a short, extremely steep valley or cleft plummeting down
from the plateau into the Yarmūk valley, meeting the Yarmūk river just
downstream from the point where it dips below the zero altitude mark. A number
of seasonal springs feed Wādī Ḥabīs but the two most important are also those
closest to the caves which form the most interesting archaeological feature at
^cAin Ḥabīs. Both are small and seasonal, the most dramatic creating an
occasional waterfall which tumbles from a niche in the edge of the plateau down a
high overhanging cliff known as ^cArāq al Ḥabīs. In this context a further
meaning of the word Ḥabīs, namely « held back » or « confined », should be
born in mind. The caves in the cliff of ^cArāq al Ḥabīs were indeed a form of
hermitage or monastic retreat long before being used as a military outpost in the
12th century. The original name of this religious settlement, perhaps a *laura*
dependant upon a larger monastery, seems to have been lost early in the Islamic
period. If, as is now generally accepted, the existing location of ^cAin Ḥabīs is
to be identified with the medieval site of Ḥabīs Jaldak or Cave de Sueth then
the term Ḥabīs has been used to describe this site since at least the 12th century.
As such it probably reflected local traditions regarding the caves rather than being
based on direct observation of Christian occupation. Jaldak is more of a
problem (1) and might reflect a personal name of Turkish origin. On the other
hand similarities with *julādhīy* « monk » and *juldh* « mole » are worth noting.

(1) P. Deschamps, « Deux Positions Stratégiques des Croisés à l'Est du Jourdain ; Ahamant et
El Habis », *Revue Historique* CLXXII (1933), p. 56, n. 3.

The actual caves at ᶜAin Ḥabīs should be seen in association with Tell Hilya to the west, plus the hillsides lying between these two positions, a fact originally recognized by Schumacher (2). Thus the site spreads over a wide area, extending about 1.2 kilometres from below Tell Yūsuf (also known as Rās al 'Alā) in the east to Tell Hilya (also known as Rās Hilya) in the west. It is, however, rarely more that 0.2 of a kilometre in breadth. In the broader historical context of the late 11th and 12th centuries ᶜAin Ḥabīs lay within a fertile and probably quite densely populated region. Northern Jordan and southern Syria, though suffering some decline during the later ᶜAbbāsid, Fāṭimid and early Saldjūk periods, were certainly not abandoned. In fact recent archaeological research suggests that the supposed agricultural, economic and population decline of this region in the early Islamic period has been both exaggerated and over-simplified. Little data is available for the Syrian (northern) side of the Yarmūk river (3) but archaeological work on the Jordanian (southern) side provides evidence of continued and even flourishing settlement during the early Islamic centuries at 'Aqraba, Ḥartā, al Rafīd, Khirbat Qaraqūsh and Khirbat Sukya, all within five kilometres of ᶜAin Ḥabīs, and at Saham, Um Qays, Bayt Rās, Sāl, Irbid and Aydūn where there are either Umayyad remains or Mamlūk mosques built on earlier, in one case probably Christian, foundations (4). A site which has been surveyed in the Yarmūk valley floor, opposite Shajarah railway station and lying approximately 0.25 of a kilometre north of ᶜAin Ḥabīs, has no apparent relevance as it yielded nothing from the Byzantine or medieval periods. Tell Qūris two kilometres to the east may, however, be more important in the strategic context, as would the area's network of Roman roads.

Although the subject has not been studied in great detail it appears that such roads, or at least the routes they traced, were still in use during the early Islamic, Crusader and Mamlūk periods. There were originally three such roads linking the Jordan valley and the south-Syrian/Transjordanian plateau. The northernmost ran just north of the Yarmūk valley having climbed the Golan Heights south of the Sea of Galilee. It then headed north-east towards Damascus. On a clear day the route is actually visible from hills above ᶜAin Ḥabīs, though at a distance of some kilometres, and would have been within what one might term the patrol area of a garrison stationed at ᶜAin Ḥabīs. This route certainly remained important throughout the early Islamic, Crusader and Mamlūk periods, perhaps second only to the direct routes from Damascus to Galilee via Banyās and Jacob's Ford. Its strategic importance remains obvious to this day. Another Roman road climbed from the Jordan valley directly up to Um Qays (Roman Gadara) and then followed the modern road towards Irbid via Bayt Rās. Such a road would similarly

(2) G. Schumacher, « Unsere Arbeiten in Ostjordanlande », Zeitschrift des deutschen Palaestina Vereins XV (1917), pp. 165-66.
(3) Correspondence from Dr. Afif Bahnassi, Director General of Antiquities and Museums, Damascus 30.9.1987.
(4) S. Mittmann, Bieträge zur Siedlungs- und Territorialgeschichte des Nordlichen Ostjordanlandes (Wiesbaden 1970), pp. 20-22 ; Yusuf Ghawānmeh, Madīnat Irbid fi'l ᶜAsr al Islām (Irbid 1986).

have been close to ᶜAin Ḥabīs and is indeed the route one takes during the first part of a journey from Irbid to ᶜAin Ḥabīs. It was in use during the early Islamic era but had probably shrunk to merely local significance by the 12th century. A third Roman road seems to have headed directly towards Irbid from the Jordan valley via the Wādī al ᶜArab and its feeder valleys. It ran a short distance south of Um Qays, was in use during the Crusader period and rose to considerable importance as a major postal road under the Mamlūks.

Most of the visible remains or significant features between ᶜAin Ḥabīs and Tell Hilya lie within the 200 and 300 metre contours on cliff faces or steep bluffs overlooking the Yarmūk river and lying from two to three kilometres east of the village of 'Aqraba. The surrounding region consists of a limestone plateau at an altitude of roughly 400 metres, cut by steep ravines leading into the major valley of the Yarmūk. The Yarmūk river actually dips below the zero altitude mark about one kilometre north-east of ᶜAin Ḥabīs. Apart from a few olive groves, the fertile and well watered plateau is today largely devoted to wheat. A few tiny wheat-fields also nestle within some feeder valleys. On the wider Syrian side of the Yarmūk valley floor market-gardening and extensive green-houses can be seen. Steep valley-sides and hills are grazed by goats while cows sometimes graze on hilltops unsuitable or too narrow for agriculture. A track of minor importance once threaded up the Yarmūk valley from the Jordan valley towards Derā'a, a route subsequently followed by the now abandoned railway. An unsurfaced road has also, apparently recently, been built on the Syrian side of the Yarmūk valley. Within this valley the frontier between Jordan and Syria follows the railway wherever this runs south of the river. Otherwise the Yarmūk is itself the international boundary. Local inhabitants stated that it took one hour to walk down to the Yarmūk river from the 'Aqraba-Ḥartā road, two hours to climb back and that the way would be virtually impassable for horses. The strategic nature of the site is still obvious when one stands on Tell Hilya. From here there are extensive views up and down the Yarmūk valley, northwestwards to the Israeli-occupied Golan Heights, across much of the level Syrian plateau towards Mount Hermon and Damascus in the north, and east towards the Jabal Aswad.

The History

Nothing specific seems to be known about the history of this site during the Roman and Byzantine periods. During the 1st century AD it lay within the Decapolis and was subsequently in the province of Palaestina Secunda though lying very close to the province of Arabia. This area seems to have been strongly influenced by Egyptian monasticism and although the only recorded early community on the east bank of the Jordan was at Mount Nebo, a monastery at Jericho lay closer at hand. In the 13th century a monastic community still existed at Dair Fiq on the lower south-western slopes of the Golan Heights (5) and may

(5) G. Le Strange, *Palestine under the Moslems* (reprint Beirut 1965), p. 429.

well have had some unrecorded connection with ᶜAin Ḥabīs in earlier centuries. If the caves at ᶜAin Ḥabīs did indeed form a *laura* then its mother-community probably lay in the Jordan valley or north of the Yarmūk. This northern area was also partly Monophysite. The early Christian writer Egeria must have passed nearby on her way from Jerusalem to Neapolis during her pilgrimage of 414-6 AD (6). Neapolis, which Egeria refers to as « Dennaba » or « Carneas » in « Ausitidis » (the land of Job) is considered to have been at Khān al Nil or Shaykh Sā'ad not far to the north-east of ᶜAin Ḥabīs and some way up the Wādī 'Alān which is itself a major tributary of the Yarmūk. While Egeria is normally considered to have travelled via Ajlūn, the fact that her narrative mentions going through the Jordan valley « for a while » and even « along the river bank itself », while a great mountain, surely Mount Hermon, eventually appeared on her left side, leaves open the possibility that her route led up into the hills east of the Jordan at some point north of Ajlūn, perhaps via one of the three Roman roads mentioned above. All would have provided a dramatic view of Hermon on Egeria's left side.

In traditional Arab legend the town of 'Aqraba, which Yāqūt identified as being « in the Jawlān province of Damascus » and thus probably with the 'Aqraba west of Tell Hilya (7), was said to be the seat of the Ghassānid kings. Although such a location seems too far to the west to be historically connected with these Christian Arab frontier allies of the Byzantine Empire the site was clearly occupied during the Byzantine era. The entire 'Aqraba promontory forms, in fact, one of the most naturally defensible sites in northern Jordan and southern Syria while Tell Hilya dominates the only practicable access to this promontory. For these reasons alone the archaeological remains on Tell Hilya demand more attention than they have so far received.

The decisive battle of Yarmūk (636AD) in which the Muslim Arabs broke the back of Byzantine power in Syria probably took place on the plateau to the north-east, almost within sight of Tell Hilya (8). During the early Islamic centuries the Yarmūk river formed a boundary between the Jund Dimashq and Jund al Urdun at this point, as it later did between the Mamlūk 'Amal 'Ajlūn and 'Amal Nawā. During the Crusader occupation the site was almost certainly known as Cave de Sueth, the Ḥabīs Jaldak of the Arabic sources, while the surrounding territory was known as the Terre de Suethe or Terra Sueta. The nearest village mentioned in the Latin sources seems to have been Arthe or Kaharthe (now Ḥartā) to the south. Other settlements in the Terre de Suethe are not always possible to identify with certainty but included Avara (Ḥawāra), Zaar (Zaḥar al Naṣarah or Zaḥar al ᶜAqaba), Beteras or Peteras (Bayt Rās), Taletarpe (Khirbat Triṭāb), Capharsalia (Kfar Sāl, now known simply as Sāl) and Casale Elleerum (tentatively identified with Ḥarīma) (9).

(6) See *Peregrinatio ad loca sancta,* trans. by J. Wilkinson as *Egeria's Travels* (London 1971).
(7) Le Strange, *op. cit.,* p. 390.
(8) Yusuf Ghawānmeh, *Maᶜrakat al Yarmūk* (Irbid 1985), passim.
(9) Mittmann, *op. cit.,* p. 250.

Throughout the historic period, and presumably also earlier, ᶜAin Ḥabīs was close to a number of significant earthquakes (659AD, 746-7AD, 1033AD in the Jordan valley ; 1546AD on the northern coast of Palestine ; 1759AD in the southern Beqā'a ; 847AD and 991AD in the northern Beqā'a) since it is not far from the Jordan valley fault-line and lies well within a seismically active zone. Any of these could have caused, or contributed to, the collapse of the ᶜArāq al Ḥabīs cliff-face, though the earthquakes of 659, 746-7 or 1033 seem the most likely candidates. Such a collapse probably led to the abandonment of the Byzantine monastic settlement. Whether the supposedly fortified structures on top of Tell Hilya date from the Roman, Byzantine or Crusader periods is as yet unknown. The late Byzantine period, perhaps even from the time of the Persian invasion (614AD) or the Islamic conquest (635-8AD), is possible and may account for the area's legendary association with the Ghassānids. An early Islamic origin is unlikely as there was little need for such defences. A Crusader date of construction also remains probable.

The use of existing caves as fortifications, with or without the addition of more orthodox defences on heights nearby, was relatively common in the medieval Middle East. The most obvious example, other than ᶜAin Ḥabīs itself, is at Hasankayf (Ḥisn Kayfā) on the upper Tigris between Mosul and Diyarbakr (10). Other passing references to caves being used either as refuges or places of ambush during the Crusader era are quite common in Latin sources (11) and are also to be found in the autobiography of Usāmah ibn Munqidh (12).

The history and function of the cave-castle at Cave de Sueth/Ḥabīs Jaldak is relatively well known and has been described in a number of articles (13). It began with the Crusaders' seizure and fortification of the lower Yarmūk valley in 1105AD. This, plus some territory on either side, was known as the Terre de Suethe, almost certainly from the Arabic term sawād meaning « cultivated zone ». In that same year the area was ravaged by the Atabeg of Damascus, a Crusader castle (Qaṣr Bardawil) near al 'Āl being razed. Subsequently the revenues of the area seem to have been shared between Damascus and the Crusader Kingdom, an arrangement confirmed by a treaty of 1109AD. Instead of provoking further retaliation by rebuilding a castle north of the Yarmūk, the Crusader Prince of Galilee garrisoned the naturally defensible site of ᶜAin Ḥabīs/Ḥabīs Jaldak further up the Yarmūk valley but on the southern side. This came to be known as the cave-fortress of Cave de Sueth. Though it was defensible, the main function of the site was clearly as an observation post, not as a major fortified position. Nor

(10) S. Ory, « Hisn Kayfā », in Encyclopedia of Islam (2nd. edit.) vol. III, pp. 524-26.
(11) Deschamps, « Deux Positions Stratégiques... » op. cit., p. 48 n. 2.
(12) Usāmah ibn Munqidh, Kitāb al l'tibār, trans. by P. Hitti as Memoires of an Arab-Syrian Gentleman (reprint Beirut 1964), at the as yet unidentified site of Zalīn near Shayzar (p. 99) and at another un-named cavern within the territory of Shayzar (p. 106).
(13) Schumacher, op. cit., pp. 164-68 ; P. Deschamps, « Une Grotte-Forteresse en Terre de Suète », Journal Asiatique CCXXVII (1935), pp. 285-99 ; Deschamps, « Deux Positions Stratégiques... », op. cit., pp. 42-57 ; Mittmann, op. cit., pp. 248-48.

could it realistically have served as a base for raids or campaigns into Muslim territory, being too small, too inaccessible and as easily observed as it in turn observed its neighbours. In reality it is possible that the area north of the Yarmūk was dominated by Damascus, that south of the river gradually falling to the Crusaders.

The modus vivendi between Franks and Damascenes only lasted until 1111AD when Tughtegin of Damascus captured Ḥabīs Jaldak and massacred its garrison, though in 1113AD the position seems to have reverted to Frankish control. In 1118AD it again fell to the Muslims but in that same year King Baldwin II successfully counter-attacked Ḥabīs Jaldak with 130 knights and then advanced to Derā'a, defeating a Damascene relieving army in the process. The entire Yarmūk valley was then held for the Prince of Galilee, serving as a base for raids and further expansion to the east and south. Another « cave-fortress » was established at Cavea Roob, probably near al Mughayir or al Shajarah where the Wādī Raḥūb meets the Wādī Shalālah fifteen kilometres south-east of ᶜAin Ḥabīs. There are, in fact, cisterns at Khirbat al Mughayir al Sharqī plus remains of an associated settlement with pottery fragments dating from various medieval periods (14). Surface rather than cliff-face caves are still used to house animals at Mughayir itself where similarly dated pottery sherds have also been found (15). Perhaps the most probable location for Cavea Roob is, however, in the tunnels of a third archaeological site, namely Tell al Muᶜallaqah, a site which as its name implies « hangs » on the edge of the fifteen to twenty metre high western escarpment of the Wādī Raḥūb. So far the most recent pottery from this site dates from the late Byzantine period (16). An iron arrowhead of typical medieval Turkish form was purchased by the author at Mughayir but no precise place of origin was available.

In 1158AD Nūr al Dīn invested Ḥabīs Jaldak but some ten or more days after the siege began Nūr al Dīn's army was completely defeated in a major battle north-east of the Sea of Galilee whereupon the siege of Ḥabīs Jaldak was abandoned. Thereafter the cave-fortress was repaired, fully resupplied and strongly garrisoned by King Baldwin III. Much of the surviving defences probably date from this time. Wooden stairs, ladders or walkways probably now linked the three levels of caves, these presumably being partially removable in time of need. In his account of these events William of Tyre described Ḥabīs Jaldak as being set in a vertical cliff, access being impossible from above or below and solely by means of a precipitous path across the mountainside. The caves themselves consisted of rooms fully supplied with the necessities of life plus plenty of good water. « *Erat autem praesidium spelunca in latere cujusdam montis arduo et admodum devexo sita : ad quam non erat vel a superioribus, vel ab inferioribus partibus accessus ; sed ex solo latere, calle nimis angusto et propter praecipitium*

(14) Mittman, *op. cit.*, pp. 8-9.
(15) Mittman, *op. cit.*, p. 9.
(16) Mittman, *op. cit.*, pp. 11-13.

imminens periculoso, ad eam veniebatut. Habebat autem interius mansiones et diversoria, quibus suis habitatoribus necessarias poterat praebere commoditates ; sed nec etiam aquae vivae et indeficientis eis vena deerat, ut quantum loci patiebatur angustia, locus satis aptus et regioni plurimum utilis haberetur... » (17). It is even possible that the garrison were supplied with meat « on the hoof » to be stabled in the lowest level of caves, shelters which are in fact still used by shepherds to this day.

In June 1182AD Ḥabīs Jaldak fell to a Muslim force under Farrūkh Shāh, Saladin's nephew and deputy in Damascus, after a mere five-day siege. This caused consternation and rumours of treachery in the Christian camp, perhaps on the part of the garrison commander Fulk of Tiberius. Farrūkh Shāh's *mamlūk* troops were, however, something of an elite unit having won an unexpected victory over the Crusaders near Belfort three years earlier. William of Tyre also mentioned reports that the enemy had mined vertically though the soft rock from the lower to the middle and thence to the upper level of caves, eventually forcing the garrison to surrender : « *...aliis vero quod ex latere speluncam effregerunt [hostes], quia lapiscretaceus erat, et facile solvebatur, et violentur ingressi stationem primam quae inferior erat, occupaverunt, dicentibus, under postmodum eos qui erant in medio et in supremo coenaculo, nam tres ibi dicebantur esse mansiones, ad deditionem compulerunt* » (18). A roughly hewn passage may, in fact, be found leading almost vertically from the second level cave next to that which originally served as a church up to the northernmost third level cave. This might have been excavated during the siege by Farrūkh Shāh's men. It seems a bit much for only five days' work but the rock is undeniably friable while Saladin's military engineers and miners were among the most highly respected of their day. It should also be noted that no tunnel would be needed to reach the second level of caves once the first level had been taken since they are only a few feet above the main ledge. The vertical tunnel also only allows access to the northernmost third level cave, there being no connention between this and a more important southern group of third level caves except by external wooden walkways of which no trace now remains. Perhaps the psychological impact of this successful mining operation and a consequent possible threat to the garrison's water supply prompted the sudden surrender.

The whole question of water supply is an important one. The waterfall of ᶜAin Ḥabīs only exists following rain. It was clearly tapped by some means to supply cisterns, almost certainly in the southern third level caves. The siege by Farrūkh Shāh also took place in the late summer, well before the rainy season, so the Crusader garrison would be relying on water stored in their cisterns. If they damaged the cisterns or poluted the water before surrendering this would be of even greater significance where the second siege of 1182AD is concerned.

(17) William of Tyre, *Historia rerum in partibus transmarinis gestarum* XVIII. c. 21, in *Recueil des historiens des Croisades : Historiens Occidentaux*, vol. I (Paris 184), pp. 855-56.
(18) William of Tyre, *op. cit.*, XX. c. 15, in *RHC : Hist. Occ.*, vol. I, pp. 1090-91.

The seizure of Ḥabīs Jaldak was the opening move in a major autumn and winter campaign during which Saladin unsuccessfully attempted to capture Beirut but then went on to conquer substantial territory in northern Iraq. During Saladin's absence in Iraq the Crusaders returned to conduct a fullscale counter-siege as part of a widespread assault on Damascene territory. Farrūkh Shāh also died at around this time but when news of the new Crusader attacks reached Saladin he is reported to have replied by saying, « *Let them, for while they knock down villages we are taking cities* » (19). William of Tyre states that the Christians brought miners who cut away rocks on top of the cliff which others then hurled down the precipice. Sharp flints embedded in the limestone damaged the tools but these were immediately repaired by yet other workers, the whole operation being defended by troops encamped on the hilltop (20) (see Appendix). A day and night bombardment was thus maintained, perhaps smashing the external wooden walkways and eventually demoralizing the garrison. William of Tyre's description seems remarkably accurate for there are still traces of what appear to be man-made excavations terrifyingly close to the lip of the cliff immediately above the ᶜAin Ḥabīs caves.

Meanwhile other warriors ventured down the narrow path leading to the ledge across the cliff-face, though whether they approached from the north, south or both directions is unclear. There they skirmished, using spears, swords, bows and crossbows, with a Muslim garrison supposedly consisting of seventy picked men. Such skirmishing presumably took place around walls whose remains can still be seen north and south of the lower caves. After three weeks the exhausted garrison, failing to see a relieving force, surrendered on honourable terms and were replaced by Christian troops. Ḥabīs Jaldak remained in Christian hands for a further five years until the entire Terre de Suethe was abandoned to Saladin after the battle of Hattin. Thereafter its military rôle seems to have disappeared until the early 1970s, the accessible caves being used only by shepherds and their flocks.

The Caves and other Structures

Remains of a small guard-house of lime-stone blocks may be seen on the western summit of Tell Hilya, in addition to the ruins of other small buildings and a cistern. There are also the possible remains of an additional building on a platform at the south-eastern end of this ridge. Rock-cut tombs and chambers of uncertain purpose exist on the eastern and south-eastern slopes of Tell Hilya and on the southern side of a saddle between Tell Hilya and the plateau. Some have recently been converted into bunkers, command-posts and store chambers for the Jordanian Army. A series of rough-hewn steps are visible where a path from the 'Aqraba road to Wādī Ḥabīs dips over the edge of the saddle near a small knoll

(19) Ibn al Athīr, *Ta'rikh al kamil* (Cairo 1953-60), 2 : 119.
(20) William of Tyre, *op. cit.*, XXII. c. 21, in *RHC : Hist. Occ.*, vol. I, pp. 1104-07.

while a further series of tombs and dwelling chambers, plus an apparent rock-cut multiniche dovecote, are visible on the slope of the plateau between the saddle and Wādī Ḥabīs. The first group of three main caves form a series of living-quarters roughly 5 to 6 metres long, 1.80 to 2 metres high and 2.5 to 4 metres deep. Some have niches for lamps or other purposes. Schumacher reported a series of nearby grave-chambers but this was not immediately obvious in 1986 or 1987 (21). A second similar group of caves lies some 100 metres to the south-east along the slope of the hill while a small structure of rough stones, perhaps a modern bunker dating from the 1970s, stands on a spur of the hillside east of Tell Hilya and somewhat below the line of the first and second groups of caves.

The third and most important group of caves lies on the eastern side of Wādī Ḥabīs and is generally referred to as the caves of ᶜAin Ḥabīs. They lie in three, or perhaps four, vertical levels across a sheer limestone cliff known as ᶜArāq al Ḥabīs. It is clear that a substantial part of this cliff has collapsed into Wādī Ḥabīs, leaving the rear walls of some caves or chambers isolated on the cliff-face. This collapse, or series of collapses, also means that all save one of the higher caves are accessible only with ladders or rock-climbing equipment. The existence of a roughly cut vertical chimney probably dating from the siege of 1182AD and linking the second level caves with one of the third level caves might suggest that the major collapse took place between the Byzantine and Crusader periods. The lowest series of three or four caves consists of natural hollows, some with lamp-niches and other small ledges, lying beneath an overhanging cliff. They are still used as shelters by goatherders and their flocks at certain times of year.

At a slightly higher elevation are two much larger man-made, or man-improved, caves, one of which was originally cruciform in plan (fig. 3A & B). Though most of its external wall has collapsed into the valley, this cave clearly had a regular cross-vaulted roof. Similarities with some of the rock-hewn Byzantine churches in Cappadocia, Turkey, immediately spring to mind. Its walls were originally smooth with carefully cut corners and the entire structure almost certainly served as a church. The lack of any traces of wall-painting, decoration or even plaster to cover such decoration may suggest that it was built or last used as a church in the Iconoclastic period. The eastern end of this « church » is, however, partly burried beneath a deep layer of animal dung and other detritus so that the area around the altar cannot be seen. A rock-cut passage about ten metres high leads almost vertically from a neighbouring man-made or improved second level cave to the northernmost of the upper register of caves. This is also a man-made structure with a flat ceiling but it is not so carefully shaped or finished as the « church » cave. Its large almost rectangular main entrance (cave-opening A) now leads onto the sheer cliff-face while two much smaller chambers are cut into its southern wall. One of these forms a low rectangular passage which opens into a moderately wide but exceedingly low rectangular chamber with a hole of uncertain depth in its floor. This is now largely filled with dust and rubble.

(21) Schumacher, *op. cit.*, pp. 165-67.

Horsfield, in his survey of c. 1933, suggested the existence of remains of a plastered water-cistern in the southern second level of caves (22). He may have been referring to a pair of large niches, one above the other, in the cliff-face, between cave-openings D & E or to the circular cave behind entrance B. As far as is known, however, Horsfield was not able to enter the southern group of third level caves and would consequently have been unaware of the shape of this circular chamber. Such cisterns, internal or cut into the face of the cliff, could have collected water via a lost channel of stone or wood leading from a point directly below the seasonal waterfall of ᶜAin Ḥabīs. Alternatively the small opening above entrance B may have funnelled water directly into the circular cistern. The seasonal waterfall actually pours down the cliff-face a metre or so from cave-opening B. The southern group of linked caves (openings B to F) are the most complete, though even here much seems to have fallen into the Wādī. All that might remain of one such collapsed room is an arched niche with a cross carved on its rear wall (fig. 4). Horsfield suggested that this niche was all that remained of an oratory dating from the Crusader occupation though Schumacher believed that it dated from the Byzantine monastic period. It may, in fact, originally have been no deeper than it is today, perhaps appearing as an angled niche in the cliff-face next to a lost exterior walkway.

The southern group of third level caves are not quite as inaccessible as was once thought. One member of a team of local treasure hunters actually reached these caves by means of ropes and a ladder constructed on the spot. Unfortunately no amount of pleading would make him allow me to use the same rickety method. The treasure-hunter found nothing of financial value but was able to supply a detailed verbal description backed up by sketches which are presented here in a clarified form (figs. 2, 3, 5 & 6). These caves were reached from a sloping ledge on which the ladder was rested. They consisted of an outer chamber (F) divided by a diagonal wall or platform from which a tunnel led into another large chamber (E) with two other exists. One led directly to the vertical cliff-face. The other was described as a small doorway opening into a second smaller chamber (D). From here a larger door led further into the cliff, to a third semicircular room with the remains of what was described as a « well » in the middle. This was reputedly about one metre deep and may actually have been a font comparable to those still seen in ruined Byzantine churches at Mādaba south of Amman. Another large doorway led into a fourth chamber (C) on one side of which was an arched alcove containing what appears to have been an opened stone tomb or ossiary, apparently of Byzantine form (fig. 5). The alcove was described as almost one and a half metres high, the tomb or ossiary being less than a metre high and open to half this depth. At the far end of chamber C was another small door leading into a fifth chamber (B), supposedly plastered and probably serving as a cistern. The observer described most of the chambers as having smooth floors and smooth white « plastered » (Arabic *jibs*) roofs and walls.

(22) Deschamps, « Une Grotte-Forteresse... », *op. cit.,* pp. 296-98.

The main ledge outside the lower level of caves is covered by a thick layer of dung but just south of the southernmost cave four courses of carefully hewn stones can be seen protruding at the edge of this ledge. The lower three courses are of a grey stone unlike rock in the immediate vicinity and the wall has the appearance of being the remains of a defensive structure built across the ledge from the cliff-face to the precipice beyond. Apparent remains of walls or a structure built of limestone can also be seen some twenty-five metres along the path leading north-west where the cliff ends and the ledge becomes a narrow track across the steep hillside. On top of the cliff of ᶜArāq al Ḥabīs, immediately above the caves of ᶜAin Ḥabīs, are a number of small caves. These may be natural formations but look more like the remains of mining activity dating from 1182AD. The upper part of the cliff-face below these small caves also appears to have a series of remarkably regular vertical fissures. Their position rules out direct erosion by the waterfall which lies further north and they are probably the result of a major cliff collapse. A geologist could presumably state whether they could also be the result of mining. If so, then part at least of the massive rock-falls which sent so much of the caves tumbling into Wādī Ḥabīs could have been initiated by military activity, the actual fall taking place some years after the siege itself. In general, however, earthquake seems the most likely cause of the collapse.

Until more detailed archaeological research is undertaken one might assume that the abondoned monastic caves at ᶜAin Ḥabīs were converted into a fortress in the following manner. The access ledge would be blocked at either end with walls, one at least of which must have had an entrance — probably the south. The ledge itself could have been protected from arrows by a simple wall or even a wooden palisade. This would also have hindered ventursome foes from scrambling up the sloping lower cliff. The rough lower caves would have had no defensive or even storage function except to shelter the duty-guard or to house animals. The second level church-cave and its neighbour would also have been virtually indefensible once an enemy gained access to the ledge. Prior to the excavation of a vertical chimney from the second to the northernmost third level cave this latter cave could only have been reached by ladders up the cliff-face. How this northerly third-level cave communicated with the southern group of third level caves is unclear. Any direct communication by wooden platforms would have had to go across the cliff-face, right beneath the seasonal waterfall. The southern group of third level caves might similarly have been reached by a ladder from the main ledge. If Horsfield's theory of a now collapsed cistern fed by the waterfall is correct, then one can imagine these caves forming a self-sufficient and virtually impregnable fortress. A small cave entrance, at the same level as the niche with a cross and smaller than any other such entrance (above entrance B on Figure 1), may have been the point where water was actually diverted via lost wooden troughs into a circular cistern (entrance B) beneath it.

124

APPENDIX

William of Tyre's description of the second siege of 1182AD (XXII, c. 21, *RHC ; Hist. Occ.*, Vol. I, pp. 104-07).

« ... *Decernunt a parte superiori caesores lapidum eisque quotquot haberent ministros necessarios simul et operum custodes, ut tute et sine irruentium periculo laborare, collocare. Erat enim spelunca in altissimo montis latere posita, non habens nisi cum multa difficultate accessum, in quo vix pediti iter esse poterat expedito, nam inferius usque in profundum subjectae vallis, ingens est et horribile praecipitium, ex latere autem ad eam accedebatur itinere unius pedis vix habente latitudinem. Erant autem in eadem spelunca mansiones tres, sibi invicem superpositae, in quibus mutuus per quasdam scalas ligneas et per quaedam angusta foramina interius ascensus erat et descensus.*

Sic ergo ea sola qua eis noceri poterat via, aggressi sunt speluncam desuper, ut praemisimus, incidere, tentantes si ad primam et superiorem speluncae habitationem incidendo sic possent penetrare. Erat igitur in eo omnis nostrorum intentio, et totus in eo labor impendebatur. Ordinatis enim ad id operis exsequendum artificibus, quotquot erant necessarii, et cooperatoribis ministris, qui lapides incisos et lapidum fragmenta per praeceps in vallum subjectam devolerent, ut sine intermissione opus procederet, visarias tam interdiu quam de nocte constituebant successiones, ut, defatigatis prioribus, novi recentesque venirent, qui operis possent et scirent pondus portare. Proficiebat ergo labor impendio, tunc ex frequentia et fervore eorum qui praedicto instabant operi, tum ex quadam habilitate quam ex se prebebat saxi, quod incidebatur, materia. Erat enim lapis cretaceus, et ad frangendum facilis, nisi quod venas durissimi silicis interpolatim habebat immixtas, quae saepius et ferrea laederent instrumenta, et his qui in opere fervebant, aliquoties ministrarent impedimentum. Porro quicquid fragmentorum, ut locus expediretur, in vallem subjectam, ut praediximus, devolvebatur, totum id qui in spelunca erant obsessi contemplabantur de proximo, unde eis timor incutiebatur amplior, tanquam qui singulis expectabant horis, incisione perfecta, ad eos violenter intraretur. Noster autem bipertitus erat exercitus, nam pars ejus, ut praediximus, in monte supremo, in quo erat spelunca, castra locaverat, ut eos qui erant opere solliciti, ab hostium protegerent insidiis, pars vero inferius residebat in plano, quibus id specialiter erat propositi, ut obsessis introitum negarent et exitum. Ii etiam nonnunquam per illam arctam, unde praemisimus, semitam, ad inferiorem ejusdem speluncae accidentes, eos qui intus erant, licet non proficerent, assultibus molestare nitebantur. Erant autem intus viri fortes et bellicosi, tam victualium quam armorum habentes copiam, quasi ad septuaginta, quos tanquam virtute probatos, de quorum fide et constantia praesumeret plurimum Salahadinus, abiens intus dimiserat, eorum diligentiae commendans municipium. Et jam eo usque ventum erat, quod qui in spelunca erant, prae frequenti et pene continua malleorum percussione, intus quiescere non poterant, videbatur enim, ad omnem ictuum ingeminationem, spelunca tremiscere et universa concuti, ita ut jam non timerent, quod ad eos nostri irrumperent violenter, sed quod tota spelunca, repetitione malleorum fatigata, subito corruens universos opprimeret. Denique quod eis subsidium ministraretur omnino sperare non licebat, nam prius noverant, ad partes remotissimas, et unde non facile redire poterat, demigrasse Salahadinum, et militares secum duxisse copias. Unde factum est, quod, postquam obsidionem tribus vel modico amplius septimanis perpessi fuerant, missa legatione ad dominum regem, per interventum domini Tripolitani comitis obtinent, ut resignato praesidio, cum armis, quae ipsi intulerant, et propria supellectili, liber eis usque Bostrum indulgeretur transitus. Sic ergo illis abeauntibus, recepto praesidio, confusionem, quam ex eodem prius videbamur induisse, auctore Domino, et per ejus surabundantem gratiam, diluimus. Porro tam domino regi quam aliis principibus curae fuit non modicae, statim, sicut expediens videbatur, ut locum resignatum et armis communirent et victualibus, et viris fidelibus, de quorum fide non dubitaretur et industria, committerent. Quo cum omni diligentia completo, noster ad propria reversus est exercitus. Factum est autem hoc, anno ab incarnatione Domini millisimo centisimo octogesimo secundo, mense octobre... ».

BIBLIOGRAPHY

GLUECK N., « Explorations in Eastern Palestine, IV », *Annual of the American School of Oriental Research* XXV-XXVIII (1951), pp. 130-1.

DESCHAMPS P., « Deux Positions stratégiques des Croisés à l'Est du Jourdain : Ahamant et El Habis », *Revue Historique* CLXXII (1933), pp. 42-57.

DESCHAMPS P., « Études sur un texte Latin énumérant les possessions musulmanes dans le Royaume de Jérusalem vers l'année 1239 », *Syria* XXIII (1942-43), pp. 87 & 99-100.

DESCHAMPS P., « Une grotte-forteresse des Croisés au-delà du Jourdain ; El Habis en Terre de Suète », *Journal Asiatique* CCXXVII (1935), pp. 285-99.

MITTMANN S., *Beiträge zur Siedlungs- und Territorialgeschichte des Nordlichen Ostjordanlandes* (Wiesbaden 1970), pp. 248-9.

REY E., « Notice sur le « Cavea de Roob » ... », in *Mémoires de la Société Nationale des Antiquaires de France* XLVI (1885), pp. 126-7.

RÖHRICHT R., « Studien zur mittelalterlichen Geographie und Topographie Syriens, I », *Zeitschrift der deutschen Palaestina Vereins* X (1887), p. 230.

SCHUMACHER G., *Across the Jordan* (1886).

SCHUMACHER G., « Unsere Arbeiten im Ostjordanlande », *Zeitschrift des deutschen Palaestina Vereins* XV (1917), pp. 164-8.

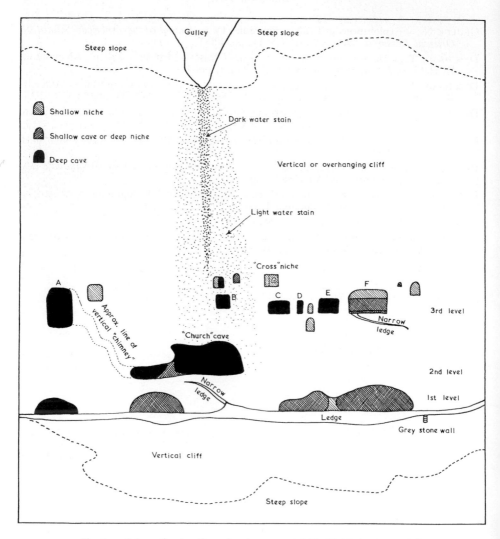

Fig. 1. — Schematic elevation of main caves at ᶜAin Ḥabīs (not to scale).

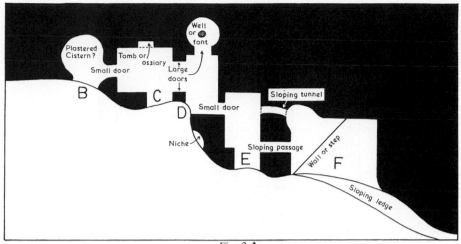

Fig. 2. ↑

One metre

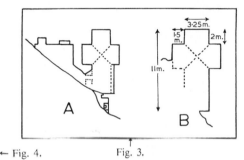

← Fig. 4.   Fig. 3.

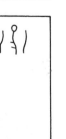

Fig. 5.   Fig. 6.

Fig. 2. — Hypothetical plan of southern group of 3rd level caves at ᶜAin Ḥabīs, from verbal reports & external photographs (not to scale).

3A. — Plan of « church » and neighbouring second level cave at ᶜAin Ḥabīs (after Horsfield).

3B. — Plan of « church » cave at ᶜAin Ḥabīs indicating how much has collapsed since the 1930s (dimensions approx).

4. — Drawing of cross-niche at ᶜAin Ḥabīs (dimensions by Schumacher).

5. — The ossiary or tomb behind cave entrance C, from verbal reports (not to scale).

6. — Graffito beside first level caves.

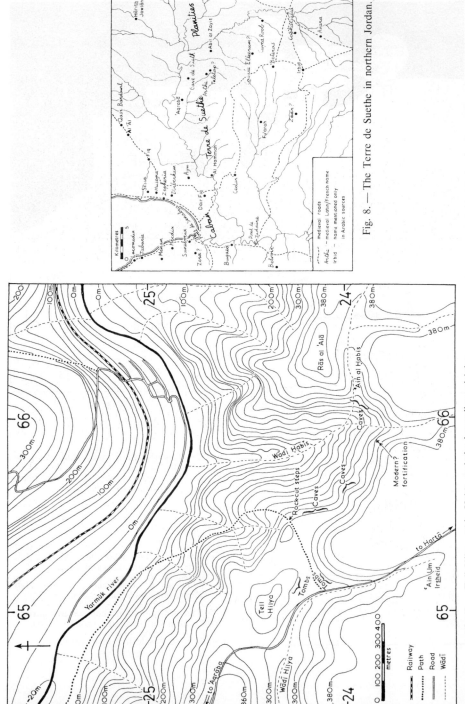

Fig. 8. — The Terre de Suethe in northern Jordan.

Fig. 7. — Tell Ḥilya, ʿAin Ḥabis and the immediate vicinity.

I. — Tell Hilya from ᶜAin Um Irsheid looking approximately north. Some caves are visible near the base of Tell Hilya and the plain of southern Syria may be seen in the distance.

II. — Wādī Ḥabīs and the Yarmūk valley from the edge of the plateau 200 metres south of ᶜAin Ḥabīs.

III. — Tell Hilya from the same position at photograph II. Three caves probably dating from the Byzantine monastic settlement are visible to the left of a cleft in the cliff through which a path passes. Some rock-cut steps still exist just above this cleft.

IV. — Wādī Ḥabīs, the summit of Rās al 'Alā (top right) and the ᶜArāq al Ḥabīs cliff (right) showing the northern end of the access path to the ᶜAin Ḥabīs caves which then proceeds across the hillside below Rās al 'Alā.

V. — The caves of ᶜAin Ḥabīs showing the access path, the lower shelterlike caves, the large second level opening of the « church » cave and its neighbour (lower centre), the isolated northernmost third level cave (upper left) and the linked series of southern third level caves (centre to centre right).

VI. — The caves of ᶜAin Ḥabīs seen from the northern edge of the access path. Note the light and dark stain created by a seasonal waterfall which pours down the cliff from of cleft (just visible at centre top), across superimposed small and large cave openings (entrance B) and thence across the collapsed face of the « church » cave.

VII & VIII. — The caves of ⁨ᶜAin Habis seen from the access path about 100 metres south-west of the beginning the ᶜArāq al Habis cliff-face. The remains of a defensive wall across the southern end of this access path (see photograph IX) are opposite the base of a ladder (lower right).

IX. — Four, or possibly five, courses of dressed stone protruding from beneath a thick layer of animal dung which covers the access path (lower centre), the lower three or four courses are of a grey stone which does not come from the immediate vicinity of the caves.

X. — The southernmost third, and possibly fourth, level caves at ᶜAin Ḥabīs showing one or two probable entrance points (centre left) through which water from the waterfall was channeled into a cistern (lower left). Also note the carefully cut rectangular niche with its small arched niche enclosing a bas-relief cross (centre).

XII. — The southernmost of the third level caves which probably formed the original entrance to the entire upper complex (upper centre left) indicating its height above the access ledge.

XI. — The overhanging cliff of ʿArāq an Ḥabīs looking southwestwards and showing the access ledge.

XIII. — The second level « church » cave with figure to indicate scale, also showing the vaulted cruciform roof and the largely collapsed western wall.

XIV. — The « church » cave showing the largely collapsed western end, a smal niche on the left side of the remaining west wall and what might be the upper corner of a door at the centre of this wall.

XV. — The eastern end of the « church » cave showing ist cruciform plan and total lack of decoration.

XVI. — The roof of the « church » cave showing the carefully cut corners and vaults.

XVII. — A cave adjacent to the « church » cave showing the collapsed western end of the « church » cave (centre right).

XVIII. — The cliff-face entrance (entrance A) of the northernmost third level cave, indicating that part of the floor of this cave has collapsed into the Wādī.

XIX. — The entrance to the northermost third level cave with figure to indicate scale. A near-vertical passage from the cave adjacent to the « church » cave and probably dating from the first siege of 1182AD has broken into this cave just behind the standing figure.

XX. — The interior of the northernmost third level cave showing the place where a vertical passage has broken in (centre right) and the openings to two subsidiary chambers (left).

XXI. — Entrances to subsidiary chambers in the northernmost third level cave, that on the left forming little more than an alcove while that on the right leads to a rectangular tomb-like structure.

XXII. — Interior of the low tomb-like chamber with a rubble-filled dip in its floor, leading off the northernmost third level cave.

XXIII. — The deepest of a number of small caves near the lip of the cliff-face above
'Ain Ḥabīs, possibly dating from the second siege of 1182AD.

XXIV. — Interior of the deepest of the small caves on the cliff above 'Ain Ḥabīs
looking across the cliff edge towards the far side of Wādī Ḥabīs.

THE MONREALE CAPITALS AND THE MILITARY EQUIPMENT OF LATER NORMAN SICILY

THE carved capitals of the Monreale Cathedral cloister near Palermo in Sicily are widely recognised as superb examples of south European Romanesque art. They have been discussed in relation to Romanesque carvings throughout Italy and southern France, and have been used to demonstrate the varying degrees of Islamic influence apparent in Sicilian and southern Italian sculpture. Their dating is reasonably certain: from 1174 to 1182 AD according to Jacquiot and King, [1] and from 1176 to 1189 AD according to G. H. Crichton. [2] The Monreale capitals are thus the last in a series of three important Italo-Norman collections of carvings to show military scenes. The others are those above the north door of the church of San Nicola in Bari which may date from 1099 to 1106 AD, and the portal above the north door of the church of La Martorana in Palermo from around 1140 to 1143 AD.

Art historians have identified Islamic elements in the San Nicola north door, [3] more specifically Fāimid Egyptian elements in the sculpted lintels of La Martorana, [4] and predominantly French [5] or predominantly Campanian [6] influences in the Monreale cloister. Others have sought to define the precise channels through which specifically Andalusian or specifically Fāṭimid influences reached Sicily. No one, however, appears to have looked at the wide range of arms and armour portrayed on these Monreale sculptures. Here one can find weaponry that clearly includes western European, Byzantine and Islamic elements and which may tell us much, not only about those who carved these capitals but also about the troops of the ruler who commissioned them.

---

[1] J. JACQUIOT & E. KING, in *Larousse Encyclopedia of Byzantine and Medieval Art,* edit. R. Huyghe, London, 1963, p. 298.
[2] G. H. CRICHTON, *Romanesque Sculture in Italy,* London, 1954, p. 147.
[3] CRICHTON, *op. cit.,* p. 155.
[4] Reference to G. MARCAIS in A. AHMAD, *A History of Islamic Sicily,* Edinburgh 1975, p. 99.
[5] JACQUIOT & KING, *loc. cit.*
[6] CRICHTON, *op. cit.,* p. 147.

The army of Norman Sicily was in many ways unique. Other countries employed both Muslim and Christian warriors, as allies or as auxiliaries, during the 11th and 12th centuries. Various Spanish kingdoms, the Duchy of Naples, certain Muslim dynasties in north Africa and Egypt, and of course Byzantium, all did so. But only in Norman Sicily did such varied contingents form the core of what was almost a professional force. According to most written sources two groups predominated. These

were the Normans themselves and the previously dominant Arabic-speaking Muslims of western Sicily. Other groups may also have played their part, such as the Greek-speaking inhabitants of eastern Sicily and Italian-speaking immigrants from Lombardy and elsewhere. This last group may, rather confusingly, also have included members of a Lombard military aristocracy that had previously dominated southern Italy much as the Arabs had dominated Sicily. There might possibly have even

FIGS. 1-12.—*Capitals in the Cloister of Monreale Cathedral*
1-12: «European» style infantry

been a small influx of newly recruited Muslim mercenaries, Berbers, Arabs or negroes, from north Africa.

All such peoples, with their traditional weapons and defences, may

FOTO II.—*Capital, Cloister of Monreale Cathedral. Saracen-Byzantine style. Scale armour, loose turban*

be illustrated in the Monreale cloister, though their precise identification is far from easy. The new Norman élite fought largely as heavy cavalry in a style comparable to that of the aristocracy of most of western Europe. The Sicilian Muslims fought for their new rulers most notably as skilled military engineers, for instance outside Capua in 1098 AD and later by erecting the fortifications of Bari. Their continued importance in the Norman kingdom may be indicated by the continued use of Arabic military titles. Many of the previous Muslim *iqṭā's,* a form of military land-holding, had been taken over and only slightly altered to form new Norman fiefs, but the old Muslim system of military organization, the *jund,* was preserved largely intact for many decades. In it Muslim soldiers fought both as infantry and as cavalry, though whether this *jund* was modified to include Christian warriors, Normans, Lombards, Italians or Greeks, is unclear. Other Muslims formed a personal guard for the sovereign, under the command of one of their own number. Another élite corps of archers protected certain aspects of government machinery. The importance of such Muslim troops had clearly declined by the end of the 12th century but it had far from disappeared. In fact these «Saracens» continued to participate in the Norman rulers' wars against Christian foes in Italy or the Balkans until the fall of the kingdom, though not against their co-religionists in north Africa.

There are five basic styles of military costume shown on the Monreale capitals. These are: full mail hauberk and helmet for both cavalry and infantry (Figs. 13, 14, 20 and Foto I); scale armour which is generally worn without a helmet by both cavalry and infantry (Figs. 18, 20-24 and Foto II); helmet but no apparent body armour, appearing only on infantry (Figs. 2, 4-6 and 17); and no apparent body armour or head protection, which again applied both to cavalry and infantry (Figs. 1, 3, 7-12, 15, 16, 19, 25 and 26). Shields include the kite-shaped shield (Figs. 2, 4-6, 11-14, 25 and 26), more «kidney-shaped» shield (Fig. 17), relatively large round shield (Fig. 20) and the small hand-held round buckler (Figs. 10, 15, 19 and 38). Weaponry is more varied and includes the long lance (Figs. 14 and 37), the short spear or javelin (Figs. 8, 11, 16 and 36), the mace (Figs. 19 and 30-32), the axe (Figs. 9 and 33), the simple short-bow (Fig. 7) and an apparently composite recurve bow (Figs. 24, 34 and 35). Swords are, however, especially varied and may, above all, reflect the mixed origins of those who carry them. Such weapons include a very broad-bladed, almost trianguler sword (Figs. 4-6 and 17), a more normal sword with a pointed or tapering blade (Figs. 2, 25, 27 and 29), and an essentially non-tapering, distinctly round-ended weapon (Figs. 10, 18 and 28). Other such weapons may be inferred from the shape of their scabbards (Figs. 12, 16, 20, 21 and 23). Of particular interest is a very crude representation of what may be a sword with a curved blade (Fig. 15 and Foto III).

The mail hauberk is represented by a series of small holes drilled into the stone (Figs. 13, 14, 20 and Foto I). This style of representation is otherwise largely confined to 12th century Italy. The closest parallel

Foto III.—*Capital, Cloister of Monreale Cathedral. Lightly protected infantry with bucklers*

to these examples at Monreale, both in form of representation and in the style of the short-sleeved hauberk, is to be found on the west front

13

14

15

Philistines
16

17

19

Massacre of the Innocents
18

20

Sleeping Guards at the Tomb

FIGS. 13-20.—*Capitals in the Cloister of Monreale Cathedral*
13-14: «European» style cavalry. 15-20: «Saracen-Byzantine» style infantry

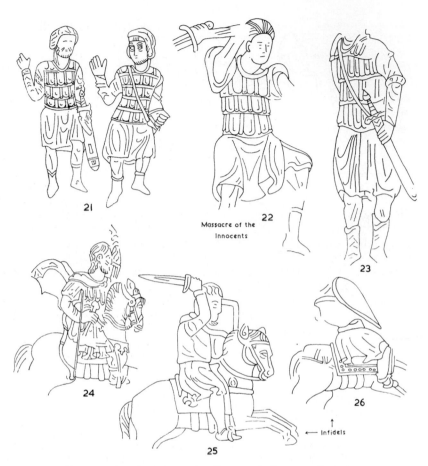

FIGS. 21-26.—*Capitals in the Cloister of Monreale Cathedral*
21-23: «Saracen-Byzantine» style infantry. 24-26: «Saracen-Byzantine» style cavalry

of the church of San Zeno in Verona (c. 1139 AD). Closer in date to Monreale are some similarly short-sleeved hauberks on the candelabrum made by Nicola d'Angelo and Pietro Vassalletto in the church of St. Peter Fuori la Mura in Rome (c. 1170 AD). Within the Norman kingdom itself short-sleeved mail hauberks, rendered in a somewhat more naturalistic style of closely spaced holes, are shown in early 12th century carvings over the north door of the church of San Nicola at Bari and on a mid-12th century carved lintel over the north door of the church of La Martorana in Palermo (Fig. 49).

Although long-sleeved mail hauberks are found in many Mediterranean lands, on both sides of the religious divide in Spain, in Languedoc, Italy and Egypt, the short-sleeved variety dominated, probably for climatic reasons. Late 12th century Norman Sicily and southern Italy may, however, have been somewhat of an exception (Figs. 40, 41 and 49). This style had become increasingly rare in the north of Europe as early as the 11th century. Nevertheless it would be wrong to imagine that the style of armour popularly associated with the «Norman knight», that is, a segmented spangenhelm, a mail hauberk and a large kite-shaped shield, was unknown in southern Italy prior to the Norman takeover. Rather this fashion was one among many to be seen in the pre-Norman Mezzogiorno. Such pre-Norman mail was again short-sleeved and ended above the knees as seen at Monreale (Figs. 20, 47, 49 and Foto I). This more limited mail protection had also often appeared on Byzantine ivories and manuscripts of the 10th and 11th centuries, either alone or in conjunction with other forms of armour. It may even be seen in a 9th century Psalter (Monastery of the Pantocrator, Mount Athos, Ms. 61, ff. 30v and 89r), and in fact there is little reason to doubt that it had been in continuous fashion since the fall of the Western Roman Empire.

The mailed horsemen of Monreale also show two other interesting features. Their saddles are secured by two girths as are those of other horsemen at Monreale (Figs. 13, 14 and 24-26), yet this was not the case at San Nicola, Bari, nor in any of the 11th century Exultet Rolls of southern Italy. First appearing in southern France in the 11th century («Atlantic Bible,» Biblioteca Laurenziana, Ms. Edili 126, Florence), this doubled girth had become almost universal throughout western Europe by the late 12th century. It is, in fact, seen in 12th century Exultet Rolls and on all the saddles of the Cappella Palatina ceiling in Palermo (c. 1140 AD). By contrast the helmets worn by these mailed riders at Monreale seem to be specifically Sicilian. They clearly include what can only be described as mailed earflaps (Figs. 13 and 14). There also seem to be no other examples even in Sicily. In Modena Cathedral, beneath the chapel at the east end, there is a 12th century carving of a prone warrior who wears a rare and very early form of sallet helmet that is roughly comparable to many helmets seen in Byzantine and other Middle Eastern illustrations. The lacing that secures this defence beneath the warrior's chin is the nearest one gets in Romanesque Europe to another helmet of the Sicilian ear-flap variety. Perhaps this style was merely a short-lived experiment even in Sicily, and one that happened to coincide with the carving of the Monreale capitals.

Whereas the mailed warriors of Monreale mostly demonstrate clear western European influence, those warriors wearing scale armour (Figs. 18 and 20-24) seem at first glance to derive from Byzantine pro-

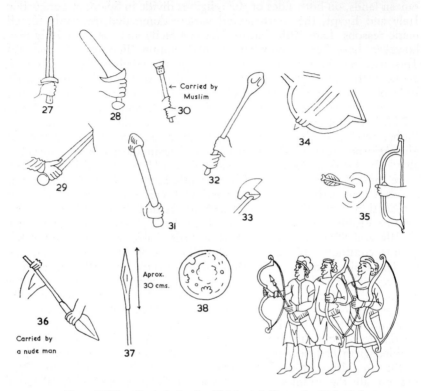

FIGS. 27-38.—*Capitals in the Cloister of Monreale Cathedral*
27-29: Swords. 30-32: Maces. 33: Axe. 34-35: Bows. 36-37: Spears. 38: Shield

totypes, as might other such examples in southern Italy (Figs. 46 and 47). While this may, in fact, be so, it is equally probable that their armours derive more immediately from the Arab world, and thus from Sicily's preceding Muslim era. Such styles of armour, at least in Egypt, Syria and north Africa, might still be traced back to a Byzantine original, either all the way to the pre-Islamic period or to Byzantine influences felt during the early Middle Ages. It is, however, equally possible that an increased use of scale armour in Byzantium from the 8th to 11th centuries was itself a result of both Muslim military pressure and Arab armour fashions. Some such defences at Monreale are worn by warriors who wear what looks like a loose turban (Figs. 18, 21, 22 and Foto II). A turban is almost certainly wound around the helmet of a sleeping warrior (Fig. 20) and is seen in other comparable sources (Figs. 39 and 45). The most noticeable feature is, however, the fact that the elements of these armours overlap downwards and are, in most cases, clearly separated by what appear to be leather straps. Hence we have here scale rather than lamellar armour. A short cuirass of this type had for some centuries been popular in Byzantium where it was generally worn with short sleeves of splinted armour. Here its individual scales were also seen overlapping upwards and were, as such, in many ways more akin to laced lamellar than to scale armour. Within the Muslim world a fashion for wearing a sleeveless cuirass that covered the abdomen, chest and shoulders, rather than simply the abdomen and chest as had earlier lamellar cuirasses in Seljuk Iran, grew in popularity in Ayyūbid and Mamlūk times, that is in the later 12th and 13th centuries. This is clearly indicated both in Ayyūbid and Mamlūk metalwork and in Syriac manuscripts from the Jazīra region of northern Mesopotamia. Most such cuirasses consisted of upwards overlapping large lamellae, although downwards overlapping forms were not unknown. A cuirass of this shape, and either of scales or lamellae, is illustrated in an 11th century Exultet Roll from Lombard southern Italy (Museo Civico, Pisa). But most of the cuirasses shown in 11th century southern Italian manuscripts, 12th century Sicilian mosaics, and 12th century Sicilian or south Italian carved ivory panels include Byzantine-style splinted sleeves and often a similarly constructed Byzantine-style skirt. The only indisputable south Italian examples of downwards overlapping scales seem, interestingly enough, all to date from the 12th century. These appear, for example, on an ivory altar-back in the Salerno Cathedral Museum as part of a cuirass that also protects the upper-arms and thighs, on bronze doors designed by Barisanus of Trani at Trani Cathedral (Fig. 46) where they are worn by St. George, and, as an exact replica of the Monreale-style of short sleeveless cuirass, being worn by a soldier in a scene of «The Betrayal» in an early 12th century Exultet Roll from Fondi (Bibliothèque Nationale, Ms. Nouv. Acq. 710, Paris).

Some of the helmets worn by otherwise unarmoured figures at Monreale seem to betray equally mixed antecedents. The first type (Fig. 2) is, by the normal standards of 12th century western Europe, very unusual indeed. Since the sculptor has gone out of his way not to indicate joints or hinges where these helmets cover cheek, neck and chin, one may assume that here is a head protection of some flexible material,

FIGS. 39-45.—*Comparative material from Sicily and southern Italy*
39: «Sicilian archers and crossbowmen,» *Chronicle of Peter of Eboli,* c. 1197 AD,
Sicilian or south Italian (Burgerbibliothek, Ms. Cod. 120/II, Berne). 40: «Constance
besieged in Salerno,» *Chronicle of Peter of Eboli,* c. 1197 AD, Sicilian or south Ita-
lian (Burgerbibliothek, Ms. Cod. 120/II, Berne). 41: «Battle between Sicilian and
Imperial Armies,» *Chronicle of Peter of Eboli,* c. 1197 AD, Sicilian or south Italian
(Burgerbibliothek, Ms. Cod. 120/II, Berne). 42: «The Emperor's Guard,» *Exultet
Roll,* 12th century Benevento, south Italian (Biblioteca Casanatense, Ms. 724, B i.
13, Rome). 43-45: Bronze door panel, late 12th century, south Italian (Trani
Cathedral)

perhaps leather. Leather, and almost certainly padded, helmets are more frequently mentioned in Arabic and Greek sources than in Latin. Al Ṭabarī describes them, for example, as do various Byzantine military manuals. Helmets of a similar sort, though harder to interpret, appear on many Byzantine manuscripts and in Muslim works of art such as Fāṭimid carved wood and ivory panels. They are also not uncommon in a south Italian context, although where they do not wrap around beneath a wearer's chin there is no reason to assume that they are not of metal (Fig. 42). Almost identical protections, characterized by the fact that they cover almost the entire head, lack visible joints or hinger, and show a distinct thickness or evidence of padding around the facial opening, are worn by Herod's soldiers on the 12th century ivory altar-back at Salerno and by a presumed 11th century ivory chess «knight» from southern Italy which is now in Paris (Cabinet des Médailles, Bibliothèque Nationale). More doubtfully they may be worn by the Army of the Emperor on an Exultet Roll from San Vincenzo al Volturno of 981-987 AD (Vatican Library, Ms. Lat. 9820, Rome). A similar form of helmet is certainly worn by both horsemen and infantry on the 11th century Byzantine ivory casket now in Troyes Cathedral.

A second type of helmet (Fig. 4) has a face-guard astonishingly similar to examples that appear on late Mozarab manuscripts from northern Spain («Beatus,» 1091-1109 AD, British Library, Ms. Add. 11695, London; and the «Avila Bible,» late 12th century, Biblioteca Nacional, Ms. ER 8, f. 324v, Madrid). These are, however, otherwise virtually unknown on either side of the Mediterranean. Another warrior wears a probably metal skull-cap that is unusual only for its broad and decorated rim (Fig. 6), while a further, somewhat worn, carving may either illustrate a soft cap or a helmet with some form of flexible neckguard (Fig. 5).

Yet another carving is, however, both clearer and much more unusual (Fig. 17). Its closest parallel is once again in a late Mozarab illumination («Beatus,» c. 1100 AD, Biblioteca Nazionale, Torino), but this latter illustration is far from clear. Helmets with neck-guards, but very rarely with crests and never with such cheek-pieces, are of course common in Byzantine manuscripts of roughly a century earlier («Smyrna Octateuque,» late 11th century, Vatican Library, Cod. Gr. 746, Rome; and «Constantinople Octateuque,» early 12th century, Topkapu Library, Ms. Gr. 8, Istanbul). Dating from a little later than Monreale are some Syriac Gospels from the Jazīra area, now in the British Library and the Vatican Library, both of which portray helmets of the same essentially Byzantine form. In Italy this shape, again lacking a crest or cheek-pieces, is clearly represented on the «Rome Casket,» a 12th century carved ivory box from Sicily or southern Italy which is now in the Palazzo Venezia Museum

IX

FIGS. 46-52.—*Comparative material from Sicily and southern Italy*
46: «St. George,» bronze door panel, late 12th century, south Italian (Trani Cathedral). 47: «St. George,» statue, late 12th century, south Italian (Portal of S. Sofia, Benevento). 48: «Centaur,» relief, c. 1153 AD, south Italian (West front, Cathedral, Bari). 49: «Hunters,» c. 1140 AD, Sicilian (North door, La Martorana, Palermo). 50: Relief, early 12th century, south Italian (West front, San Nicola, Bari). 51: «Demons,» relief, late 12th century, south Italian (Exterior, Cathedral, Barletta).
52: «Merman,» relief, 1175-1200 AD, south Italian (Nave, Cathedral, Bitonto)

in Rome. The shield carried by the Monreale warrior is also of interest (Fig. 17). It is an almost exact replica of that carried by a demon on a 12th century Frankish capital in Nazareth that portrays a «Believer with the Queen of Faith.» These shields may well be of leather and perhaps had a north African origin. If so, then they are early versions of the famous kidney-shaped Adarga shield that was subsequently carried by almost all «Moors» in late 13th to 15th century Spanish art.

The equipment carried by unarmoured figures at Monreale is relatively straightforward. One horseman (Fig. 25) clearly has a tall shield with a flatish top and, since he is in combat with a mailed figure, he probably represents a lightly armed north African, Berber or Arab cavalryman. In other words he is some form of «infidel.» This interpretation is supported by the fact that he is armed only with an almost triangular sword of a type that is carried by those Monreale infantrymen who could well be Sicilian Muslims. Another such «infidel» horseman does, however, carry an ordinary round-topped kite-shaped shield, of a type common in other sources from this region (Figs. 40-42 and 50).

One infantryman, with his tall shield and short broadbladed thrusting or throwing spear (Fig. 11), could have come from almost any country bordering the Mediterranean. In these areas, from the 11th century onwards, such a tall infantry shield was normally associated with the spear rather than the sword. Examples of armoured or unarmoured such foot soldiers are numerous (Figs. 40 and 49). For instance in the «Liber Testamentorum Regium» of 1126-1129 AD from Oviedo (Oviedo Cathedral Library), on a late 12th century fresco from the Castilian church of San Baudelio de Berlanga (Museum of Fine Art, Boston), on a 12th century relief of «The Betrayal» in Pistoia Cathedral Crypt, in the late 11th century carving over the north door of San Nicola at Bari, on a fragment of 11th century Fāṭimid lustre ware now in the Victoria and Albert Museum, London, and in the early 12th century ivory book-covers of «Queen Melisende's Psalter» in the British Museum. At this time and in this area lightly protected sword-armed infantry normally carried a smaller, hand-held rather than arm-supported, shield commonly referred to as a buckler (Figs. 10, 15, 50 and Foto III). Although there are exceptions to this general rule, the evidence in its favour is very strong.

Mention has already been made of both the simple short-bow and the recurve composite bows that appear at Monreale. These seem to have shared the field in the Mediterranean region (Figs. 34, 35, 39, 40, 43, 45, 48 and 49) until the Turkish style of composite bow virtually took over Muslim archery. At this time, of course, the long-bow and cross-bow were competing to oust the simple short-bow in north-west Europe.

Both these weapons may also appear in southern Italy at the very end of the 12th century (Fig. 38).

This leaves the axe and the mace. Around the Mediterranean the former weapon (Figs. 9 and 33) was more common in Spanish and Byzantine sources. An axe very similar to those at Monreale appears, together with a sword, in the hands of a turbaned foot soldier on the Cappella Palatina ceiling of c. 1140 AD, but in general the simple axe seems to have been relatively rare as a weapon of war in Sicily.

The same cannot be said of the mace. These are, interestingly enough, more often placed in the hands of heretics, demons, Herod's troops and other such undesirables than into the hands of Christians, by both Byzantine and Italian Romanesque artist. The weapon also appears, though not very frequently, in Fāṭimid art. In Norman Sicily, meanwhile, it is grasped by apparently negroid warriors at Monreale (Fig. 19) and by a man whose costume probably identifies him as a Muslim (Fig. 30). A mace is also carried by a Centaur on an 11th century ivory oliphant from Salerno (Museum of Fine Art, Boston), by a camel-riding Arab on the Cappella Palatina ceiling, by a number of demons on carved friezes at Barletta Cathedral (Fig. 51), by a two-tailed merman in Bitonto Cathedral (Fig. 52) and by a pair of warriors, one with closely curled and somewhat African hair, on the late 12th century bronze doors of Trani Cathedral (Fig. 44). In all these south Italian examples, where shields are carried, they are of the small round hand-held variety. Once again the circumstances in which the mace appears in the Norman kingdom suggest that the mace was primarily an «infidel» weapon.

Now to return to that strange curved sword or knife (Fig. 15). The curved blade had long been known in the east and in the nomadic zones of the Eurasian steppes. Knives that were long enough to be regarded as swords, with long hilts and no quillons just as at Monreale, are shown in the hands of Chaldeans in a 9th century Byzantine «Book of Job» (Vatican Library, Cod. Gr. 749) and in other similarly dated Greek manuscripts. Comparable weapons appear on 9th and 10th century Cappadocian frescoes that also betray a strong Islamic costume influence (Kokar Kilise, Peristrema Valley, Hasan Dag) and in 11th century Byzantine manuscript illustrations of Arabs and Turks. In Egypt a true sword with a slightly curved blade appears on two paper fragments from Fustāt («Two Warriors,» 11th-12th century, Museum of Islamic Art, Cairo; and «Jazrafīl who rides an Elephant,» c. 1200 AD, Department of Oriental Antiquities, British Museum, London). In western Europe at a rather earlier date the curved knife with long hilt and long blade but no quillons, appears in the south French «Beatus of St. Sever,» 1028-1072 AD (Bibliothèque Nationale, Ms. Lat. 8878, f. S, Paris). In Sicily a comparable but smaller weapon is used to slay a Muslim child in the «Chronicle of Peter of Eboli,» c. 1197 AD (Burgerbibliothek, Ms. Cod. 120/II, Berne). In Europe these weapons possibly had Byzantine or Muslim antecedents and may themselves have been the forerunners of the heavy, single-edged Falchions that grew in popularity with the warriors of 13th century Europe.

BIBLIOGRAPHY

Recent publications on medieval Sicily have been few and of a mixed degree of originality, while earlier studies remain essential reading for all those interested in the Norman Kingdom of southern Italy and Sicily and in its background. The most useful generally available such works are as follows:

AHMAD, A.: *A History of Islamic Sicily,* Edinburgh, 1975.
AMARI, M.: *Biblioteca Arabo-Sicula,* Turin-Rome, 1880-1881.
— *Storia dei Musulmani di Sicilia,* Catania, 1933.
ARATA, G. V.: *L'Architettura Arabo-Normanna e il Rinascimento in Sicilia,* 1925.
BELLAFIORE, G.: «The Cathedral of Monreale,» *Connoisseur,* March, 1975.
BERTAUX, E.: *L'Art dans l'Italie Méridionale,* vol. I, Paris, 1904.
CHALANDON, F.: *Histoire de la Domination Normande en Italie et en Sicile,* Paris, 1907.
GABRIELI, F.: «La Politique Arabe des Normands de Sicile,» *Studia Islamica,* IX, 1958.
GARTON, T.: «Islamic Elements in Early Romanesque Sculpture in Apulia,» *AARP,* IV, 1976.
GAY, J.: *L'Italie Méridionale et l'Empire Byzantin,* Paris, 1904.
JAMISON, E.: *Admiral Eugenius of Sicily,* London, 1957.
— «The Sicilian Monarchy in the Mind of Anglo-Norman Contemporaries,» *Proceedings of the British Academy,* XXIV, 1938.
JONES, D.: «Romanesque, East or West?», *Connoisseur,* April, 1976.
NORWICH, J. J.: *Kingdom in the Sun 1016-1130,* London, 1967.
— *The Normans in the South 1130-1194,* London, 1970.
SARRE, F.: «L'Arte Musulmana nel sud d'Italia e in Sicilia,» *Archivio Storico per la Calabria e la Lucania,* Rome, 1933.
SCHETTINI, Fr.: *La Scultura Pugliese dall'XI al XII Secolo,* Bari, 1946.
VENTURI, A.: *Storia dell'Arte Italian,* vol. III, Milan, 1902.
WACKERNAGEL, N.: *Die Plastik des XI und XII Jahrhunderts in Apulien,* Leipzig, 1911.

X

THE CAPPELLA PALATINA CEILING AND THE MUSLIM MILITARY INHERITANCE OF NORMAN SICILY

THE CEILING; ITS STRUCTURE, STYLE AND DATE

THE Cappella Palatina was the royal chapel of the Norman rulers of Sicily and southern Italy. It stood within their palace in their chief city of Palermo. Built for king Roger II (1130-1154) between the years 1132 and 1143,[1] the chapel still has as one of its greatest glories a painted wooden ceiling. This ceiling, which is constructed in an Islamic style, is widely believed to have been begun around 1140.[2] The chapel itself falls into three sections: a nave and two flanking aisles. The ceiling of the nave, formed of *muqarnas* or superimposed suspended quarter-domes, arches, squinches and niches, has attracted most attention from art historians because of its splendid surface decoration and because it is an early example of the *muqarnas* style.[3] Nevertheless, the ceilings over the two aisles, each formed of a sequence of beams and recessed curved panels, were apparently built and decorated at around the same time.[4]

Each ceiling was originally coated with a thin layer of plaster which was then painted with naturalistic scenes, decorative motifs and inscriptions.[5] Though damaged in many places, and with layers of painted plaster flaking away in even more, these paintings are among the most extensive still surviving from the 12th century as well as being virtually unique in style and content. It is also worth noting that the degree of 15th century overpainting appears to have been exaggerated,[6] and is,

---

[1] DALU JONES, «The Cappella Palatina in Palermo: Problems of Attribution,» in *Art and Archaeology Research Papers*, I (1972), p. 41.

[2] R. ETTINGHAUSEN, *Arab Painting* (Geneva 1962) p. 44.

[3] JONES, *op. cit.*, p. 45.

[4] R. H. PINDER-WILSON and C. N. L. BROOKE, «The Reliquary of St. Petroc and the ivories of Norman Sicily,» in *Archaeologia*, CIV (1973), p. 290.

[5] JONES, *op. cit.*, pp. 41-42.

[6] JONES, *op. cit.*, p. 42, follows U. MONNERET DE VILLARD, *Le pitture musulmane al soffito della Cappella Palatina* (Rome 1950), pp. 221-222, in believing that most

in the opinion of the author, very obvious where it has been done. The panels illustrated in this article (figs. 1-26) seem almost entirely free of such later overpainting, although a few other military or otherwise mounted figures have clearly been tampered with.

It is not the intention of this article to discuss the structural origins, decorative style or iconographic intentions of this splendid ceiling, and only to a limited extent to consider the question of artistic attribution. These issues have been thoroughly argued by a number of scholars,[7] although many questions still remain unresolved. Here I hope merely to draw attention to the military equipment illustrated on the three sections of ceiling, including horse harness and certain features that could have had ceremonial military associations.

Panels showing military subjects are, in fact, relatively few when one considers the emphasis on royal authority, power and triumph seen in the overall decoration of the Cappella Palatina.[8] This was, of course, the Royal Chapel and so the number of military saints and Christs Triumphant seen on the Byzantine-style wall mosaics, plus the courtly life, hunting scenes and powerful symbolic animals on the ceiling, should come as no surprise.[9] On the other hand, the very fact that the repertoire of scenes and decorations was almost entirely Islamic,[10] though drawn from both the east and west of the Muslim world,[11] meant that the artists could use an extremely wide selection of symbolic motifs. Meanwhile their Christian European contemporaries tended more often to fall back upon the reality of power or authority in the medieval world by illustrating warriors or priests.

Before looking at the details of military figures on the ceiling one needs to review the leading opinions on attribution and artistic origins. These must have a bearing, not only on the style of painting but also on

of what can now be seen is really 15th century overpainting. PINDER-WILSON and BROOKE, *op. cit.*, p. 293, note 1, state that there has been a lot of overpainting of faces on the ceiling but that there is no reason to suppose that major, as opposed to purely stylistic, alterations were made.

[7] A. PAVLOVSKY, «Décoration des plafonds de la Chapelle Palatine,» in *Byzantinische Zeitschrift*, II (1893); U. MONNERET DE VILLARD, *Le pitture musulmane al soffito della Cappella Palatina in Palermo* (Rome 1950); R. DELOGLU and V. SCUDERI, *La Reggia dei Normanni e la Cappella Palatina* (Florence 1969); SIMON-CAHN, *The ceiling of the Cappella Palatina in Palermo and its Program* (Unpub. thesis, Columbia University, New York, 1971).

[8] ETTINGHAUSEN, *op. cit.*, pp. 44-45 and 50.

[9] *Ibid.*

[10] PINDER-WILSON and BROOKE, *op. cit.*, pp. 290-291.

[11] *Ibid.;* Monneret de Villard also sees many non-Islamic elements on the ceiling, *op. cit.*, pp. 34-47; Jones similarly sees some clear Romanesque features, *op. cit.*, p. 43.

the content, at least as far as costume, arms and harness are concerned. Monneret de Villard regarded the question as ultimately unanswerable, but expressed a preference either for a Fāṭimid, presumably Egyptian, artist working with local Muslim help or for artists from Edessa or Diyarbakr.[12] Ettinghausen quotes André Grabar as disliking both Christian or even Sicilian connections,[13] and then goes on to state his own preference for an artist or artists rooted in Fāṭimid traditions but cut off from current mid-12th century Fāṭimid developments in Egypt. Thus he suggests a Tunisian connection since elements of earlier Iraqi ʿAbbāsid styles may have survived longer in this Muslim province, a province which lay under very strong Siculo-Norman political influence at the time that the Cappella Palatina was being built.[14] Dalu Jones refines this latter argument further. She points out that Sicily's links with Fāṭimid Egypt were both attenuated and long past, that the Norman domination of Sicily had lasted long enough for a distinctive artistic style to have developed, that its cosmopolitan character meant that its art was unlikely to have been an off-shoot of any one school and that there is surviving architectural evidence to support a strong cultural link between post-Fāṭimid North Africa and Norman Sicily.[15] She also draws attention to the cultural links that had existed between Muslim Sicily and Muslim Spain, as well as arguing that there is no valid reason why Christian Sicilians should not have participated in the essentially Islamic decoration of the Cappella Palatina ceiling. They and their forebears would have been fully conversant with Muslim art and culture following almost two hundred and fifty years of Muslim rule.[16] Why then should this magnificent and singular piece of 12th century art not be a truly Sicilian creation, reflecting the characteristically mixed influences on that island's culture?[17] There is certainly nothing in the arms, armour, harness or ceremonial regalia illustrated on the Cappella Palatina ceiling to dispute such a conclusion and, by contrast, much to support it.

Other aspects of Sicilian and southern Italian art confirm a process of enthusiastic cross-fertilization and the borrowing of motifs from other cultures. The artists who worked on the Cappella Palatina ceiling were fully conversant with Arabic script[18] and motifs. But the earlier crafts-

---

[12] MONNERET DE VILLARD, *op. cit.*, pp. 48-49.
[13] A. GRABAR, in ETTINGHAUSEN, *op. cit.*, p. 50.
[14] ETTINGHAUSEN, *loc. cit.*
[15] JONES, *op. cit.*, pp. 44-45.
[16] *Ibid.*, p. 46.
[17] *Ibid.*, p. 47.
[18] *Ibid.*, p. 46.

men who carved that series of ivory oliphants which are generally attributed to 10th or 11th century Apulia, Amalfi or Salerno used Islamic decorative motifs wrongly, though clearly being aware of them. [19] Sicilian painted ivory boxes from rather later than the Cappella Palatina ceiling, probably from the late 12th or early 13th centuries, bear inscriptions that are so accurate that their craftsmen are generally assumed to have been Muslims. [20] Also from early 13th century Sicily comes a Latin copy of *The Book of Fixed Stars* by 'Abd al Raḥmān al Sūfī (Bib. Arsenal Ms. 1036, Paris) which, by its faithful adherence to an Islamic original is proof that Christian illuminators copied from Muslim artists. [21] It is particularly unfortunate that, of those slightly earlier illuminated manuscripts so far given a Siculo-Norman attribution, [22] none include military figures that might have parallels with those on the Cappella Palatina ceiling.

The very fact that differing cultures probably influenced the decoration of the ceiling means that the figures appearing on that ceiling could in turn shed light on the costume, armaments and perhaps even tactics of regions neighbouring Norman Sicily as well as upon the Siculo-Norman kingdom itself. The figures that are to be discussed in this article can be divided into five main groups: Military but Unarmoured Horsemen (figs. 1-11), Clearly Armoured Horsemen (figs. 11-13), Mounted Huntsmen (figs. 14 and 15), Infantrymen (figs. 11 and 16-23) and Miscellaneous Riders who include those on camels and elephants (figs. 24 26).

THE MILITARY TRADITIONS OF NORMAN SICILY

Since the ceiling and its decoration must, essentially, be seen as a Muslim work of art produced under Siculo-Norman rule, it would be advisable to take a brief look at the Muslim warriors of pre-Norman Sicily and their descendants who served the Norman kings up to the time that the ceiling was painted.

It was the Berbers, above all men from the Huwwārah tribe, [23] who

---

[19] PINDER-WILSON and BROOKE, *op. cit.*, p. 297.

[20] *Ibid.*, p. 290.

[21] *Ibid.*, p. 293.

[22] H. BUCHTAL, «A school of miniature painting in Norman Sicily,» in *Late Classical and Medieval Studies in honor of Albert Mathias Friend Jr.* (Princeton 1955), pp. 312-339; H. BUCHTAL, «The beginnings of MSS. illumination in Norman Sicily,» in *Papers of the British School at Rome,* XXIV (1956), pp. 78-85.

[23] M. AMARI, *Storia dei Musulmani di Sicilia* (Catania 1933), vol. I, pp. 394-395.

played the leading role in the Muslim conquest of Sicily from the Byzantines in the 9th century.[24] Two centuries earlier the backward Berbers had differed from their Muslim Arab conquerers more in their relative lack of military equipment than in the forms or styles of such weaponry. Around 903 AD, however, and within a year or so of the completion of the conquest of Sicily, an Arab geographer could write that the Berbers now fought with Arab horses, Arab camels and Arab bows.[25] He was probably referring to the tribal leadership or élite, as there is plenty of later evidence suggesting that the mass of Berber warriors still fought on foot with the javelin as their favourite weapon.[26]

While the Berbers subsequently won a dominant political position in the Maghrib, they never achieved the same in Sicily. The Kitama and later the Ṣanhāja tribes at various times and in various provinces provided the backbone of Fāṭimid armies,[27] but in Sicily the Kitama, having virtually conquered the island for the Fāṭimids in 917 AD,[28] degenerated into little more than a harrassed minority under subsequent autonomous Arab Kalbite rule.[29] The Berber community in Sicily remained, however, a troublesome and apparently warlike one until the Norman conquest.[30] It retained a distinct identity under early Norman rule,[31] but thereafter seems to have been absorbed into the island's general Muslim population.

Although the Ṣanhāja are rarely mentioned in a Sicilian context, they may provide a good example of Berber military organization and equipment at this time. As the dominant force in what is now Tunisia, they could, in the 11th century, field a small élite of lance — armed and armoured cavalry. Most of their horsemen would, however, have been more lightly equipped.[32] Such an élite, or at least its leadership, have been described as wearing *kazāghand* mail-lined jerkins and helmets or coifs.[33] Perhaps the majority of Berber armoured cavalry would have

[24] Aziz Ahmad, *Storia della Sicilia Islamica* (Catania 1977), p. 62.

[25] Ibn al Faqih al Hamadhānī, «Kitāb al Buldān,» extracts in *Description du Maghreb et de l'Espagne au IIIe-IXe siècle*, edit. M. Hadj-Sadok (Algiers 1949), pp. 40-41.

[26] Beshir Ibrahim Beshir, *The Fatimid Caliphate 386/996-487/1094* (Unpub. Ph. D. Thesis, London Univ., 1970), pp. 67-70; M. Brett, «The Military Interest of the Battle of Ḥaydarān,» in *War, Technology and Society in the Middle East*, edit. V. J. Parry and M. E. Yapp (London 1975), pp. 83-84.

[27] Beshir, *op. cit.*, pp. 28-34.

[28] Ahmad, *op. cit.*, pp. 78-79.

[29] *Ibid.*, p. 84.

[30] *Ibid.*, pp. 62 and 92.

[31] *Ibid.*, p. 140.

[32] Brett, *op. cit.*, p. 84.

[33] *Ibid.*, pp. 84-85.

worn quilted or buff-leather protections, as their descendants wore in the 14th century.[34] A relative poverty in armour might have decreased the effectiveness of Berber cavalry, which was rarely noted for its striking power either in the Middle East or in the Iberian Peninsula. But it seems to have had little influence on Berber infantry which generally enjoyed a higher military reputation than did its mounted counterparts. The most characteristic North African and Saharan item of equipment was, of course, the large leather *lamṭ* shield which, being a body-covering defence, meant that armour was largely unnecessary.[35]

Some Berber troops in Fāṭimid North Africa were described as being dark-skinned and virtually indistinguishable from Black Africans.[36] Negro soldiers, particularly an élite guard unit commanded by a Muslim, are subsequently recorded in Norman Sicily.[37] As yet, however, the origins of these latter troops are unknown. They may have been descended from those Muslim negroes who lived in Sicily before the Norman conquest[38] or have been Sudanese *mamlūk* or *ʿabīd* slave-recruited warriors[39] such as those who had earlier served in Aghlabid and Zīrīd armies.[40]

While Arab troops played a secondary role, numerically speaking, in the Muslim conquest of Sicily,[41] Arabs certainly took a leading role politically, culturally and in the command of most military forces.[42] Hence their importance to the development of Siculo-Muslim armies, and the military traditions inherited by the Normans must not be underestimated. Muslim battle tactics during their 9th cenury conquest of the island were essentially those that had won the Umayyads an empire from the Atlantic to Central Asia. In other words they were fundamentally passive with the Muslims adopting a static defensive position and only counter-attacking with cavalry and infantry after the latter had absorbed the shock of an enemy's initial charge.[43] Combined with a

---

[34] Ibn Khaldūn, trans., *Histoire des Berbères* (Paris 1934), vol. III, pp. 118-119; Anon., *Chronique du Bon Duc Loys de Bourbon,* edit. A. M. Chazaud (Paris 1876), pp. 218-257.
[35] H. T. NORRIS, «The Hauberk, the Kazāghand and the ʿAntar Romance,» in *Journal of the Arms and Armour Society,* IX (1978), pp. 98-99.
[36] BESHIR, *op. cit.,* pp. 28-34.
[37] F. CHALANDON, *Histoire de la Domination Normande en Italie et en Sicile* (Paris 1907), vol. II, p. 739.
[38] AHMAD, *op. cit.,* p. 62.
[39] BESHIR, *op. cit.,* pp. 38-44.
[40] BRETT, *op. cit.,* p. 82.
[41] AHMAD, *loc. cit.*
[42] *Ibid.*
[43] AMARI, *op. cit.,* vol. I, p. 397.

broader offensive strategy of raiding and sieges, such defensive tactics remained highly effective among many Muslim armies and were even echoed in the great Ottoman conquests. [44]

Arab influence, plus a continuing strong political and cultural connection with the Arab Middle East, probably accounted for the fact that Siculo-Muslim armies were recruited and organized along Middle Eastern lines rather than along the quasi-feudal lines apparent in Muslim al Andalus. [45] Troops of servile or slave origin, plus mercenaries, played a vital role [46] although the introduction of the *iqtā* and regional *jund* systems of military land-holding to parts of Sicily did produce some aspects of feudalism, [47] as they did in Egypt, Syria and elsewhere.

Both these forms of military organization persisted under the Normans. The *iqtā* were transmuted with little apparent difficulty or alteration into Norman fiefs for the new Christian élite. Meanwhile the *jund* system of western Sicily, with its territorial militias based upon the *iqlīm* or district, continued to provide the Norman rulers with reliable Muslim troops.

In equipment the admittedly sparse evidence seems again to point towards similarities with the east, above all with Fāṭimid Egypt, rather than with al Andalus. Such parallels refer, however, to urban-based or professional troops rather than to those tribal auxiliaries who also played an important role in Sicilian forces. Sicily was a rich agricultural and urbanized island and as such its warriors were likely to mirror those of the Nile Valley, perhaps Syria and almost certainly Ifrīqīyah (Tunisia) more than those of the nomad-dominated semi-desert and steppe. Differences in arms and armour are, however, likely to have been ones of quantity and perhaps quality rather than of type or style. Christian sources indicate that light troops and light arms predominated, but armour is certainly recorded by Muslim authors and was worn not solely by leaders or commanders. [48] The very fact that the entire Muslim population, not merely a warrior élite, had, and often exercised, military responsibilities may account for many such fighters not possessing armour. There was also the characteristic Muslim fashion for covering

[44] V. J. PARRY, «La manière de combattre», in *War, Technology and Society and the Middle East,* edit. V. J. Parry and M. E. Yapp (London 1975), pp. 218-219 et seq.

[45] F. GABRIELI, «Gli Arabi in Spagna e in Italia,» in *Ordinamenti Militari in Occidente nell'alto Medioevo. Settimane di Studio del Centre Italiano di Studi sull'Alto Medioevo,* XV (Spoleto 1968), vol. II, p. 717.

[46] *Ibid.*

[47] AHMAD, *op. cit.,* pp. 64, 73 and 93.

[48] GABRIELI, *op. cit.,* p. 718.

one's mail or scale armour with another garment such as a *burd,* a striped upper garment, which was typical among the Fāṭimids as early as the 10th century.[49]

It is clear that by the end of the 10th century at least a sizeable minority of Fāṭimid horsemen, perhaps forming a hard-core of shock troops as had been the case even in later Umyyad times, used armour including mail hauberks, helmets and *tijfāf* horse-bards of felt.[50] Sword and javelin remained the preferred weapons of cavalry as well as of infantry.[51] Nevertheless a possible decline in the popularity of the javelin among Fāṭimid horsemen by the mid-12th century probably reflected an increasing use of armour. The wearing of armour would, of course, have made throwing a javelin more difficult while the armour worn by an opponent similarly made such a weapon less effective.[52]

Fāṭimid infantry forces were basically divided into spear- and sword-armed men, many of whom wore armour, and archers who were generally not protected.[53] Lightly equipped and extremely mobile infantry archers were, of course, to be among the most effective Siculo-Muslim troops available to their Norman overlords.[54] The highly sophisticated communications system, probably of beacons, that characterized Fāṭimid defensive strategy[55] also seems to have been mirrored in Muslim Sicily. A pidgeon-post that linked the island of Pantelaria to Ifriqīyah in 1088 AD is similarly likely, at least originally, to have been but one link in a chain of comparable communications between Sicily and the African coast.[56]

Nor had Muslim Sicily been isolated by war or religious differences from the Italian mainland during these centuries. The island's mixed population made cultural contacts almost inevitable, but there were also a surprising number of friendly military links despite frequent and continuing outbreaks of hostilities. A fluctuating alliance between Muslim

---

[49] MUḤAMMAD IBN HĀNIᶜ AL ANDALUSĪ, edit. ZĀHID ᶜALĪ, *Tabyīn al Maᵓānī fī sharkh dīwān Ibn Hānī* (El Cairo 1934), vol. I, pp. 686-687; M. CANARD, «L'Imperialisme des Fatimides et leur Propagande,» in *Annales de l'Institut d'Études Orientales de la Faculté des Lettres d'Alger,* VI (1942-1947), p. 168.

[50] BESHIR, *op. cit.,* p. 71.

[51] *Ibid.,* pp. 67-70.

[52] ZAKARIA MUSBAH GHAITH, *The Crusades in Arabic Poetry up to the Death of Nūr al Dīn* (Unpub. M. Litt. thesis, Edinburgh University 1970), *passim.*

[53] BESHIR, *op. cit.,* pp. 76-79.

[54] C. FITZ-CLARENCE, «Mémoire sur l'emploi des mercenaries mahométans dans les armées chretiennes,» in *Journal Asiatique,* XI (1827), p. 47.

[55] J. F. VERBRUGGEN, *The Art of War in Western Europe during the Middle Ages* (Oxford 1977), p. 292.

[56] *Ibid.*

Sicily and the virtually independent quasi-Byzantine city-state of Naples was a major factor in southern Italian politics during the 9th and 10th centuries.[57] Many Muslims even fought as mercenaries for Athanasius II, Bishop of Naples, alongside local militia forces and a small Byzantine contingent.[58] While many Sicilian Christians adopted Islam after the Muslim conquest of their island, numbers of Arabs in the Benevento area settled down and turned Christian after the failure of Muslim attacks on southern Italy in the 10th century.[59] Further south, in the Byzantine *theme* of Lucania, the situation was even more fluid. Here, in he 10th century, a great many Arabs were recruited as soldiers and enjoyed, for a while,[60] the same atmosphere of toleration that enabled the southern Italian Jewish community to become one of the most flourishing in the so-called Dark Ages.[61] Later these Arab soldiers abandoned Islam and were absorbed by the local community. Perhaps even more convoluted was the fate of a band of 10th century Byzantine Greek soldiers who, having adopted Islam, seized the stronghold of Pietrapertosa and operated as free-booters in the *theme* of Lucania until they also seem to have been absorbed into the surrounding Christian population. It would also be interesting to know more about the origins of the Masnada, a band of mercenaries who remained largely responsible for Papal security until the mid-12th century.[62] Their name sounds astonishingly Arabic and makes one think of *masnad,* a prop or support, and *musānadah,* meaning help or assistance, all of which are terms not inconsistent with their role in Papal Rome.

Christians remained a majority in Sicily throughout the years of Muslim rule and herein lie other possible cultural links with the outside world, this time with North Africa. Latin-speaking Christian communities, almost certainly town-orientated as they had been since Byzantine times, survived in Ifrīqīyah at least until the late 9th century.[63] Some were, perhaps, involved in that slave-trade from Europe in which North

[57] A. R. LEWIS, *Naval Power and Trade in the Mediterranean, AD 500-1000* (Princeton 1951), p. 134.

[58] J. GAY, *L'Italie Méridionale et l'Empire Byzantin* (Paris 1904), p. 137.

[59] F. E. ENGREEN, «Pope John the Eighth and the Arabs,» in *Speculum,* XX (1945), p. 320.

[60] A. GUILLOU, «L'Italia byzantina, douleia e oikeiôsis,» in *Bulletino dell'Instituto Storico Italiano per il Medio Evo,* LXXVIII (1967), p. 11.

[61] A. GUILLOU, «Inchiesta sulla popolazione greca della Sicilia e della Calabria nel Medio Evo,» in *Rivista Storica Italiana,* LXXVI (1963), p. 56.

[62] P. PARTNER, *The Lands of St. Peter* (London 1972), p. 195.

[63] W. H. C. FREND, «North Africa and Europe in the Early Middle Ages,» in *Transactions of the Royal Historical Society,* 5 ser., V (1955), p. 76.

African Christians played a prominent role.[64] Though long in decline, the Christian agricultural population of Ifrīqiyah only went into eclipse following invasion by the nomadic Banū Hilāl in the 11th century.[65] Even up to 1140 the rulers of present-day Tunisia employed Christians and recent Christian converts to Islam in their armies.[66]

Differences in culture and religion were clearly not as yet the barriers to communication, both physical and cultural, that they were later to become. Muslim Sicily was part of a wider world with contacts to the north and south. In military terms its associations were, naturally enough, largely with Muslim North Africa. As such it had a relatively highly militarized population, at least as far as the Muslim community was concerned. This community probably reached a maximum of aproximately half a million under Kalbite rule in the 11th century.[67] So it was hardly surprising that the Normans found their conquest of the island a far tougher and lengthier business, some thirty years, than had been their progress in southern Italy. In Sicily the Norman conquerors faced a population of soldiers, Arabs, Berbers, local converts and others, who were prepared to defend their existing political supremacy.[68]

Before looking at the Normans themselves, the Italians and Byzantines should first be fitted into the military context, even if only for comparison. Both would have an influence on the development of the Norman army, certainly on the mainland and to some extent even in Sicily.

The demilitarization of the local population under Byzantine rule applied to the rural rather than urban sections of society.[69] It seems to have been more typical of the early Byzantine centuries than the later and, as such, might have meant that the Greek population of eastern Sicily retained a demilitarized status under Muslim rule while the Greeks of the mainland gradually tended to lose theirs. Evidence for increasing local participation in regional defence in the Byzantine *themes* of Langobardia (Apulia), Lucania and Calabria portrays land-owners leading their own forces in support of Imperial units sent from Constantinople, even in the 10th century.[70] As these regions developed economically, they became administratively more self-sufficient. Around 1040 the full-time *theme* armies were disbanded and defence devolved to local urban

---

[64] ENGREEN, *op. cit.,* p. 321.
[65] FREND, *op. cit.,* p. 78.
[66] FREND, *op. cit.,* p. 78, note 3.
[67] AHMAD, *op. cit.,* p. 92.
[68] GUILLOU, «Inchiesta sulla popolazione greca,» pp. 63-64.
[69] *Ibid.*
[70] A. GUILLOU, «L'Italia bizantina,» p. 12.

militias stiffened by occasional units sent from the Byzantine capital.[71] Such urban, largely infantry, militias tended to show greater loyalty to their own locality and to local interests than to the Byzantine Empire as a whole. Subsequently they came to terms with the Norman invaders and helped eject the Byzantine authorities.[72]

Such Byzantine local militias were not, of course, necessarily Greek. The population of Calabria may have been predominantly so, but that of Lucania was extremely mixed while that of Langobardia, with the exception of the Salento area on the very tip of the heel of Italy, was largely Italian.[73]

A very similar system operated in those areas under Lombard authority in the duchies of Capua, Benevento and Salerno,[74] almost certainly reflecting Byzantine infuence.[75] These turbulent minor states were not feudally organized and their rulers relied primarily on urban militias, the local aristocracy having, by the 10th century, largely lost the military interests that it had shown in the preceding two centuries.[76] In the countryside fortified positions such as castles were garrisoned by servile troops recruited by the castle's owner.[77] In coastal cities like Naples there already existed, by contrast, a class of citizens whose status and military obligations, probably as cavalry, were sufficiently impressive for the Normans to enfeif them as knights within a few years of taking control of the city.[78] A similar situation was seen in certain Adriatic towns, including Bari.[79] Mounted troops were also fielded by the major ecclesiastical authorities and land-owners.[80] Many, if not most, such Church troops seem to have been mounted and armoured in normal European fashion. Such expensive equipment was probably made possible because church estates were, in general, more feudalized than were those of neighbouring secular land-owners.[81] Secular militias included armoured horsemen, though they were probably few, as well as light cavalry and numerous infantry.[82]

---

[71] A. GUILLOU, «Italie méridionale byzantine ou Byzantins en Italie méridionale?», in Byzantion, XLIV (1974), pp. 174-175.

[72] Ibid.; D. P. WALEY, «'Combined Operations' in Sicily, AD 1060-78,» in Papers of the British School at Rome, XXII (1954), p. 121.

[73] GUILLOU, «L'Italia bizantina,» p. 11.

[74] C. CAHEN, Le Régime Féodal de l'Italie Normande (Paris 1940), p. 72.

[75] CAHEN, Le Régime Féodal, p. 68.

[76] J. BEELER, Warfare in Feudal Europe 730-1200 (Ithaca 1971), pp. 64-65.

[77] CAHEN, Le Régime Féodal, p. 74.

[78] E. CURTIS, Roger of Sicily (London 1912), p. 356.

[79] CURTIS, op. cit., pp. 357-358.

[80] CAHEN, Le Régime Féodal, p. 65.

[81] CAHEN, op. cit., pp. 65 and 72.

[82] CAHEN, op. cit., pp. 72-73.

The bulk of such Italian troops were militiamen whose primary economic interests lay outside their military duties. They are, therefore, unlikely to have provided those Christian troops who reportedly served in Fāṭimid and other Muslim North African armies. A large contingent of Christians had marched eastward from Tunisia with Jawhar in 1005 during the Fāṭimid conquest of Egypt. Jawhar was, in fact, himself of Christian Sicilian origin. A Christian fleet from Amalfi also helped in this operation.[83] While some of these troops may simply have been European mercenaries, such as those later reported in Zīrīd Ifrīqīyah,[84] others could have been numbered among those North African Christians previously mentioned as serving various Tunisian rulers.[85] Equally they were just as likely to have been natives of Sicily or Sardinia, both of which were then under some degree of Fāṭimid control.

These then were the military circumstances into which the Normans erupted so violently and so successfully in the 11th century and which they were soon to inherit. The Normans themselves were mostly armoured horsemen of the normal north European type.[86] The feudal military obligations that provided the foundation of the expanding Norman state were similarly typical, consisting of forty days of duty with «hauberk and destrier» and a suitable feudal following.[87] The number of such «one hauberk» knight's fees was to grow quite large, three thousand four hundred and fifty-three on the mainland alone according to the *Catalogus Baronum*. This referred to the years between 1154 and 1166 and excluded the region of Calabria.[83] New knight's fees created in Sicily tended to be small,[89] which could indicate that they followed the pattern of the previous Muslim *iqta* military land-holdings. Perhaps they were, as a consequence of their small size, large in number. Elsewhere there is mention of non-noble freeholders, probably new settlers and colonists, whose land tenure was on condition of military service.[90] Such an essentially feudal structure was, nevertheless, firmly rooted in the pre-Norman administrative system. Variations between provinces also betrayed the pre-Norman foundation. In Apulia and Ca-

---

[83] C. CAHEN, «Un texte peu connu relatif au Commerce Oriental d'Amalfi au Xe siècle,» in *Archivio Storico per le Province Napoletane*, n. s. XXXIV (1955), pp. 64-65.
[84] BRETT, *op. cit.*, pp. 82-83.
[85] FREND, *op. cit.*, p. 78, note 3.
[86] WALEY, *op. cit.*, p. 121.
[87] CAHEN, *Le Régime Féodal*, pp. 62-64.
[88] CURTIS, *op. cit.*, p. 351.
[89] BEELER, *op. cit.*, p. 72.
[90] *Ibid.*, p. 74.

pua Lombard elements were visible,[91] in Calabria Byzantine and in Sicily, most noticably of all, Islamic.

The Norman rulers could not, however, rely solely on such feudal resources.[92] There was, for example, a theoretical widening of military obligation so that the entire adult male population could be called upon to fight.[93] The serfs, *servientes defensati,* were expected to provide their own equipment[94] while in Sicily the villein class, whether of Lombard, Italian, Greek or Muslim origin, had to undertake specific local garrison duties.[95] In reality, however, the growing centralization and wealth of the Norman government seems to have led to a steady decline in such a reliance on local levies, particularly in traditionally well administered ex-Byzantine and ex-Islamic areas like Calabria and Sicily.[96] In turn there was a rapidly increasing reliance on paid professional mercenaries.[97]

This increased employment of paid professionals introduced yet more elements into an already complex military situation. Troops as well as sailors were recruited from northern Italian states like Pisa and Genoa, being used to garrison coastal cities as well as to man the fleet.[98] It has, in fact, been suggested that the Norman rulers of Sicily relied on strictly Italian troops far more than has normally been realized.[99] Non-Muslim as well as Siculo-Muslim troops were, of course, needed to support the feudal core of the Norman army. The Normans made war on almost all their neighbours at various times, including the rulers of North Africa. It was here that the non-Muslims were required since it seems to have been agreed that the Normans' Muslim troops would not be sent against their co-religionists.[100] Altogether the Norman field army could consist of heavy and light cavalry, some of the latter being armed with the bow though probably not fighting in Turkish Central Asian horse-archer fashion, plus heavily armoured and more lightly equipped infantry. Other contingents of volunteers fought without pay, but for

[91] E. Jamison, «The Norman Administration of Apulia and Capua,» in *Papers of the British School at Rome,* VI (1913), p. 266.

[92] Beeler, *op. cit.,* p. 62.

[93] *Ibid.,* p. 74.

[94] Chalandon, *op. cit.,* vol. II, p. 535.

[95] Curtis, *op. cit.,* p. 365.

[96] Cahen, *op. cit.,* p. 118.

[97] Cahen, *op. cit.,* p. 76.

[98] E. Jamison, *Admiral Eugenius of Sicily* (London 1957), p. 114.

[99] Waley, *op. cit.,* p. 121.

[100] F. Gabrieli, «La Politique Arabe des Normands de Sicile,» in *Studia Islamica,* IX (1958), pp. 92-93.

booty alone. [101] These latter *rizico* seem to recall those *muṭṭawwiʿ* volunteers who figured so prominently in the Muslim armies of the period.

A Muslim landed aristocracy also survived, at least in western Sicily. Although probably depleted and in decline, it still seems to have held a number of castles and to have fielded its own military forces of both infantry and cavalry until the early 13th century. [102] Most of the Muslim troops serving the Norman rulers were clearly professionals paid by the Treasury rather than a part-time militia. Though paid, their service was in a way a quasi-feudal duty performed in return for the religious toleration extended towards Islam by the Norman government. Such troops formed a standing army that included light cavalry, a corps of skilled siege-engineers and numerous infantrymen of whom the archers were renowned for their speed of movement and rate of shooting. These Muslim troops were organized along lines that reflected the pre-Norman *jund* system and were led by men of their own faith. [103] An élite, significantly drawn from the ranks of the infantry archers, formed a guard for the Royal Treasury or Camera. [104]

Muslim troops, the most reliable part of the ruler's military potential, were reputedly led by their own *quwwad* (sing. *qāʾid*). [105] This explanation has, however, recently been placed in some doubt. The title merely indicated leadership but carried no particular rank. Many *quwwad* were, in fact, legally registered as serfs. [106] The first such leaders seem to have survived from the preceding Kalbite military hierarchy. Later others were of higher social rank, but this status bore no apparent relationship to the title of *qāʾid*. In fact the title was probably little more than an honourific which could also be given to Christians. [107]

The Siculo-Norman court and its ceremonial

The élite Muslim Treasury guards may, to some extent, have also had ceremonial functions. Siculo-Norman court ceremonial was among the most complicated and splendid in western Europe. King William II,

---

[101] AMARI, *op. cit.*, vol. III/2, p. 547.

[102] E. LÉVI-PROVENÇAL, «Une héroïne de la Résistance Musulmane en Sicile au début du XIIIᵉ siècle,» in *Oriente Moderno*, XXXIV (1954), p. 286.

[103] BEELER, *op. cit.*, pp. 74-75; FITZ-CLARENCE, *op. cit.*, pp. 46-47.

[104] JAMISON, *Admiral Eugenius*, p. 39.

[105] CURTIS, *op. cit.*, pp. 371-372; BEELER, *op. cit.*, p. 75.

[106] LÉON-ROBERT MENAGER, *Amiratus-L'Émirat et les Origines de l'Amirauté (XIᵉ-XIIIᵉ siècles)* (Paris 1960), p. 88, note 1.

[107] *Ibid.*

during the latter part of the 12th century, presided over a palace where Muslim forms of ceremony seem to have predominated, although Byzantine fashions may earlier have been more important. [108] Many court officials were Muslims and ceremonial dress seems to have been a mixture of Byzantine and Muslim styles. [109] The source of such Muslim inspiration must surely have been either the memories of surviving Kalbite officials or the contemporary courts of Ifrīqīyah and Egypt. The former were, incidentally, almost certainly a provincial variation of the latter. If so, then one should logically look to Cairo for the originals of any elements of Muslim court ceremonial in Norman Palermo. That, in fact, is precisely what seems to be indicated on those Cappella Palatina panels which illustrate ceremonial scenes. Not all the elements known to have featured in Fāṭimid ceremonial are, however, to be seen on the Palermo ceiling

Fāṭimid official ceremonial was, even as early as the end of the 10th century, more sophisticated than that of any other court with the exception of the Byzantine Empire. [110] Symbols of military rank included collars or necklaces and decorated staffs or wands. [111] In procession various military functionaries carried the Caliph's weapons and other symbols of authority including a parasol, sword, glaive, spear and shield. [112] Decorated staffs of rank were covered with silver. Some were also gilded. To these were fastened embroidered streamers, while their tops were surmounted by gilded silver balls. [113] The ruler's own flags and banners were of assorted shapes and sizes. The most important «Banners of Glory,» of which there were two, seem to have been carried furled. But numerous other smaller silk flags, embroidered with Koranic inscriptions, were flown from simple bamboo shafts. Large wind-socks in the form of lions were also prominent. [114] Although no such devices appear on the Cappella Palatina ceiling, they were known in Carolingian Europe and were probably of ultimate Central Asian origin (fig. 370). The senior «Men of the Sword,» who were the military rather than civilian or administrative élite of the Fāṭimid state, were distinguished

---

[108] CHALANDON, op. cit., vol. II, pp. 738-739.
[109] Ibid., pp. 738-740.
[110] M. CANARD, «Le Cérémonial Fatimite et le Cérémonial Byzantin,» in Byzantion, XXI (1951), p. 355.
[111] CANARD, «Le Cérémonial», p. 367.
[112] Ibid.
[113] CANARD, «La Procession du Nouvel An chez les Fatimides,» in Annales de l'Institut des Études Orientales de la Faculté des Lettres d'Alger, X (1952), pp. 370-371.
[114] CANARD, «La Procession du Nouvel An,» pp. 383-386.

by a special *muḥannak* turban.[115] This, as its name implied, went under the wearer's chin like a bridle. Certain troops also wore parade arms which were normally kept in a separate arsenal, the *khizān al tajammul*.[116] These would presumably have included those gilded swords, helmets with shagreen-covered aventails or neck-guards, shagreen-covered maces, javelins with silvered shafts decorated with silk tassels and shields with silvered bosses that appeared during important processions.[117] Not surprisingly, the saddles and horse-harness of senior officers were similarly magnificent. Gold, silver, enamelling and insetting with precious stones were all used as decoration, while some horses also wore collars of gold chain or amber and even gilded bracelets around their legs. Brocade and silk fabrics decorated certain saddles on which a senior man's insignia, rank and even official number or *'idād* was inscribed.[118]

It is worth noting that symbolic camel litters, or *'ammārīyāt,* were also used as emblems of rank in Fāṭimid Egypt.[119] These were apparently unoccupied, unlike those illustrated on the Cappella Palatina ceiling. But their brocaded sides, silk streamers and silver-decorated leather rails were otherwise reminiscent of those in Palermo[120] (figs. 24 and 26).

ARMS PRODUCTION AND TRADE IN THE NORMAN KINGDOM

The Norman rulers of Sicily and southern Italy inherited a flourishing, although probably small-scale, local armaments industry. As yet, however, it is impossible to say how the products of such industries differed from, or were similar to, the arms and armour of neighbouring arms manufacturing regions in Western Europe, Byzantium, North Africa or the Middle East.

It is also unfortunate that we do not know how many, and to what degree, various late Roman arms manufacturing centres continued production during the so-called Dark Ages. In the present context it would be particularly useful to know the fate of the Roman *fabricae* at Benevento which, although it appears to have been of minor importance pro-

[115] CANARD, «La Procession du Nouvel An,» p. 374; ID., «Le Cérémonial,» p. 368.
[116] CANARD, «Le Cérémonial,» p. 355.
[117] CANARD, «La Procession du Nouvel An'» pp. 367-370.
[118] *Ibid.,* pp. 374-375.
[119] *Ibid.,* p. 371.
[120] *Ibid.*

ducing unspecified arms, [121] was situated in a city whose political importance grew rather than declined during those confused centuries. Some ex Roman centres probably continued production under barbarian rule, particularly those in the Rhineland and upper Danube provinces [122] which were to become Europe's most important sword-making regions. A similar survival has been suggested for Pisa and Lucca, [123] the latter city having had a *fabricae* making swords in the 4th and 5th centuries. [124]

Muslim Sicily was not only rich in iron from around Messina and Palermo [125] but also in the timber needed to provide the energy for metal-working. Armourers were, in fact, reported to have been active in late 9th century Palermo, [126] Muslim Sicily certainly seems to have shared the general economic expansion, both agricultural and industrial, that was seen in the western provinces of Islam from the 8th to 11th centuries. [127] In North Africa a growing metallurgical industry far outstripped anything seen in Classical times, largely because the Romans had enjoyed access to other more easily exploited mineral-rich regions. [128] Under the Fāṭimids this expansion also involved an arms industry, highquality leather shields and rather less renowned swords being specifically mentioned. [129]

A comparable, though perhaps less dramatic, process of economic expansion was taking place in southern Italy from the 7th to early 11th centuries. There was a growth of wealth and production in both the Byzantine provinces and the Lombard duchies which involved industry and agriculture. [130] Although silk production was the most vital industrial sector, there was also plenty of mining, metal-working and shipbuilding. [131]

[121] O. SEECK, *Notitia Dignitatum* (Berlin 1876).
[122] M. TODD, *Everiday Life of the Barbarians, Goths, Franks and Vandals* (London 1972), pp. 116-117.
[123] D. M. BULLOUGH, «The Early Medieval City in Western Europe» (Unpub. paper delivered to the colloquium on *The Early Medieval City*, Edinburgh University, 6 may 1978).
[124] A. H. M. JONES, *The Later Roman Empire, 284-602 AD* (Oxford 1964), p. 834.
[125] M. LOMBARD, *Les métaux dans l'ancien monde du Vᵉ au XIᵉ siècle* (Paris 1974), p. 162.
[126] AHMAD, *op. cit.*, p. 95.
[127] LEWIS, *op. cit.*, pp. 161-167.
[128] LOMBARD, *op. cit.*, pp. 159-162; G. MARCAIS, *La Berbérie Musulmane et l'Orient au Moyen Âge* (Paris 1948), pp. 79-80.
[129] BESHIR, *op. cit.*, pp. 55-62 and 67-70; Murḍā ibn ʿĀlī ibn Murḍā al Tarsūsī, trans. and edit. C. CAHEN, «Un Traité d'Armurerie composé pour Saladin,» in *Bulletin d'Études Orientales*, XII (1947-48), pp. 106 and 127.
[130] GUILLOU, «Italie méridionale byzantine,» pp. 166-167.
[131] *Ibid.*, p. 170.

The lively Mediterranean trade of coastal cities like Amalfi during these centuries is perhaps better known, although the importance of this latter maritime republic declined steadily in the face of Pisan and Genoese competition from the 10th century onwards.[132] Nevertheless, it is worth noting that trade between the southern Italian ports of Amalfi and Salerno, particularly in their traditional cargoes of wood and iron, revived immediately after their occupation by the Normans. Thereafter it continued until relations with Egypt were ruined by Siculo-Norman attacks on the Nile Delta in 1153.[133] In this context it should be pointed out that the Norman rulers of Sicily and southern Italy continued their predecessors' strict state monopoly over the exploitation of forests and iron mines, and hence over arms production, as well as over the export of primary products.[134]

EQUIPMENT ILLUSTRATED ON THE CEILING

The arms and armour illustrated on the Cappella Palatina ceiling is as varied as one would expect in such a culturally mixed island as 12th century Sicily. Yet Islamic elements predominate and it may even prove to be the case that those aspects which at first glance appear very European may, in fact, also have been known in western Islam.

All the swords on the ceiling are straight, but within this limitation they show a great deal of variety. Only one weapon (fig. 1 left) could be described as a typical 12th century European sword with its gradually tapering outline, sharp point, prominent quillons and heavy pommel. Similar weapons survive in a number of western European countries (figs. 302, 323 and 334) and their various features are shown in much mid-12th century Italian art (figs. 248, 250, 257, 263 and 267). Interestingly enough, the Cappella Palatina horseman who is carrying this perhaps sheathed sword is, judging by his costume, not intended to be a Norman or indeed a Christian.

Swords with non-tapering blades having rounded, blunt ends predominate on the Cappella Palatina ceiling and could be regarded as showing Islamic characteristics (figs. 3, 8, 13 and 23; possibly also 17, 18 and 20 to 22). Such weapons were certainly typical of much of the

[132] S. M. STERN, «A document from the Fāṭimid Chancery concerning Italian Merchants,» in *Studi Orientalistici in Onore di Giorgio Levi della Vida* (Rome 1956), pp. 534-537.

[133] CAHEN, «Un texte peu connu,» pp. 64-65; M. CANARD, «Une lettre du Calife Fāṭimide al Ḥāfiz (524-544/1130-1149) à Roger II,» in *Atti del Convegno Internazionale di Studi Ruggeriani* (Palermo 1955), pp. 125-127.

[134] BEELER, *op. cit.*, p. 74; CURTIS, *op. cit.*, p. 370.

Muslim and Byzantine worlds prior to the adoption of the curved Central Asian sabre. That is from the late-Roman period to the 12th century (figs. 93, 123, 126, 127, 141, 145, 146, 148, 155, 158, 188, 201, 203, 210, 276 and 346) and beyond. They are also clearly described by such Muslim authors as al Kindī, [135] who also pointed out that European swords differed by having tapering blades. [136] Essentially the same weapons were, however, to be seen in parts of western Europe, particularly those having close cultural, commercial or political links with the Muslim world in the 11th (figs. 221 C, 233, 280 C, 282 and 312) and even 12th centuries (figs. 238 A, 242, 243, 254, 286, 292, 299, 318, 324 and 325).

Perhaps apparently single-edged weapons might be a more specific pointer to one or other influence (figs. 1 and 11 right). Those with a single curved edge and blades that are too thin to be termed falchions and too late to be regarded as *scramasaxes* appear to have been characteristic of Byzantium and some of its neighbours in earlier centuries (figs. 140, 147, 217 and 348). Yet they were confined almost entirely to Sicily and Italy by the 11th and 12th centuries (figs. 31, 61 and 223).

The design of quillons has traditionally been used as a guide by those studying swords and representations of swords. They come in a greater variety than do blades while at the same time tending to be more easily recognized and categorized than the often crudely represented swordblades of much medieval art. Quillons are also normally visible even when a sword is in its scabbard. On the Cappella Palatina ceiling there are four major categories of quillons. The first is, paradoxically, a lack of apparent quillons (fig. 1). Although missing from most daggers and knives in both Islam and Christendom, the absence of quillons from weapons long enough to be called swords does, by the 11th and 12th centuries, seem strongly associated with western Islam and the immediately neighbouring Christian regions (figs. 31, 32, 35, 61, 69, 71, 84, 96, 113, 115, 120, 224 and 277). One might have been tempted to speculate on a specifically North African, Maghribī origin for this style, given that it seems to be present even in the probably 7th century *Ashburnham Pentateuch* (figs. 76 and 77), had it not been for the clear presence of quillons in later, Islamic, sources from the Maghrib (figs. 79, 81 and 87).

Thick quillons which extend only slightly beyond each side of the blade are the most characteristic of all those illustrated on the Cappella

---

[135] AL KINDĪ, «Al Suyūf wa Ajnāsuha,» edit. A. R. Zaki, *Bulletin of the Faculty of Letters, Fouad I University*, XIV (1952), pp. 9-11.
[136] AL KINDĪ, *op. cit.*, pp. 32-33.

Palatina ceiling (figs. 3, 4, 8, 19 and 21). They are also seen throughout the 12th century Mediterranean world, though perhaps most often along the southern shore. Asymmetrical quillons are quite another matter. Shown once very clearly (fig. 13) and twice in a more debatable form (figs. 19 and 23), such asymmetrical quillons are, without doubt, an Islamic characteristic and an eastern one at that. Their origins are probably to be found in eastern Iran or Transoxania (figs. 191, 368 and 371) and their presence strongly suggests either a single-edged weapon or the slashing style of sword-play that would later be associated with sabre-fencing. The migration of this form westwards may have preceded the coming of Islam (figs. 142 and 143) but was certainly stimulated by that event (figs. 136, 139, 160, 161, 177, 181, 182, 198, 307 and 348). Turkish tribal migrations similarly took asymmetrical quillons westward along a northern axis (fig. 343). Nowhere, outside the Iberian peninsula, have I been able to find a representation of this type of asymmetrical quillons in Christian western Europe.

The langet, or projection from the quillons down the blade, similarly reached Europe via Islam. This feature was known in many parts of Europe in the 12th century but was not widely adopted until the 15th. It is clearly, though only once, shown on the Cappella Palatina ceiling (fig. 20). During the 12th century such langets may have formed part of most swords in Egypt (figs. 125 and 126), many in the Iberian peninsula (figs. 295, 296 and 299) and a few such weapons in southern France (fig. 324). Such a langet could have developed from an almost triangular style of quillons which, having its apparent origins in India, spread across Islam and Byzantium from the 7th to 10th centuries, eventually being represented in southern Italian manuscripts of the 11th century (fig. 226).

Four figures on the ceiling appear to be ceremonial guards and, judging by their very Islamic costume, could represent those élite Muslim units that protected the Norman ruler and his Treasury (figs. 17 and 20 to 22). Their stylized stance probably had its iconographic origins in Iranian art and it mirrors that adopted by supposed «guard» figures in courtly art from other Islamic lands from the 8th to 13th centuries (figs. 103, 157, 169, 187, 193, 204 and 271). The Cappella Palatina ceiling is not the only example from Sicily or southern Italy (fig. 29) and another example may even illustrate Islamic iconographic influence almost at the centre of 9th century Christian Europe (fig. 218).

Spears appear six times on the Cappella Palatina ceiling, but only on three occasions are they in use, twice with a single-handed downward thrust (figs. 1 and 12) and once in that two-handed technique seen in most Islamic art (fig. 7). The two downward thrust pictures, although realistic and perfectly feasible, should be treated with caution because both figures are obviously posed so that they fit the constricted space of half a semi-dome. Of greater interest is the third horseman (fig. 7). I have attempted to discuss the question of medieval European and Islamic cavalry spear techniques elsewhere.[137] The two-handed technique with a long lance was obviously extremely ancient, long preceding the adoption of stirrups. Yet it persisted in the Middle East and North Africa at least until the end of the medieval period. Such a survival is evidenced not only by the illustrated sources, of which other Sicilian examples are known (figs. 64 and 65), and where iconographic conventions might have been expected to persist, it is also described in written sources such as *furūsīya* cavalry training manuals.[138]

Here, however, we are more concerned with the weapons rather than the way in which they were used. Where visible most of the spears have normal diamond-shaped blades with sharply angled edges (figs. 2, 10 and 25). Such would seem to have been preferred in western and central Islam from the 11th to 13th centuries, although broader leaf-shaped spear-blades were also illustrated. In Europe, meanwhile, there was a gradual move away from diamond-shaped cavalry spear-heads with angled edges towards a narrower version of the leaf-shaped blade. This trend probably reflected the increasingly widespread possession of armour among European horsemen. Two clearly illustrated and, from a European viewpoint, unusual features do, however, demand comment. The first is an elaborately shaped, almost fleur-de-lys, spear-head wielded by an armoured horseman (fig. 12). This I have not found in a strictly European context and, in fact, the only apparent parallels all date from the 12th century and stem either from Sicily (fig. 63) or western Iran (figs. 174, 175 and 178). Large spear-blades with a waisted or barbed outline having, in effect, two cutting angles on either side are, however, seen in Egyptian art from around this time. They appear on javelins as well as true spears or lances (figs. 105, 106, 108 and 130). These would be widely illustrated in Syria and Mesopotamia during the following century. Nevertheless, where such small details are concerned too much

---

[137] D. NICOLLE, «The Impact of the European Couched Lance on Muslim Military Tradition,» in *Journal of the Arms and Armour Society,* X (1980), pp. 6-40.

[138] MUHAMMAD AL AQSARĀᵀ, *Nihāyat al Suʾl waʾl Umnīya fī Taʿlim Aʿmāl al Furūsīya* (Ms. Or. 3631, British Library, London); anon. *Kitāb Majmūʿ fī al Rumḥ wa Ghayrihi* (Revan Ksku Coll., Istanbul); IBN AKHĪ KHAZZĀM, *Kitāb, ʿIlm al Furūsīya waʾl Bayṭara* (Ms. Arabe 2824, Bib. Nat., Paris). For other important *furūsīya* manuscripts see HASSANEIN RABIE, «The Training of the Mamlūk Fāris,» in *War, Technology and Society in the Middle East,* V. J. Parry and M. E. Yapp, edits. (London 1975), p. 154, note 6 et seq.

can be read into what might have been little more than a slip of the artist's hand or a product of his imagination.

The same might be true of the spherical protuberance clearly illustrated beneath the blade of a spear carried by a camel rider on the Cappella Palatina ceiling (fig. 25). On the other hand comparable protuberances are also seen within a clearly defined geographical region. They could have served the same function as so-called «boar-spear» lugs which were characteristic of many spears from early medieval Europe, Byzantium and Islam. Such devices ensured that the weapon did not penetrate too far into a victim and thus risk either breaking the shaft or being difficult to extract. Spherical, or at least not lug-shaped, anti-penetration devices seem to be illustrated with varying degrees of clarity from 8th or 9th century eastern Turkistān (fig. 370) to 13th century Iberia (figs. 303 and 304). Its apparent migration westwards is very erratic and it would be dangerous to suggest that this form of anti-penetration device was of Turkish origin, thereafter being introduced to other peoples via Islam (figs. 98, 105, 154, 162, 163, 190, 227, 283, 308, 313, 360, 361 and 362). That such a feature was a reality rather than an artistic device might be confirmed by its presence on surviving later Islamic weapons (fig. 186).

Attached to two spears on the Cappella Palatina ceiling are flags or pennons (figs. 2 and 10). Neither could be described as typically European although there was, of course, plenty of variety in the flags, banners and pennons of 12th century Europe. The first is a long triangular flag with a vertical decorative band which, in a more specifically Muslim context would probably have born a Koranic inscription (figs. 196 and 197). Certainly the *rāya,* normally considered to be a large banner when compared with the *liwā',* often carried pious inscriptions in Fāṭimid Egypt. [139] This I would take as the most obvious source of inspiration for those artists working on the Cappella Palatina ceiling.

Large triangular flags are extremely rare in early medieval European art, and where they are shown they tend either to be associated with infidel foes or are illustrated in contexts having strong Islamic or Central Asian links. Examples include Mozarab manuscripts from Spain (figs. 273, 274, 279 and 284), a Spanish manuscript illustrating a Babylonian army (fig. 306), a 12th century Russian manuscript in which such banners predominate (fig. 344), Sicilian and south Italian sources (figures 54 and 237A), enemies overthrown by the Maccabees in an early 10th century manuscript from St. Gallen (fig. 331), and a manuscript illuminated in the Crusader States (fig. 330) which also betrays many

---

[139] CANARD, «La Procession du Nouvel An,» pp. 383-384.

other minor Islamic features. Interestingly enough, this latter source is one of the few in European art to show streamers of a sort referred to in Fāṭimid Egypt as *maʿājir*. [140] The second standard on the Cappella Palatina ceiling does look more like three such streamers than it does a rectangular flag with a trifurcated edge. Although such an obvious form of decoration as a streamer is shown in many countries it does, around the period in question, seem to have been more popular within the Islamic orbit than within Christendom (figs. 108, 165-168, 172, 176, 268, 313 and 360). The question of Islamic flags and banners has caught the attention of many scholars but still remains highly complex. [141]

The only other weapons that appear on the Cappella Palatina ceiling are a supposed mace (fig. 9) and two forms of axe (figs. 16 and 23), although in the latter case two of the objects in question (fig. 16) could also be interpreted as fans. The supposed mace, apart from apparently being in the process of having its haft broken, is also a very basic weapon. As such it would equate with the Arabic *dabbūs* which, in most original sources, seems to indicate a simple mace rather than the winged form of *ʿamūd*. [142] Maces had long been common in Muslim armies, particularly those of the richer eastern and central provinces where armour was abundant. The mace was, of course, primarily an armour and helmet-breaking weapon. Maces were prominent during Fāṭimid ceremonial parades, [143] clearly caught the attention of European warriors who faced them during the later 12th century [144] and were widely adopted by Byzantine cavalry from the 10th century onwards. [145] But they did not become important in western Europe until the 12th or 13th century. [146]

Simple maces similar to those seen on the ceiling appear regularly, if not particularly frequently, in pre-Islamic and Islamic art from the 7th to 12th centuries (figs. 94, 97, 144, 149, 157, 185, 192, 194, 195,

[140] *Ibid.,* pp. 370-371.
[141] M. GIERS, «Sur la question des drapeaux arabes,» (in Russian) *Zapiski Kollegii Vostokoviédov,* V (1930), pp. 342-365; A. R. ZAKI, *Al Aʿlam waʾl Sharat al Mulk fī Misr (Flags and Coats of Arms in Egypt)* (Cairo 1948); also the relevant entries in *The Encyclopedia of Islam,* second edition.
[142] AL ṬARSŪSĪ, *op. cit.,* pp. 117 and 139.
[143] CANARD, *op. cit.,* pp. 367-369.
[144] Anon., *Itinerarium Peregrinorum,* trans. K. Fenwick (London 1958), pp. 64, 78, 93 and 131-132.
[145] J. F. HALDON, «Some Aspects of Byzantine Military Technology from the Sixth to the Tenth Centuries,» in *Byzantine and Modern Greek Studies,* I (1975), p. 39.
[146] E. OAKESHOTT, *The Archaeology of Weapons* (London 1960), pp. 178 and 258; P. MARTIN, *Armour and Weapons* (London 1967), p. 244.

209, 363 and 369). They also appear in Byzantine sources, though generally in the hands of Biblical villains, infidels or, more specifically, Bedouin Arabs. This association of the simple mace with the Muslim world is also seen in western European art where such weapons are almost invariably found in provinces under varying degrees of Muslim influence (figs. 216, 220, 225, 240, 241, 273, 280, 280 B, 285, 298, 301 and 314). In 12th and early 13th century Sicily itself this weapon was particularly abundant (figs. 41, 44, 60 and 73).

As to the Palermo axes, one appears to be a perfectly normal war-axe (fig. 23) that would not have looked out of place in the hands of a northern European warrior (figs. 332, 335, 340 and 342). The only feature that distinguishes the Cappella Palatina axe is that its «beard», or the extension of its blade, clearly projects up rather than down the haft as was normal with asymmetrical forms of European war-axe. As such it is of a form not generally seen outside 12th century Sicily and southern Italy (figs. 62 and 241) although it will be clearly shown in later Spanish sources (fig. 305). It could, in fact, be misleading to assume any north European influence on these particular Sicilian and south Italian weapons. War-axes were certainly not uncommon among Mediterranean warriors, both Muslim and Christian during this and preceding centuries (figs. 228, 231, 232, 241, 245, 280 A, 281, 288, 291, 309, 311, 315, 317, 326, 328, 353, 355 A and 357). They are also prominent in Sicilian art of the 12th century (figs. 36, 40, 46, 47, 59, 62, 70 and 72). The popularity of various war-axes in this region at around this time lends support to the interpretation of the two objects on the Cappella Palatina ceiling (fig. 16) as axes rather than as fans. Broad, half-moon-shaped axes in which the two ends of the blade almost touch the haft are to be found among the other Sicilian weapons figured above. They were also not unknown in Islamic art from the 9th to 14th centuries (figs. 131, 137 and 195), often in a ceremonial context just as they are on the Cappella Palatina ceiling. This, in addition to their shape, leads one to assume that the weapons in question are examples of the nāchakh or nājikh. In 13th century Muslim India this was considered a «noble» weapon suitable for princes, [147] and an Indian origin seems to be suggested. [148] In Egypt, during the preceding century, the nājikh was stated to be of eastern, perhaps Persian, origin and often to have a highly decorated blade. [149] Similar axe-blades are certainly placed

---

[147] MUḤAMMAD IBN MANṢŪR FAKHR AL DĪN MUBARAKSHĀH, Adab al Ḥarb wa al Shujāʿah, edit. A. S. Khwānsārī (Tehran 1969) pp. 260 and 268.

[148] MUBARAKSHĀH, op. cit., p. 272.

[149] AL ṬARSŪSĪ, op. cit., pp. 118 and 140.

in the hands of the Hindu deities Ganesa and Durga by Indian artists both in continental India (figs. 372 and 373) and the East Indies (fig. 374). Broad axe-blades fastened to their hafts at two points rather than the normal single fixture are rare, but again not unknown (figures 152, 163 and 241).

It is worth noting that one particular weapon is missing from the Cappella Palatina ceiling, namely the bow and arrow. This might seem strange given the importance and high status of Muslim archers among the Norman rulers' élite guard units. On the other hand, bows seem to have had no ceremonial status in Islamic lands that lacked a dominant Turkish or Turkified military aristocracy. The weapons are, however, widely illustrated in other Sicilian and neighbouring sources from this period (figs. 34, 37, 42, 43, 45, 51, 52, 56, 66, 82, 123, 130, 220, 233, 238B, 247 and 262). The majority of such weapons have angled «ears.» These are the unbending outer parts of a bow which are also illustrated in an interesting Sicilian manuscript from a century later (fig. 75). This may, however, have been a case of a Latin scribe directly copying an earlier original, just as might have been true of the Moroccan artist who produced a similarly dated Arabic edition of the same manuscript (fig. 91).

A minority of the presumed warrior figures on the Cappella Palatina ceiling clearly wear helmets (figs. 5, 9, 11 left, 12 and 13). Others probably do so (figs. 2, 3, 4, 8, 16 and 19), although in some of these latter cases their headgear could be non-protective hats. The most clearly delineated helmet (fig. 5) is worn by a horseman with a kite-shaped shield. It is of a tall conical form commonly seen throughout 11th and 12th century Europe. Here there is no evidence of a segmented spangenhelm construction, but by the mid 12th century helmets beaten from a single piece of iron were common. Though more rarely illustrated than in contemporary Europe, pointed helmets, some clearly of a segmented structure, were seen throughout most of the Muslim world (figs. 113, 114, 138, 155, 156, 158, 199, 205-208, 364 and 365). This is true even if one excludes Iberia where, of course, pointed helmets of a thoroughly European form predominate among those illustrated in Mozarab, Castilian and Catalonian manuscripts. A particularly clear Muslim representation of a pointed spangenhelm is to be found in the early 13th century Moroccan manuscript mentioned earlier (fig. 90). This is of great interest as so few illustrated sources are known from medieval North Africa, a region in close cultural and political contact with both Muslim and Norman Sicily. This manuscript is of further interest in the present discussion because it also illustrates a figure wearing a turban wrapped around a helmet or hat that is drawn in almost exactly the same manner as is the spangenhelm in the manuscript (fig. 89). Might one not be justified in assuming that the headgear partially hidden by turbans on the Cappella Palatina ceiling (figs. 8 left, 16 left and 19) are also pointed helmets, as might be a similar form of headgear seen on a Fāṭimid Egyptian dish (fig. 112)? This is, however, mere speculation. So is the interpretation of other pointed headgear on the ceiling as helmets rather than hats. One might have a form of nasal (fig. 4) but this is too confusingly drawn to identify the headgear without question as a helmet. The very large nasal of the first helmet is in itself of interest. These were highly characteristic of 12th century Italy (figs. 246, 249, 255, 256 and 263), as they were of many other parts of Mediterranean western Europe. Substantial nasals also appear in 11th century perhaps Islamic-influenced southern Italian ivorywork (figure 221 C), Mozarab manuscripts from Spain (fig. 278), an earlier and more obviously Islamic ceramic fragment from Andalusia as well as on 10th century frescoes from Nubia (fig. 138) and Iran (fig. 200).

One other helmet on the Cappella Palatina ceiling is of sufficiently distinctive shape to merit comment. It appears to have a forward-angled crown (fig. 13), although lacking the smooth outline normally associated with 12th century European helmets with such forward-angled crowns (figs. 257, 290, 327, 337 and 339). Such forward-angled crowns, which almost certainly indicated that the front part and top of the helmet were thicker than the sides and rear, are a distinctively western European feature. Even when it does appear in Middle Eastern sources it betrays European influence, either because the piece of art was executed under Crusader domination or because Crusaders were the subject of the illustration (fig. 130). The abrupt, almost knob-shaped angle on the Cappella Palatina helmet need not pose a problem, however. Similarly abrupt forward tilts on a helmet's crown are widely shown in 12th century European sources. Most come from Italy or Spain, which may itself be significant as far as the Cappella Palatina illustration is concerned (figs. 245, 251, 255, 289, 293, 294 and 300).

The headcovering with the previously discussed possible nasal (figure 4), if it is indeed a helmet rather than a soft pointed cap, has a reverse-angled crown. Such a shape is rarer for a helmet than a forward-angled crown but is not unknown in the art of the period. It appears on 12th century headcoverings that clearly were real helmets, both in Sicily (figs. 49, 53 and 58), Italy (fig. 260 B) and as far away as western Iran (fig. 178).

Hauberks are twice clearly illustrated on the Cappella Palatina ceiling (figs. 11 left and 13). Such armour may also be worn by a third, less clearly defined, horseman (fig. 12). All these armoured men are, it should be noted, horse riders. They all also wear helmets and carry kite-shaped shields. The representation of armour on the two well-preserved illustrations poses the classic problem of whether mail or scale is intended. The use of a repeated scalloped line looks at first glance more like scale, but there is evidence from other painted rather than carved sources in southern Italy, as elsewhere, to suggest that such a pattern was often used to indicate mail (figs. 54, 227, 228, 260 A and 261). The device was not popular in Egypt where the best-known representation of 12th century mail is rendered as a series of random dots (fig. 130) very similar to that just visible on the third, perhaps armoured, Cappella Palatina cavalryman (fig. 12). Otherwise it would seem that Egyptian artists used a series of tightly packed small circles to represent mail (figs. 101 and 105), a convention that was also popular in eastern Islamic painted sources. A third and more debatable Egyptian system of representing mail appears on a recently published 12th century ceramic fragment (fig. 129), but this has a parallel on the Cappella Palatina ceiling.

The case for scale armour cannot entirely be ignored, however. Such armours were certainly known in Italy and Sicily. Sometimes they are almost unmistakable (figs. 44, 238, 239 E, F and G, 246, 249 and 265) and at other times are less certain (figs. 55, 57, 221 and 269). Although I have argued elsewhere that the relatively frequent appearance of scale armour in Mediterranean Europe probably reflected strong Arab influence during the so-called Dark Ages, [150] surviving representations of supposedly Sicilian Muslim warriors from this and the immediately preceding century almost certainly indicate that mail was worn quite extensively (figs. 27-32, 74 and 224). North African illustrative material from this period is executed in a very crude style but I believe that we do have one reasonably clear representation of mail (fig. 78). Another probably shows the padded, quilted soft-armour widely associated with North Africa and the Sahara (fig. 81) while others almost defy interpretation, although they could represent mail (figs. 86 and 102). A fragmentary but clear illustration from Egypt shows a horseman wearing a scale or lamellar hauberk over his mail (fig. 101). The details of the representation seem to point to lamellar, while the still westward-looking orientation of Fāṭimid recruitment and military organization perhaps points towards scale armour.

A feature of two of the Cappella Palatina armoured riders is the apparent slit up the sides of their hauberks (figs. 12 and 13). A horseman's hauberk was, of course, normally slit up the front and back for

[150] D. NICOLLE, *Islamische Waffen* (Graz 1981), p. 17.

ease of riding, and is generally illustrated as such. But hauberks slit at the sides are not unknown (figs. 234, 258 and 267). Such a style must surely have been intended for fighting on foot as it would not only have been uncomfortable when riding but would make a horseman's legs vulnerable. Despite the fact that it is twice shown being worn by men on horseback, as it is on the Cappella Palatina ceiling, it should be born in mind that this fashion seems to be restricted to Italy. Here, from the 10th to 12th centuries and particularly in the pre-Norman south, urban infantry militias rather than feudal cavalry may have played a dominant role in local warfare. [151]

It might also be noted that one of the armoured riders has a decorative band around his upper arm (fig. 13). This may be taken as a *ṭirāz* such as those worn by various other figures on the ceiling (figs. 1 left, 4, 10, 12, 18, 21, 22, 25 and 26). Some of these, plus other figures, have sleeve decorations that may, however, be more satisfactorily interpreted as the borders of a sleeveless outer garment (figs. 2, 3 left, 14, 15, 16 left, 20, 21 and 22). The whole question of the Muslim *ṭirāz* remains vexed. [152] Essentially the term *ṭirāz,* in a medieval Islamic context, could refer to an embroidered garment normally signifying rank or honour, or to a garment bearing an inscription demonstrating loyalty or allegiance, or to the embroidered band on which this inscription was placed. [153] Some fabrics had woven tapestry or brocaded cotton ornamental bands applied to them, but in Egypt under the Fāṭimids the tapestry version became more popular and was manufactured, often for export, in Alexandria, Cairo and Tinnīs. [154] A workshop, the *khizānah al malikiyah,* specializing in the making of fabrics known as *ṭirāz al malik* existed under Norman patronage in 12th century Palermo and apparently continued to operate into the 13th century. [155] For this reason alone the appearance of the *ṭirāz* on the Cappella Palatina ceiling comes as no surprise. Yet the fashion of wearing decorative bands around the upper arms of ceremonial costumes may have been adopted both in Byzantium and Italy before the establishment of the Siculo-Norman realm (figs. 226 and 347), almost certainly as a result of Islamic influen-

---

[151] BEELER, *op. cit.,* pp. 66 and 192-194; VERBRUGGEN, *op. cit.,* pp. 103 and 125-126.

[152] A. GROHMANN, «Ṭirāz,» in *Encyclopedia of Islam,* first edition, vol. IV, pp. 785-792; L. GOLOMBEK and V. GERVERS, «Ṭirāz Fabrics in the Royal Ontario Museum,» in *Studies in Textile History, in Memory of Harold B. Burnham* (Toronto 1977); M. MAZROUK, «Ṭirāz Institution in Medieval Egypt,» in *Studies in Islamic Art and Architecture in Honour of Prof. K. A. C. Creswel* (Cairo 1965).

[153] GOLOMBEK and GERVERS, *op. cit.,* p. 82.

[154] *Ibid.,* pp. 82-83.

[155] GROHMANN, *op. cit.,* p. 790.

ce. The fashion may also have survived the collapse of the Norman kingdom (fig. 244). Certainly the application of a *ṭirāz* type of band over a hauberk was unusual, but again it was not unknown. Sometimes it is clearly illustrated (figs. 131, 170 and 213), at other times less certainly so (figs. 134, 265 and 329).

A further costume feature is also interesting enough to demand comment. This is a scarf or cloak slung across the chest and over the arm of the horseman who is wielding his spear in the supposedly «bedouin» two-handed style (fig. 7). Such cloaks may also be draped across the shield of a second horseman (fig. 8 right) and be used as rudimentary protections by two huntsmen (fig. 1). This manner of draping a cloak or sash over one shoulder and beneath another, rather as rolled blankets were carried by certain 19th century infantrymen, is characteristic of the 12th and 13th century Middle East (figs. 132-135, 151, 159, 164, 165, 168, 170, 171, 211 and 214) but disappeared in the 14th century. Interestingly enough it also appears in 11th century Italy (figs. 222 and 230B).

Such evidence is too thin for any theories to be based upon it, yet a general eastward spread of this fashion does seem to be indicated. Almost every representation of a Coptic warrior saint in both Egypt and Nubia, from the 8th to 13th centuries, portrays a substantial cloak over one arm. But this iconographic convention never shows cloaks going beneath an arm. Perhaps the fashion developed, barely recorded in surviving art sources, in Egypt and then spread across the central providences of Islam in the wake of Ayyūbid expansion (figs. 93, 100, 115 and 124).

The turbans illustrated on the Cappella Palatina ceiling are of two main types, those with (figs. 7, 8 left, 17, 20 and 22) and those without (figs. 9, 16 left, 23 and 25) the *muḥannak* loose loop of cloth slung beneath the chin. As mentioned earlier, the *muḥannak* style of wrapping a turban was a mark of senior military rank in the Fāṭimid Caliphate. Here it appears, paradoxically, to have been less frequently illustrated (figs. 108, 112 and 118) than the turban lacking a chin loop. Turbans of this latter style, essentially similar to those in Palermo, both with and without a trailing end or *rafraf* hanging at the back, are seen in 10th to 13th century art from Egypt to Morocco (figs. 83, 86, 88, 91, 101, 103, 105, 106, 119, 120 and 128), and of course beyond.

Three quite distinctive forms of shield appear on the Palermo ceiling. These are the ordinary kite-shaped, so-called Norman shield (figs. 3, 5, 8, 9, 10, 11 left, 12 and 13), a kite-shaped shield with a flat base (fig. 9) which, judging by its proportions, may also have originally appeared on another damaged and now incomplete picture (fig. 8 left), and small, round, hand-held bucklers (figs. 4, 11 right and 25). It is now widely accepted that the so-called Norman kite-shaped shield was known in Byzantium and parts of the Muslim world before the First Crusade. It cannot, therefore, have been introduced to the area by the north European warriors of that expedition. Known in the Arab world as the *ṭāriqah,* this shield was primarily considered an infantry defence suitable for siege-warfare. [156] In Persian-speaking regions it was known as the *sipar-i shūshak* or lute-shaped shield. [157] Apart from those well-known carvings on Cairo's al Naṣr Gate (fig. 117), the *ṭāriqah* also appears on a possibly 10th century Fāṭimid ceramic fragment (fig. 107), in large and small forms on a comparable 12th century fragment (figure 130), on a late 12th century Coptic Egyptian Gospel (fig. 126) and on the probably 12th century *Warka wa Gulshāh* manuscript from Azarbāyjān (figs. 173 and 178-180). There is, therefore, no reason to insist on a Norman or even Christian inspiration for the Cappella Palatina kite-shaped shield, despite the fact that they are widespread in southern Italian and Sicilian art from the immediately preceding decades (figures 221 B, 229, 230 A, 236-239 and 242).

Of perhaps greater significance is the flat-bottomed shield (fig. 9). Known in Islam as the *janūwīyah,* it was specifically considered an infantry protection ideal for foot soldiers lined up in defensive array behind their shield-wall. [158] Clearly shown in both Christian and Muslim art from the Middle East (figs. 122, 126, 212 and 364), it only appears in Europe in Palermo (fig. 9) and Rome (fig. 259). In the former instance an Islamic inspiration is perfectly feasible while in the latter it would not be inappropriate since soldiers at Christ's crucifixion could well be represented as pagans, infidels or other sorts of undesirables.

The round shields on the Cappella Palatina ceiling are of the small, hand-held variety more accurately referred to as bucklers. Such shields abound in both Christian and Islamic art throughout the Middle Ages. So it may only be worthwhile drawing attention to a few examples from neighbouring regions, cultures and centuries (figs. 27, 28, 31, 32,

---

[156] BESHIR, *op. cit.,* p. 74, note 210; AL HARAWĪ, «Les Conseils du Šayḫ al Harawi a un Prince Ayyūbide,» trans. J. SOURDEL-THOMINE, *Bolletin d'Études Orientales,* XVII (1961-62), pp. 205-210; E. REHATSEK, «Notes on Some Old Arms and Instruments of War, chiefly among the Arabs,» in *Journal of the Bombay Branch of the Royal Asiatic Society,* XIV (1880), pp. 242-243; AL ṬARSŪSĪ, *op. cit.,* pp. 114 and 137.

[157] MUBARAKSHĀH, *op. cit.,* p. 242.

[158] AL HARAWĪ, *loc. cit.;* REHATSEK, *op. cit.,* p. 227; AL ṬARSŪSĪ, *loc. cit.;* ʿIMĀD AL DĪN AL KĀTIB AL IṢFAHĀNĪ, *Conquête de la Syrie et de la Palestine,* edit. Le Comte Carlo de Landberg (Leiden 188), pp. 68, 77 and 191.

78, 81, 85, 98, 100, 224, 226 and 240-242). These often have a very convex shape and as such might, at least in the Arab world, be examples of the *daraqah* or «bulbous» shield which would normally have been of leather.

A final form of rudimentary shield shown on the Cappella Palatina ceiling is a cloak slung over the left arm (fig. 1) in a manner that would later be associated with southern European cloak-and-dagger duelling techniques. [159] That the technique was known in the 11th century Mediterranean world, and probably beyond, is confirmed by the reminiscences of a Nordic warrior who served for some years in the Byzantine Varangian Guard. [160] It is also seen, sometimes clearly, sometimes less so, from the 4th century onwards in many works of art (figs. 92, 219, 275 and 345).

This leaves only horse furniture to be analyzed. The bridles all incorporate a nose-band (figs. 1-3 and 7-14). With the possible exception of Moorish Spain and a couple of representations on an Egyptian painted paper fragment, one of which illustrates a European (fig. 130), all 11th and 12th century Islamic bridles, including those from Egypt and North Africa, have nose-bands (figs. 83, 86, 102, 104, 108, 110, 111, 113, 115, 116 and 120). The majority, though not all, of European 12th century bridles were of a new form, lacking a nose-band, that was to remain popular for a further two centuries. It probably resulted from the adoption of a more savage form of curb bit (figs. 237 A-C, 253, 257, 266, 267, 286, 316, 320-322 and 333). The most obvious exceptions to this 12th century trend, outside Byzantium and Byzantine-influenced eastern Europe, was to be found in southern Italy and Sicily. Here the majority, though again not all, of bridles continued to incorporate nose-bands (figs. 221 A and B, 222, 227, 229, 234, 236, 239, 243 and 260 A). I venture to suggest that this could indicate a lingering Islamic and perhaps also Byzantine influence.

Where still visible, the horse-bits on the Cappella Palatina ceiling (figs. 2, 10, 12 and 14) seem to be of the curb variety, having a cross-piece or chain beneath the animal's chin to join the lower ends of the two cheek-pieces. Two other pictures are more difficult to interpret (figs. 7 and 8 right) but show no certain evidence of having illustrated snaffle, rather than curb, bits. The curb bit was probably introduced into Europe from the east during the so-called Dark Ages, perhaps via

[159] R. Martínez del Peral Forton, *La Navaja Española Antigua* (Madrid 1979), *passim*.
[160] S. Blondal and B. S. Beneditz, *The Varangians of Byzantium* (Cambridge 1978), p. 212.

the Muslims in Spain and southern Europe [161] as well as via the Turks in eastern Europe. [162] But it does not seem to have been widely adopted throughout most of western Europe until the 14th century. [163]

Straightforward curb bits, lacking the linking chain or semi-rigid crossbar, had long been known in the pre-Islamic Iranian and Turkish worlds. They appear in Islamic art from the very beginning and shortly thereafter also in Byzantine sources. Their probable first appearance in the immediate vicinity of Sicily is, not surprisingly, on a fragment of 10th or 11th century Fāṭimid ceramic from Tunisia (fig. 78). They are, however, seen in the more abundant surviving Egyptian sources a century or so earlier (figs. 95, 98, 101, 102, 270 and 272). Here I am leaving aside a pair of dubiously dated, but supposedly early 8th century, curb-bits form Spain, one in the Real Armería in Madrid and the other in the Metropolitan Museum of Art in New York (No. 47.100.24). As far as the rest of Europe is concerned, one must await the 11th century to see clear representations of the curb-bit, firstly in southern Italy under strong Islamic influence (figs. 221 A and B, and 222), then gradually progressing up the peninsula (figs. 229, 236 and 237), thence to Norman England (fig. 336) and, around the turn of the century to France (fig. 310). It is interesting to note how relatively soon the crossbar curb-bit was seen in the Norman realm of the north. Could this have been a result of contact with their cousins to the south, in Sicily? It is particularly unfortunate that the only 11th century Sicilian source to show a horseman is fragmented and lacks the animal's head (fig. 33). The curb-bit, with and without a linkage between its cheek-pieces, is, however, clearly shown in 12th century Sicilian ivorywork (figs. 64 and 68), as well as on the mainland (figs. 243, 260 A and 266).

Some pieces of horse furniture, or perhaps more accurately decorations, that betray Middle Eastern influence are horse-collars shown somewhat unclearly on the Cappella Palatina ceiling (figs. 1 left, 5, 7-10 and 11 left). This *qilādah* was essentially a broad strap running around the horse's throat but not apparently attached to the throat-lash. The origins of this fashion are obscure, but it has been suggested that decorative horse-collars were copied by the Muslims from the Turks in Central Asia. [164] While this may have been true, there is also pictorial evidence to suggest that similar decorations were known in Yemen, Par-

[161] BEELER, *op. cit.,* p. 170; L. LOURIE, «A Society Organized for War: Medieval Spain,» in *Past and Present,* XXXV (1966), pp. 68-69.

[162] A. KIRPITCHNIKOFF, *The Equipment of Rider and Horse in Russia from the 9th to 13th centuries* (Leningrad 1973), pp. 138-139.

[163] V. NORMAN, *The Medieval Soldier* (London 1971), pp. 233-234.

[164] M. LOMBARD, *The Golden Age of Islam* (Oxford 1975), p. 168.

thian and Sassanian Iran, Palmyra and the eastern regions of the Roman and Byzantine Empires during the pre-Islamic era. Exceptionally rich horse-collars, some even decorated with gold or amber, were a feature of Fāṭimid ceremonial harness, [165] while under the later Mamlūk Sultans of Egypt comparable scarves would act as emblems or means of identification. [166] Decorated collars also featured in the Marīnid army of early 14th century Morocco. [167]

As far as those shown in mid-12th century Sicilian sources are concerned, however, the most obvious antecedents and parallels are to be found on the one hand in Egypt and the Maghrib from the 10th century onwards (figs. 83, 102, 109, 120, 129 and 130) and on the other hand in Byzantium during that same period (figs. 351, 353, 355 B, 356 and 359). Such collars do not appear in Europe outside Sicily and the Iberian peninsula, except on Italo-Saracenic ivories (fig. 222), until the 12th century. Even then there is only a single instance from Norman Apulia (fig. 239G), plus the 12th century «Song of Roland» stained-glass window at Chartres where Moors are represented (fig. 321). The fashion was not, in the event, to be adopted in medieval Europe.

The saddles illustrated on the Cappella Palatina ceiling are all of basically the same Middle Eastern type. They have rounded skirts, normally two girths and a moderately high flared cantle, though not of the wrap-around type associated with the European high or war saddle. The pommels, though only visible in a few panels, are clearly low and provide no protection to the groin or thighs as did the pommel of the later European war saddle. One may, therefore, fairly assume that all these seats were of the wooden, or in some cases bone, framed leather-covered type that had its origins in Central Asia (fig. 341). Such saddles were standard throughout the medieval Muslim world and were the direct ancestors of all forms of modern saddle, especially of the high and supportive so-called Cowboy saddle. They were also the original of the normal «peace» saddle of medieval Europe.

The skirts of such saddles did not, of course, have to be rounded. Their shape and size varied acording to current fashion which was itself often governed by political factors such as the rise and fall of military élites from differing ethnic backgrounds. Suffice to say that rounded rather than squared saddle-skirts were characteristic of Byzantium (figs. 349, 350, 354, 356, 358 and 359). In Egypt and North Africa

---

[165] CANARD, «La Procession du Nouvel An,» p. 375.
[166] L. A. MAYER, *Mamluk Costume* (Geneva 1956), glossary.
[167] IBN FADLALLĀH, «Masālik al Abṣāṛ,» trans. J. SAUVAGET, in *Historiens Arabes* (Paris 1946), p. 135.

saddles having rectangular skirts retained their popularity (figs. 80, 102, 109, 113 and 120). A sharp increase of the rounded from in provinces slightly further east during the 11th and 12th centuries leads one to speculate that this fashion had been introduced, or at least encouraged, by the Saljūq Turks (figs. 153 and 366). However, it equally cannot be denied that such forms of saddle appear in Italian art from the 8th or 9th century to the 11th, predating any possible Saljūq influence. Perhaps in Italy the fashion survived from earlier Lombard days when again it was probably a reflection of Central Asian, Hunnish or Avar, influence (figs. 215, 222 and 235). Elsewhere in 12th century Italy, as in the rest of Europe, saddles for both peace and war normally had rectangular skirts and were quite unlike those shown on the Cappella Palatina ceiling (figs. 239 B-G, 243, 254, 257, 266 and 267).

A further feature that places these saddles on the frontier between Byzantino-Islamic fashion and that of western Europe is that some are secured by both breast and crupper straps (figs. 2, 4, 10 and 15) while others only have the former (figs. 1 right, 3, 5 and 7-9). During the first half of the 12th century, throughout most of western Europe including the Iberian peninsula, the crupper strap was gradually abandoned (figs. 252, 260 A, 266, 267, 287, 297, 319, 320, 333, 336, 338 and 339). In Italy, particularly in the south, there is evidence to indicate that the crupper strap was abandoned more reluctantly (figs. 54, 67, 239 A-D and 257). The continued use of the crupper strap in the Muslim and Byzantine worlds is, meanwhile, very obvious (figs. 83, 86, 120, 155, 183-185, 189, 358 and 359).

The sum total of evidence gained by a detailed analysis of the arms, armour, horse furniture and certain costume details illustrated on the Cappella Palatina ceilings points strongly towards an Islamic inspiration for most of the subjects shown. Where European elements can be isolated, they can generally also be found in western Islamic countries, particularly Egypt and North Africa. Other evidence already suggests that, in general, these provinces of the Muslim world had much in common with their Christian neighbours along the northern shores of the Mediterranean. In fact, one may be tempted to see, painted on the Cappella Palatina ceiling, representatives of a long-established early medieval Mediterranean military culture. This culture had, by the mid-12th century, all but been swamped by newer northern European styles on the Italian mainland, southern France and to a lesser degree Christian Spain. In Egypt it would soon be mixed with, though not entirely swamped by, those essentially Turkish military styles that already dominated most of the rest of the Middle East and which would also take over Byzantine military culture.

I would also venture to suggest that this interpretation of the subject matter on the Cappella Palatina ceiling in no way contradicts the theory that these panels were painted by local Sicilian craftsmen working within an established artistic heritage. This had its first roots in the golden age of 'Abbāsid civilization and its more immediate roots in a Fāṭimid school of art transmitted and transmuted by the provincial but vibrant culture of Muslim Ifriqīyah (Tunisia). A strictly European, and more immediately Norman, influence is almost impossible to pinpoint even in those items of military equipment where one would most expect to find it.

PHOTO 1. Painted ceiling panel, ca. 1140 (*in situ,* Cappella Palatina, (Palermo). Military unarmed horseman.

Photo 2. Painted ceiling panel, ca. 1140 (*in situ,* Cappella Palatina, Palermo). Military armed horseman.

PHOTO 3. Painted ceiling panel, ca. 1140 (*in situ,* Cappella Palatina, Palermo). Turban-dressed rider on camel.

1-26. Painted ceiling panels, c. 1140 (*in situ,* Cappella Palatina, Palermo). Monneret de Villard photograph numbers (Dept. of Oriental Antiquities, British Museum, London) are shown in brackets below.

1. Nave (M. de V. 2861).
2. Nave (M. de V. 26987).
3. Nave (M. de V. 27030).
4. Nave (M. de V. 27042 and 27057).
5. Nave (M. de V. 2882).
6. Nave (M. de V. 2782).

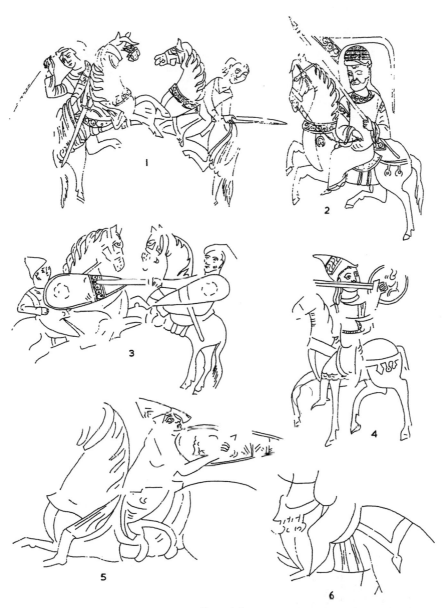

FIGS. 1-6

X

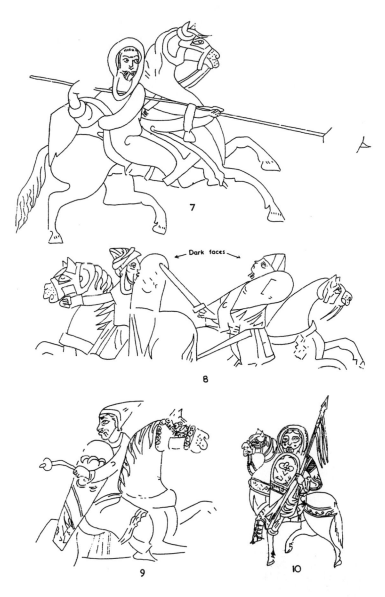

Dark faces

Figs. 7-10

Claws

11

12

13

14

15

FIGS. 11-15

Figs. 16-26

27-29. Carved figures on an ivory box, Sicily or southern Italy, 1050-1100 (Inv. 17.190.241, Met. Museum of Art, New York).
30. Carved figure on an ivory box, Sicily, 11th century (Inv. K.3101, Staat. Museum, West Berlin).
31. Carved figure on an ivory oliphant, Sicily or southern Italy, late 11th century (Musée Crozatier, Le Puy-en-Velay).
32. Carved figure on an ivory oliphant, Sicily or southern Italy, 11th century (Inv. 04.3.177, Met. Museum of Art, New York).
33. Fragment of Siculo-Muslim ceramic, probably from Erice, 11th or 12th century (Russo Perez Coll., State Ceramic Museum, Caltagirone).
34-43. Carvings on capitals, late 12th century (*in situ,* Cloisters of the Cathedral, Monreale).

FIGS. 27-43

44. Carving on a capital, late 12th century (*in situ*, Cloisters of the Cathedral, Monreale).
45. Carved panel over north door, mid-12th century (*in situ*, La Martorana, Palermo).
46. «The Betrayal,» mosaic, 1180-1190 (*in situ*, Cathedral, Monreale).
47. «The Crucifixion» (*as above*).
48. Shield of «St. Demetrius,» mosaic, mid-12th century (*in situ*, Cappella Palatina, Palermo).
49. «Siege of Salerno, defenders,» Sicily or southern Italy, early 13th century (f. 116a, *Chronicle of Peter of Eboli*, Cod. 120/II, Burgerbib., Berne).
50. «Henry VI's entry into Palermo» (f. 134a, *as above*).
51. «Siculo-Muslim archer» (f. 131, *as above*).
52. «Constance besieged in Salerno» (f. 117a, *as above*).
53. «Sicilian crossbowmen» (f. 131, *as above*).
54. «Richard of Acerra captures Capua» (f. 124a, *as above*).
55. «Siege of Mopsvestia,» Siculo-Byzantine, early 13th century (f. 151v, *Skylitzes Chronicle*, Cod. 5-3, N2, Bib. Nac., Madrid).
56. «Al Maʿmūn's siege of Amorium» (f. 59v, *as above*).
57. «Emir Chabdan defeated by Bardas Phocas» (f. 136v, *as above*).
58. (*as above*).

FIGS. 44-58

59-60. «Emir Chabdan defeated by Bardas Phocas» (f. 136v, *as above*).

61. «Hispano-Arabs in Crete» (f. 39v, *as above*).

62-63. (*as above*).

64-65. Painted figures on an ivory box, Sicily, 12th century (Museo Nazionale, Florence).

66. Painted figure on an ivory box, Sicily, 12th century (Treasury, Cappella Palatina, Palermo).

67. Painted figure on an ivory box, Sicily, 12th century (Musée de Cluny, Paris).

68. Painted figure on an ivory box, Sicily, 12th century (formerly in the J. Brummer Coll., New York).

69. «David beheads Goliath,» carved ivory box, Sicily or southern Italy, late 12th century (Palazio de Venezia Museum, Rome).

70-71. «Diopuldo fights villagers,» Sicily or southern Italy, early 13th century (f. 130a, *Chronicle of Peter of Eboli,* Cod. 120/II, Burgerbib., Berne).

72. «Constance flees Salerno,» (f. 119a, *as above*).

73. «Traveller,» (f. 101a, *as above*).

Figs. 59-73

X

74. Carved figure on an ivory box, Sicily, 12th or early 13th century (Museum Dahlem, West Berlin).
75. «Sagittarius,» Sicily or southern Italy, 1220-1250 (Latin translation of Al Sūfī's *Book of Fixed Stars,* Ms. 1036, Bib. Arsenal, Paris).
76. «Pharoah's guard,» North Africa, 7th century (f. 50a, *Ashburnham Pentateuch,* Ms. Nouv. Acq. Latin 2334, Bib. Nat., Paris).
77. «Pharoah's army drowns» (f. 68a, *as above*).
78. Ceramic fragment, Tunisia, 10th-11th century (Inv. 11762, Benaki Museum, Athens).
79. Ceramic fragment, Tunisia, 10th-11th century (Inv. 11761, Benaki Museum, Athens).
80. Bas-relief of huntsmen, Morocco, 1050-1100 (Bardo Archaeological Museum, Algiers).
81-82. Ceramic plaques from the Palace of Sabra, Tunisia, mid-11th century (Bardo Museum, Tunis).
83. Ceramic fragment from Sabra, Tunisia, 11th century (Bardo Museum, Tunis).
84-85. Ceramic fragments from Sabra, Tunisia, 11th century (Provincial Museum, Qairouan).

Figs. 74-85

X

86. Fragments of a ceramic plate from Sabra, Tunisia, 11th century (Inv. 10, Museum of Islamic Arts, Dār Hussayn, Tunis).
87. «Perseus,» northern Morocco, 1224 (Al Sūfī, *Book of Fixed Stars,* Ms. Ross 1033, Vatican Lib., Rome).
88. «Bootes» (*as above*).
89. (*as above*).
90. «Cepheus» (*as above*).
91. «Sagittarius» (*as above*).
92. «Ares,» Coptic ivory figurine, 4th-5th century (Dumbarton Oaks Coll., Washington).
93. «Sacrifice of Jeptha's daughter,» fresco, 7th-8th century (*in situ,* Bema, St. Catherine's Monastery, Sinai).
94. «Midianite buys the boy Joseph,» Coptic textile, 7th century (Hermitage, Leningrad).
95. «St. Theodore,» carved wooden door panel, Coptic, 9th century (*in situ,* Church of Abu Sarga, Cairo).
96. «St. Theodore,» Coptic, 9th-10th century (f. 287v, *Homilies,* Ms. Copt. 66, Vatican Lib., Rome).
97. Ceramic fragment, Egypt or Iraq, late 9th-early 10th century (Inv. 227, Benaki Museum, Athens).
98. Papyrus fragment, Egypt, 10th century (Rainer Coll., Bib. Nat., Vienna).
99. Lustre-ceramic fragment, Egypt, 10th-11th century (Victoria and Albert Museum, London).
100. Original fragments in now-restored lustre bowl, Egypt, 10th-11th century (Museum of Islamic Art, Cairo).

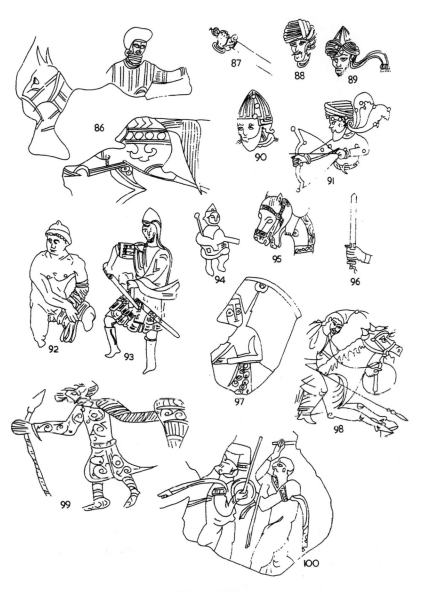

Figs. 86-100

X

101. Painted paper fragment, Egypt, 10th century (Inv. I.8, Keir Coll., London).
102. Ceramic fragment, probably North African, 10th-11th century (Museum of Islamic Art, Cairo).
103. Ivory plaque, Egypt, 10th century (Louvre, Paris).
104. Painted paper fragment, Egypt, 11th (?) century (Keir Coll., London).
105. Painted paper fragment, Egypt or Iraq, 11th-12th century (Museum of Islamic Art, Cairo).
106. Painted paper fragment from Fusṭāṭ, Egypt, 11th-12th century (Inv. 12801, Museum of Islamic Art, Cairo).
107. Painter paper fragment, Egypt, 11th-12th century (Louvre, Paris).
108. Painted paper fragment, Egypt, 11th-12th century (Museum of Islamic Art, Cairo).

104

Figs. 101-108

FIGS. 109-120

Figs. 121-130

FIGS. 131-142

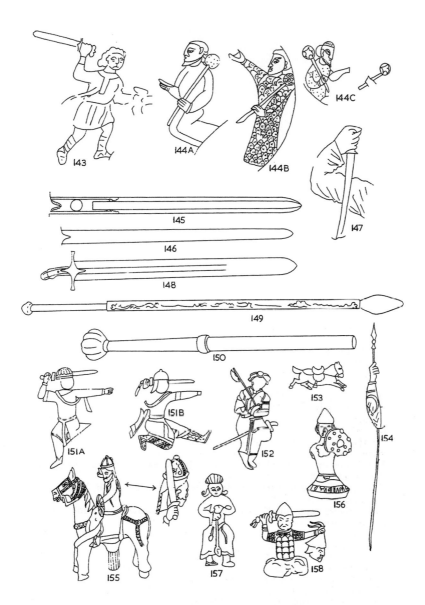

FIGS. 143-158

159. «St. Bahnām,» carved stone relief, c. 1164 (*in situ,* Convent of Mār Bahnām, nr. Mosul).
160. «Trial of Jesus,» Syriac Gospel from Jazīra region, 1216-1220 (Ms. Add. 7170, British Lib., London).
161. «Guard at Christ's Tomb» (f. 160r, *as above*).
162. «The Betrayal» (f. 143v, *as above*).
163. «The Betrayal» Syriac Gospel from Tur Abdīn, Jazīra, 1226 (formerly in the Bishop's Library, Midyat).
164. Figure on an inlaid metal writing-box, Jazīra, early 13th century (Franks Bequest, British Museum, London).
165-169. Figures on an inlaid metal bottle, Jazīra, early 13th century (Inv. 41.10, Freer Gallery of Art, Washington).
170. Figures on a carved gateway, 1233-1259 (recently collapsed, Bab al ʿĀmādiya, ʿĀmādiya).
171. Inlaid figure on a metal ewer, Jazīra, 1232 (*Blacas Ewer,* inv. 66.12-29.61, British Museum, London).
172-173. «Army of Yemen,» manuscript from Azarbāyjān, late 12th century (f. 37/35a, *Warka wa Gulshāh,* Ms. Hazine 841, Topkapu Library, Istanbul).
174. «Rabī wounds Warka» (f. 18/18b, *as above*).
175-176. «Rabī fights Warka's father» (f, 13/15a, *as above*).
177. «Rabī fights the Banū *Shayba*» (f. 12/13b, *as above*).
178. «Battle of Banū Zabba and Banū *Shayba*» (f. 10/12a, *as above*).
179. «Rabī's night attack» (f. 3/6a, *as above*).
180. «Yemenīs fight Bahrayn and Aden» f. 40/38b, *as above*).

FIG. 159-180

181. «Yemenīs defeat Bahrayn and Aden» (f. 41/39b, *as above*).
182. Figure on a carved relief from Kubachi, 13th century (?) (Hermitage, Leningrad).
183. Dani*sh*māndid coin from Felitene, early 12th century (Cab. des Médailles, Bib. Nat., Paris).
184. «The Magi,» Christian fresco painted under Saljūq rule, 1150-1200 (*in situ*, Carikli Kilise, Cappadocia).
185. «Kilij Arslan II,» stucco relief, Saljūq, 1156-1188 (Museum of Turkish Art, Istanbul).
186. Javelin, Ottoman, 17th century (Museo Civico, Bologna).
187. Fresco fragment from Throne Room, Sāmarrā-Jawsaq, ʿAbbāsid, 836-839 (Museum für Islamische Kunst, West Berlin).
188. Lustre dish, Iraq, 10th century (Keir Coll., London).
189. «Book of Antidotes,» Jazīra, 1199 (Ms. Arabe 2964, Bib. Nat., Paris).
190. «Bedū lances,» Iraq, 1230 (Ms. S.23, Oriental Institute, Leningrad).
191. «Sun and Moon gods,» east Iranian fresco, 7th-8th century (*in situ*, Ghorband Valley, Funduqistān).
192. Mace on an engraved silver dish from Kulagysh, east Iran, 7th-8th century (Hermitage, Leningrad).
193. Sassanian-style coin of Hajjāj ibn Yūsuf, Iran, early 8th century (Cab. des Médailles, Bib. Nat., Paris).
194. Figure on an engraved silver dish, *Kh*urāsān or Tuskistān, 9th-10th century (Hermitage, Leningrad).
195. Figure on a carved ivory chess-piece, Sind or eastern Iran, 9th century (Inv. 311, Cab. des Médailles, Bib. Nat., Paris).
196. Lustre bowl, ʿAbbāsid, 9th-10th century (Louvre, Paris).

FIGS. 181-196

X

118

Figs. 197-214

215. Relief carving, Lombard, 8th-9th century (*in situ,* Cathedral, Civita Castellana).
216. «King Arthur,» Italo-Byzantine mosaic, 9th-10th century (*in situ,* Church of the Pantocrator, Otranto).
217. «Crucifixion,» Italo-Byzantine, 9th-10th century (*Exultet Roll, Ms.* 2, John Rylands Lib., Manchester).
218. «Donor figure,» fresco, early 9th century (*in situ,* Church of San Benedetto, Malles, Trento).
219. Manuscript, southern Italy, 10th century (*Avatea, Ms.* 3, Library, Monte Cassino).
220. Carved altar panels, southern Italy, 11th-12th century (*in situ,* Santa Maria in Valle Porclaneta).
221. Ivory chess-pieces, southern Italy, 11th century (Cab. des Médailles, Bib. Nat., Paris).
222. Figure on a carved ivory oliphant from Amalfi, mid-11th century (Cab. des Médailles, Bib. Nat., Paris).
223. «Crucifixion,» figure on a carved ivory box from Farfa, c. 1071-1072 (Treasury, S. Paolo fuori le Mura, Rome).
224. Figure on a carved ivory oliphant, Sicily or southern Italy, late 11th century (Private loan to the Victoria and Albert Museum, London).
225. «Centaur,» figure on a carved ivory oliphant from Salerno, 11th century (Inv. 57,58L, Museum of Fine Arts, Boston).
226. Manuscript from Benevento, 11th century (f. 192, *Leges Langobardorum,* Cod. 4, Archives, Badia della Santissima Trinita, Cava).
227. «Pharoah's army drawns,» manuscript from Gaeta, 11th century (*Exultet Roll* No. 2, Cathedral Archives, Gaeta).

FIGS. 215-227

228

230A

230B

231

232

229

233

236

234

235

FIGS. 228-236

237.A-D. «Legend of King Arthur,» carved relief, 1099-1106 (*in situ,* Porta di Pescheria, Cathedral, Modena).
238A-B. «Defenders of Jerusalem?,» carved relief of the First Crusade (?), early 12th century (*in situ,* north door, Church of San Nicola, Bari).
239A-D. «Attackers of Jerusalem?» (*as above*).

237A 237B 237C

237D 238A 238B

239A 239B

239C 239D

FIGS. 238-239D

239E-H. «Attackers of Jerusalem?» (*as above*).

240. «Merman,» carved relief, 1175-1200 (*in situ,* Cathedral nave, Bitonto).

241. «Demons,» carved reliefs, late 12th century (*in situ,* exterior of the Cathedral, Barletta).

242. Carved relief, early 12th century (*in situ,* west front, Church of San Nicola, Bari).

243. «Pharoah in the Red Sea?» (*as above*).

244. Carved capital, early 13th century (*in situ,* Cathedral, Matera).

245. Carved reliefs on stone candelabrum, central Italy, c. 1170 (San Paolo fuori le Mura, Rome).

246. Carved relief of a knight, early 12th century (*in situ,* west front of Cathedral, Lucca).

247. Carved relief of «Centaur», 1153 AD (*in situ,* west front of Collegiata Cathedral, Bari).

248. Sword carried by unarmoured infantryman, carved relief from the Porta Romana in Milan, mid-12th century (Sforza Castle Museum, Milan).

249. Armoured infantryman, carved relief from the Porta Romana in Milan, mid-12th century (Sforza Castle Museum, Milan).

239E 239F 239G 239H 240 242 241 243 244 245 246 247 248 249

Figs. 239E-249

X

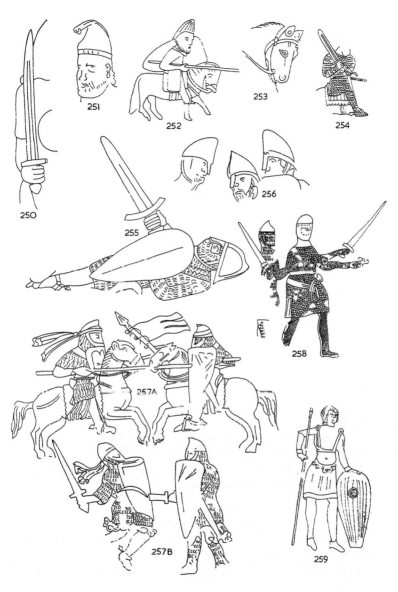

FIGS. 250-259

FIGS. 260-267

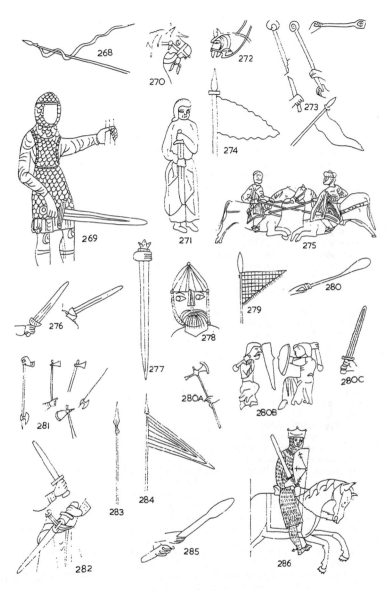

Figs. 268-286

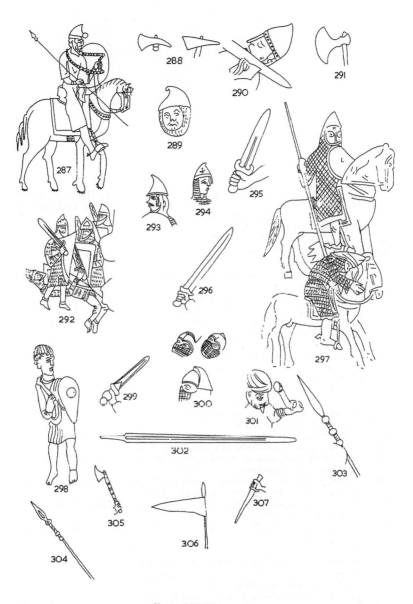

FIGS. 287-307

135

308. «Triumph,» carved ivory plaque, France, 9th century (Bargello, Florence).
309. «Guards at Christ's Tomb,» carved capital, France, late 11th-early 12th century (*in situ,* Church, St. Nectaire).
310. «Horsemen of the Apocalypse» (*as above*).
311. «The Betrayal», (*as above*).
312. Carved capital, southern France, 1087-1119 (*in situ,* Cloisters of Ste. Foy, Conques).
313. «Illustrated Bible,» northern France, early 11th century (Bib. Munic., Arras).
314. «Expulsion of Moses' mother,» southern France, late 11th century (f. 27r, *Atlantic Bible,* Ms. Edili 125-126, Bib. Laurenziana, Florence).
315. «Cutting Sampson's hair,» carved capital from Cathedral of Notre Dame des Doms, Avignon, 12th century (Inv. 1922.132, Fogg Art Museum, Boston).
316. «Abisme slain by Turpin,» carved relief, early 12th century (*in situ,* lintel of west door, Cathedral, Angouleme).
317. «Entry into Jerusalem,» carved capital, 1100-1150 (*in situ,* Cloisters of La Daurade).
318. «Generosity,» carved capital, c. 1155 (*in situ,* Notre Dame du Port, Clermont-Ferrand).
319. «Templer,» fresco, mid-12th century (*in situ,* Templer Church, Cressac).
320. «Roland,» stained glass window, 12th century (*in situ,* Cathedral, Chartres).
321. «Fleeing Moors» (*as above*).
322. Ivory chess-piece, southern France, 12th century (Bargello, Florence).
323. Sword, France, 1130-1170 (Private Coll., London).
324. «Siege of Carcassonne,» carved relief, early 13th century (*in situ,* Church of St. Nazaire, Carcassonne).
325. «Massacre of the Innocents,» carved pillar, 12th century (*in situ,* eastern section of the Cloisters, St. Trophime, Arles).
326. «Judas Macchabeus,» Syriac Bible perhaps from Antioch, late 12th century (f. 208v, Ms. 01.02, University Library, Cambridge).
327. Coin of Baldwin II of Edessa, Crusader States, 1100-1118 (Cab. des Médailles, Bib. Nat., Paris).
328. «The Betrayal,» manuscript from Acre, 1131-1143 (f. 7v, *Queen Milisende's Psalter,* Ms. Egerton 1139, British Library, London).
329. Ceramic fragment from Al Mina, Crusader States, early 13th century (Archaeological Museum, Antioch).
330. «Amazons fight Alexander,» manuscript from Acre, late 13th century (f. 86v, *Universal History of William of Tyre,* Ms. 562, Bib. Munic., Dijon).

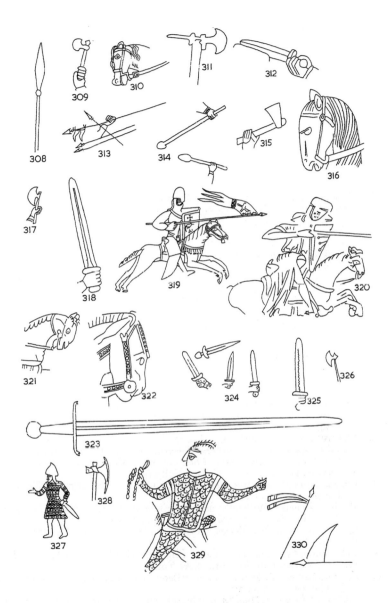

Figs. 308-330

X

Figs. 331-340

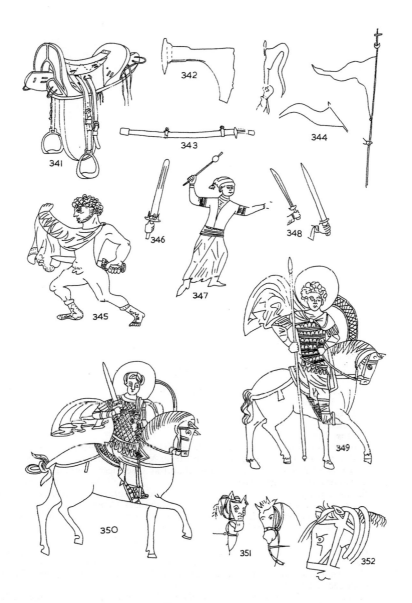

FIGS. 341-352

141

FIGS. 353-365

366. «St. Theodore,» fresco, Georgia, 1096 (*in situ,* Church, Iprari).
367. «Judgement of Pilate» and «Guards at Christ's Tomb,» Armenia, c. 1270 (ff. 184 and 194, *Four Gospels,* Ms. 32-18, Freer Gallery of Art, Washington).
368. «Hindu deity,» fresco fragment from Hu-Kuo convent, Khotan, 7th-10th century (British Museum, London).
369. Pottery figurines from Afrāsiyāb-Kafir Kala region, Turkistān, 7th-8th century (Hermitage, Leningrad).
370. «Hindu deities,» fresco, Turkistān, 8th-9th century (*in situ,* Cave 19, Kumtara, Sinkiang).
371. Frescoes, India, late 5th century (*in situ,* Cave 1, Ajanta).
372. «Ganesa,» statue, eastern India, 11th century (Inv. 1872.7-1.61, British Museum, London).
373. «Ganesa,» statue, eastern India, 11th century (Inv. 1872.7-1.54, British Museum, London).
374. «Durga slaying Mahisha,» statue, central Java, 10th century (Inv. 17.1014, Museum of Fine Arts., Boston).

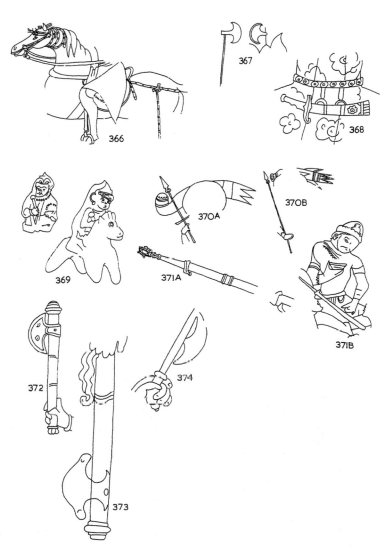

FIGS. 366-374

ARMS, ARMOUR AND HORSE HARNESSES IN THE PARMA BAPTISTERY PAINTED CEILING

These paintings are believed to have been made between 1248/9 and 1251/2 AD.[1] There is clearly a strong Byzantine influence in their artistic style as well as strong parallels with the Byzantine or Byzantino-Balkan art of Serbia and Macedonia.

Four panels contain military figures or weaponry. These include two of the panels which illustrate the Story of Abraham on the first level below the Dome (plates A and B), plus two panels which show the Story of John the Baptist on the second level below the Dome (plates C and D). Whereas the scenes showing John the Baptist before Herod (plate C) and the beheading of John the Baptist (plate D) are easy to interpret, those concerning Abraham are more difficult. They probably illustrate an episode in the Book of Genesis (Chapter 14: verses 1–16) and might need some explanation. The first panel (plate A) could show Abraham's brother Lot being captured by Chedorlaomer, leader of an alliance of Four Kings who rebelled against King Bera of Sodom and his alliance of Five Kings (Gen. 14: 12). The picture portrays two unarmoured figures being dragged away by a group of armoured men, perhaps the most senior of whom is on foot and is wearing pseudo-Roman armour. Ahead are three men on camels, which was an artistic device to identify the army in question as desert folk or "infidels". In the second military panel which deals with the story of Abraham (plate B), the army of the Four Kings with their camels are pursued by another force of armoured horsemen while also being bombarded with rocks by a group of unarmoured figures

---

[1] The Romanesque Baptistery which stands next to the Duomo in Parma is regarded as one of the finest of its kind in Italy. It is an octagonal building of red marble from the region of Verona and construction reportedly began in 1196 under the direction of Benedetto Antelami. Restoration of the interior was completed not many years ago, but has caused some controversy. For a modern general study of the paintings inside the dome, see: A. Bianchi, "Il ciclo pittorico del Battistero di Parma: La cupola", *Felix Ravenna*, CXXXI–CXXXII (1986); also published as a separate booklet (Ravenna 1987).

behind a hill. This probably represents the battle in which Abraham *"divided himself against them, he and his servants, by night, and smote them and pursued them..."* (Gen. 14: 15). Thereafter Abraham rescued his brother Lot and was blessed by Melchizedek, the priest-king of Salem, in a ceremony involving bread and wine. This formed the highly significant culmination of an otherwise minor Biblical battle.

The main items of military interest are as follows: long round-topped kite-shaped shields of an old fashioned form; the heraldry on these same shields; long-sleeved mail hauberks with short hems, plus coifs; a mail hauberk with only one integral mitten; forward-angled helmets with nasals; a round-topped helmet with a nasal; a round helmet with a neck-protecting extension; a brimmed war-hat or *chapel-de-fer* worn with "antique" armour; a separate mail coif apparently being worn without a hauberk; a sword with a nut-shaped pommel and slightly curved quillons; a *gonfanon* or lance-pennon with a triple tail; bridles with curb bits but without nose-bands; round edged saddles with moderately raised cantles (the rear of a saddle); doubled girths to secure these saddles; camel riders apparently wielding clubs; and a bell around a camel's neck. These items of interest are now discussed in detail:

1 – Round-topped long kite-shaped shields of old fashioned form (in the picture of John the Baptist before Herod, plate C)
The clearest shields in all the military panels are those held by Herod's guards. Shields shown in the two battles of Chedorlaomer are largely obscured but appear to be of the long kite-shaped type, one possibly having a flattened top. This is carried by the leading figure in Abraham's army (plate B) who probably represents Abraham himself. Since the flat-topped kite-shaped shield is essentially a later or more up-to-date form, it has presumably been given to the hero of this episode. The ordinary round-topped, so-called "Norman" shield was very common in 12th-century Italy, as in most parts of Europe. It is also seen throughout the 13th century in Italy,[2] where it may have persisted for longer than in most

---

[2] Relief on the central portal of the Basilica of San Marco, Venice, c. 1240; silver altar panels illustrating the life of St. James, by Andrea di Jacopo d'Ognibene, end of the 13th century (*in situ* Pistoia Cathedral); stone mosaic illustrating the Fourth Crusade, early 13th century (*in situ* Church of S. Giovanni Evangelista, Rome); *Conquista dell'oltremare*, manuscript from Pavia castle, end of the 13th century (Bib. Nat., Cod. 2631, f. 21r., Paris); "The Philistines capture the Ark", wall painting, c.1250–55 (*in situ* Crypt of the Cathedral, Anagni).

parts of 13th-century Europe. Comparable shields are also seen seen in Byzantium and in the arts of areas under strong Byzantine influence such as Sicily, the Crusader States of the Middle East and Russia.[3] The manner in which the shields of Herod's guards are being held on the Parma ceiling is commonly seen in the art of late 12th- and 13th-century Italy,[4] Byzantium including the Christian art of those Anatolian provinces which had fallen to the Turks, in Sicily, the Crusader States and Russia.[5] It is also seen, though to a lesser extent, in France and Germany. Such shields are, therefore, too common and widespread to be very significant except that they reinforce a general impression of military similarity between Italy and Byzantium.

2 – Heraldry on shields (in the picture of John the Baptist before Herod, plate C)
The term heraldry may be premature in this context, yet the patterns on these two shields are very distinctive. The lower chevron on the left hand shield appears in a 12th-century *Exultet Roll* from Benevento,[6] while the diagonal stripes appear with minor variations at Novara and Rome in the early 13th century.[7] However, such early forms of heraldic pattern cannot be seen as purely western European, for the same designs appear in the

---

[3] Ceramic vase from Istanbul, Byzantine 12th to 14th century (Benaki Museum, Athens); "St. George", stone relief, Russian, 1234 AD (*in situ* Cathedral of St. George, Yureve-Polskom); *Psalter of Simonovko Khludovskiya*, Russian, c.1300 (location unknown); seal of Henry I, Latin Emperor of Constantinople, early 13th century (Bib. Nat., Cabinet des Médailles, Paris); *Chronicle of Peter of Eboli*, Sicily or southern Italy, end of the 12th or early 13th century (Burgerbib., Cod. 120/11, Bern); *Skylitzes Chronicle*, Sicily in Byzantine style, late 12th or early 13th century (Bib. Nac., Cod. 5–3. N2, Madrid).
[4] Relief on the central portal of the Basilica of San Marco, Venice, c. 1240.
[5] "St. George", carved alabaster plaque, Byzantine, 12th century (Archaeological Museum, inv. 1000, Plovdiv); *Barlaam and Joasaph*, Byzantine manuscript, end of the 12th or early 13th century (Monastery of Iviron, Cod. 463, Mount Athos); "St. George", wall painting, Christian art under Seljuk Turkish domination, 1283–95 (*in situ* Church of Kirkdam Alti, Belisarma, Cappadocia, Turkey); "St. George", stone relief, Russian, 1234 AD (*in situ* Cathedral of St. George, Yureve-Polskom); "St. Cnut", wall painting on a column, Crusader Palestine, 12th century (*in situ* Church of the Nativity, Bethlehem); "St. George", mosaic, Sicily in Byzantine style, 12th century (*in situ* Cathedral, Cefalù); "Guard outside the wall of Damascus during the escape of Paul", mosaic, Sicily in Byzantine style (*in situ* Cappella Palatina, Palermo).
[6] "Protospatius of the Emperor", in an *Exultet Roll*, southern Italy, 12th century (Bib. Casanatese, Cod. 724 B1.13, Rome).
[7] "Knights leaving a castle", wall painting, 13th century (*in situ* Broletto old town hall, Novara); "The Fourth Crusade", stone mosaic, early 13th century (*in situ* Church of S. Giovanni Evangelista, Rome).

Byzantine-style art of 12th- and 13th-century Sicily and in Russia[8] though I have yet to find it in Byzantine art from within the Byzantine Empire. One might guess that these sources reflect western military influence upon the late 12th- and 13th-century Byzantine world rather than being an example of Byzantine artistic influence in Parma.

3 – Long-sleeved mail hauberks with short hems, plus coifs (Chedorlaomer captures Lot, and Abraham rescues Lot, figs. A and B)
These long-sleeved mail hauberks are worn by all the mailed figures except one in Chedorlaomer's army, who may have mid-length sleeves. There are also two figures in Abraham's army who might not actually be wearing complete mail hauberks. Such armour was the most common form of protection among fully armoured troops throughout western Europe in the 12th and 13th centuries. Long-sleeved hauberks had been common in Italy since at least the mid-12th century and were also seen in Byzantium where, as in the Islamic world, long sleeved mail hauberks had been known before they appeared in the West. Integral mail coifs had also been standard equipment since the 11th century in most parts of western Europe but were rapidly being replaced by separate mail coifs during the late 12th and 13th centuries. Such separate mail coifs had again been known in Byzantium and the Islamic world before spreading to western Europe. Thus such forms of armour were much too common and widespread by the mid-13th century to indicate any particular military influence, one way or the other.

4 – Hauberk with only one mitten (Chedorlaomer captures Lot, plate A)
This highly distinctive fashion, which is worn at Parma by a member of Chedorlaomer's army, seems to have been characteristic of Italy where it appears in a number of late 12th- or early 13th-century sources.[9] The fact that the single mail mitten is worn on the left hand at Parma but on the right elsewhere is explained by the fact that the Parma horseman has been reversed for reasons of artistic composition. As a result he holds his lance in his left hand and has his shield on the right. It would, however, be

---

[8] *Psalter of Simonovko Khludovskiya*, Russian, c.1300 (location unknown); *Chronicle of Peter of Eboli*, Sicily or southern Italy, end of the 12th or early 13th century (Burgerbib., Cod. 120/II, Bern).

[9] "Assassination of Thomas à Becket", wall painting, late 12th or early 13th century (*in situ* Church of SS. Giovanni e Paolo, Spoleto); wall painting of a knight, late 12th century (*in situ* Palazzo della Ragione, Mantua).

extremely interesting to find other examples of the single mail mitten, particularly if they appeared outside Italy.

5 – Forward-angled helmets with nasals (Chedorlaomer captures Lot; Abraham rescues Lot, figs. A and B)
This form of helmet was again common throughout most of western Europe during the 12th century and may even have been known in the late 11th. It was similarly seen in the Middle East and could have been invented in this technologically more advanced area. In Europe the form became rarer during the 13th century, particularly after 1250, although it was still seen occasionally. Once again this feature is too common to be significant.

6 – Round topped helmet with nasal (Abraham rescues Lot, plate B)
Three of the five horsemen in Abraham's army wear round-topped helmets whereas none do so in Chedorlaomer's force. Plenty of round-topped helmets appear 12th- and early 13th-century western European art, particularly from the Mediterranean lands. Some have "buttons" on top while others do not. Round-topped helmets with nasals or even full visors are generally a later feature but are found in late 12th- and 13th-century Italian and Sicilian sources.[10] Similar helmets are also seen in art from Byzantium and regions under Byzantine artistic influence but here nasals remain virtually unknown, or at least very rarely appear in the pictorial sources. Surviving helmets with crowns that are sufficiently flattened to be regarded as round topped rather than pointed do, however, include both those with and those without nasals.[11] The

---

[10] Relief carving of warriors, early 12th century (*in situ* west front of the Cathedral, Lucca); relief carving of the city militia of Milan, from the Porta Romana, 1167 (Museo del Castello Sforzesco, Milan); "Assassination of Thomas à Becket", wall painting, late 12th or early 13th century (*in situ* Church of SS. Giovanni e Paolo, Spoleto); "army of the Maccabees", mosaic, 110–50 (*in situ* Church of San Colombano, Bobbio); "knights leaving a castle", wall painting, 13th century (*in situ* Broletto old town hall, Novara); *Chronicle of Peter of Eboli*, Sicily or southern Italy, end of the 12th or early 13th century (Burgerbib., Cod. 120/II, Bern).

[11] Helmet from the grave of a nomad warrior at Moscu, Moldavia, probably Kipchaq, 12th or 13th century (see V. Spinei, *Moldavia in the 11th–14th centuries*, Bucharest 1986, plate 18/11); helmet from Yasenovo near Stara Zagorsk, Bulgarian or Byzantine, 9th or 10th century (Historical Museum, inv. 200, Kazanlik); "Helmet of Jaroslav Vsevolodovich", lost during the battle of Lipets in 1216 (Kremlin Museum, Lykovo no. 20, Moscow); helmet found near Orel, c.1200 (State Hermitage Museum, Nikolskoye no. 25, St. Petersburg); helmet found near Kiev, early 13th century (Historical Museum, Kiev no. 27, Kiev).

majority have distinct "buttons" or small finials on top and must represent the reality behind the "buttoned" helmets which are so common in Byzantine art. The giving of such essentially Byzantine or eastern European helmets to Abraham's army and not to Chedorlaomer's might suggest Byzantine artistic influence. Or it might merely indicate that round-topped helmets were regarded as a more modern and thus more prestigious form of protection.

7 – Round helmet with neck extension (Abraham rescues Lot, plate B)
Two helmets of this type are shown being worn by a leading figure who may be regarded as Abraham, and by one of his followers. Such helmets with apparent neck-guards had been almost universal in Byzantine and Byzantine-style art for several centuries. But here there is evidence to suggest that the neck extension was, in reality, part of a hood or cover worn over the helmet and its coif or aventail. Such a practice probably had its origins in Iran or the Caucasus as early as the 8th century.[12] Rudimentary neck-protecting extensions are found in 12th- or 13th-century helmets of probable steppe nomadic origin, but these helmets are distinctly pointed rather than round and the neck-extensions are also straight and as well as being much shorter.[13] As such they compare with helmets in various Islamic art-sources of the 12th to 14th centuries. Helmets more or less similar to these on the Parma ceiling are common in art from 12th and 13th century Italy and Sicily but are virtually unknown elsewhere in western Europe.[14] The very realism of some of these sources

---

[12] Hood with leather stiffening, from a grave at Moshchevaya Balka, northern Caucasus, Alano-Saltove, 8th or 9th century (State Hermitage Museum, St. Petersburg).

[13] Helmet from Kovali near Kiev, Kipchaq or Mongol Golden Horde, late 12th to mid-13th century (Historical Museum, Moscow); helmet from Lipovitz near Kiev, Kipchaq or Mongol Golden Horde, late 12th to mid-13th century (Historical Museum, Moscow); helmet found at the battlefield of Kulikovo, Russia, late 13th or 14th century (Battlefield Museum, Kulikovo).

[14] Carved capital, Siculo-Norman, late 12th century (*in situ* Cloisters of the Cathedral, Monreale); *Skylitzes Chronicle*, Sicily in Byzantine style, late 12th or early 13th century (Bib. Nac., Cod. 5–3. N2, Madrid); so-called "Rome Casket", carved ivory box, Sicily or southern Italy, late 12th century (Museo di Palazzo Venezia, Rome); *Encyclopedia of Maurus Hrabanus*, southern Italy, 1023 (Monastery Library, Cod. 132, Monte Cassino); so-called "Chess Set of Charlemagne", southern Italy, Islamic Sicily or North Africa, 11th or 12th century (Bib. Nat., Cabinet des Médailles, Paris); carved stone relief probably illustrating the "Siege of Jerusalem by the First Crusade", start of the 12th century (*in situ* north door, Church of S. Nicola, Bari); carved stone relief illustrating the "Gesta di Floovant", c.1148 (*in situ* west front of the church of S. Maria della Strada, Molise); armoured figure beneath a lion, carved column-base, late 12th century (*in situ* Cathedral, Modena); "Protospatius of

suggests that they represented a form of helmet that actually did exist, and that they were not merely a Byzantine artistic convention. As such they are further evidence for military similarity and perhaps mutual influence between 12th- and 13th-century Italy and the Byzantine world. Perhaps it is here, as well as in the art of the Islamic Middle East, that we should look for the origins of the widespread *bascinet* type of western European helmet which clearly came into existence at the end of the 13th century.

8 – War-hat worn with "antique" armour (Chedorlaomer captures Lot, plate A)
Only one example of the brimmed *chapel de fer* or war-hat appears in the Parma paintings and it is worn by the presumed figure of Chedorlaomer himself. The "evil king" otherwise wears antique or pseudo-Roman armour of a clearly anachronistic type. As such the brimmed helmet could be dismissed as merely an artistic convention rooted in Byzantine iconography. On the other hand such helmets are only rarely associated with unrealistic pseudo-classical armour. War-hats with rudimentary sloping brims had appeared in highly realistic Italian sources since the end of the 12th century, and they continued to do so throughout the 13th century. Meanwhile they also appeared in less realistic sources in a style known as "the Greek Manner".[15] Some are shown with an apparent segmented construction while others are shown as having been forged from one piece, as here in Parma. Brimmed war-hats appear much earlier in Byzantine art or in art under strong Byzantine influence, strongly

---

the Emperor", in an *Exultet Roll*, southern Italy, 12th century (Bib. Casanatese, Cod. 724 B1.13, Rome); wall painting probably illustrating an Italian knight pursuing a Hungarian, late 12th or early 13th century (*in situ* Crypt of Massenzio, Basilica, Aquileia); relief carving of the infantry militia of Verona, mid-12th century (*in situ* on tympanum of west door, Church of S. Zeno, Verona); "Pharoah's Guards", mosaic, Venetian in Byzantine style, 13th century (*in situ* Basilica of S. Marco, Venice); silver alter panels illustrating the life of St. James, by Andrea di Jacopo d'Ognibene, end of the 13th century (*in situ* Pistoia Cathedral); "The Milanese capture Napo della Torre at Desio", wall painting, end of the 13th century (*in situ* Rocca Borromeo, Angera).
[15] Fragmentary wall painting, late 12th or early 13th century (*in situ* Crypt of Massenzio, Basilica, Aquileia); relief carving on the Tomb of Guillame Balnis, c.1289 (*in situ* Convento dell'Annunziata, Florence); "Crucifixion" in the *Missale Romanum*, probably German in Byzantine style from Styria, 13th century (Museo Archeologico Nazionale, Cod. LXXXVI, Cividale); silver altar panels illustrating the life of St. James, by Andrea di Jacopo d'Ognibene, end of the 13th century (*in situ* Pistoia Cathedral); *Conquest of Jerusalem*, Venetian manuscript, late 13th century (Bib. del Seminario, Padua); "The Philistines capture the Ark", wall painting, c.1250–55 (*in situ* Crypt of the Cathedral, Anagni); "The Milanese capture Napo della Torre at Desio", wall painting, end of the 13th century (*in situ* Rocca Borromeo, Angera).

suggesting that this type of helmet originated in Byzantium[16] or the
Middle East.[17] The fact that such a helmet is only worn by Chedorlaomer
at Parma suggests that the style was still associated with Byzantines or
"infidels" in the minds of some mid-13th-century northern Italian artists.

9 – Separate mail coif (Abraham rescues Lot, plate B)

The mail hauberks on the Parma ceiling may all be of the separate type,
since a dividing line around the wearer's neck was not necessarily shown.
Separate coifs are, however, clearly being worn by two figures in Chedorlaomer's army and one in Abraham's army. Two are worn with
pseudo-Classical armour, as very often done in Byzantine art, but one is
worn without any armour other than a helmet. Plenty of hauberks
without coifs appear in late 12th-and 13th-century Italian art but this
form of armour had been illustrated much earlier in Middle Eastern Late
Roman, Byzantine and Islamic art. The only doubt concerns the possibility that, as in some Byzantine and Islamic sources, apparently separate
mail coifs worn with helmets were in reality representations of mail
aventails fastened directly to the rims of helmets. By the 14th century this
would often be the case even in western Europe. Here at Parma,
however, such a feature might indicate Byzantine influence although by
the mid-13th century the fashion was again too widespread to have much
significance.

---

[16] "Arrest of David" in a Byzantine *Psalter*, 9th century (Library of the Monastery of
the Pantocrator, Cod. 61, Mount Athos); "Soldiers of Joshua", carved ivory box,
Byzantine, 9th to 11th century (Victoria and Albert Museum, inv. A.542–1910, London);
"Philistine soldier" in the *Smyrna Octateuch*, Byzantine, 9th to 11th century (Vatican Library,
Ms. Gr. 746, Rome); "Crucifixion", wall painting, Byzantine, early 10th century (*in situ*
Church of Tokali, Göreme, Cappadocia, Turkey); *Menologion of Basil II*, Byzantine
manuscript, c.1017 (Bib. Marciana, Venice); "The Betrayal", wall painting, Cypriot-
Byzantine under Crusader domination, c.1200 (in situ Hermitage of S. Neofito, Ktima,
Enkleistra); *Works of John Chrysostom*, Byzantine manuscript, 12th century (Bib. Nat., Cod.
Gr. 806, Paris); "Goliath" in a Byzantine *Psalter*, 12th century (Bodleian Library, Ms.
Barocci 15, Oxford); "Islamic horseman", painted panel in Islamic style, c.1140 (*in situ*
Cappella Palatina, Palermo); *Skylitzes Chronicle*, Sicily in Byzantine style, late 12th or early
13th century (Bib. Nac., Cod. 5–3. N2, Madrid); "Resurrection", Armenian *Gospels*, 11th
century (Bib. di S. Lazzaro degli Armeni, Ms. N. 141/102, Venice); "Jesus before Pilate",
Armenian *Gospels*, c.1270 (Freer Gallery, Ms. 32–18, Washington); *Chronicle of Georgi
Amartola*, Russian, 1318–27 (Lenin Library, N. 126, Moscow); "St. Mercurios", wall
painting, Byzantine, 1295 (*in situ* Church of Sv. Kliment, Ochrid); Russian helmet, 13th
century (Kremlin Armoury, Moscow).

[17] "Siege of a fortification", fragment of a wall painting from Khirbat al-Mafjar,
Umayyad Islamic, 743–4 (Palestine Archaeological Museum, Jerusalem).

10 – Sword with "nut" shaped pommel and slightly curved slender quillons (Execution of John the Baptist, plate D)

The nut-shaped pommel was more common in 12th-century Europe than in the 13th, having become known from at least by 11th century. Two swords of this type have also been found in Russia, although both were almost certainly imported from western Europe.[18] The style does not appear in Byzantium despite the fact that swords, or at least unmounted blades, were being imported from western Europe by this period – as they were into the Islamic world.

In European art such a "nut"-shaped of pommel is not normally associated with slender curved quillons, as it is shown here in Parma. Nevertheless slender curved quillons of the Parma type were relatively common in 11th-century Byzantine art and continued to be seen throughout the 12th and 13th centuries, by which time they had also appeared in Russian, Sicilian and Italian sources. The evidence it too confused to make clear judgements but there does appear to be a general pattern. This might suggest that long, slightly curved quillons had their origins in the southern or Mediterranean Europe rather than in northern Europe, possibly in the Byzantine Empire or Italy or, in a more general way, in both. They may also be associated with a more sophisticated form of fencing which, having developed in the pre- and early Islamic Middle East, then spread to the Mediterranean world, both Christian and Islamic.

11 – Gonfanon with triple tail (Chedorloamer captures Lot, plate A)

Only one flag or lance-pennon appears in these scenes and it is in the hands of Chedorlaomer's army. Thus the fact that the banner is of a type common throughout 12th- and 13th-century Europe is unlikely to have any significance. Fewer large lance pennons appear in Byzantine art although those that do are generally of this three-tailed form.[19]

---

[18] Sword from Kamenetz-Podolsk, c.1000–50 (see D. Nicolle, *Armies of Medieval Russia, 750–1250*, Oxford 1999. p. 36); sword from the battlefield of Kulikovo (Battlefield Museum, Kulikovo).

[19] *Cynegetica* by Pseudo-Oppian, Byzantine manuscript, 11th or 12th century (Bib. Marciana, Cod. Gr. 497, Venice); so-called *Seraglio Octateuch*, Byzantine manuscript, early 12th century (current whereabouts unknown); *Chronicle of Georgi Amartola*, Russian, 1318–27 (Lenin Library, N. 126, Moscow).

12 – Bridles with curb bits but no nose-bands (Chedorlaomer captures Lot, and Abraham defeats Chedorlaomer, figs. A and B)

This type of bridle was a distinctively western European form and was widespread during the 12th and 13th centuries, although the curb-bit itself did not become so common in pictorial sources until the later 12th and 13th centuries. It was also shown in a much-damaged early 12th-century wall painting in Kiev[20] and in late 13th-century Byzantine-style wall painting in Cyprus.[21] Elsewhere the bridles shown in Byzantine or Byzantine-style art almost invariably have nose bands, often also with doubled cheek straps, and are thus much closer to the horse-harness traditions of Central Asian nomads. Meanwhile the fact that bridles lacking nose-bands are shown being used by Muslims and others in 12th-century Siculo-Norman art probably indicates northern European influence.[22] The style only appears in Italy from the mid-12th century onwards and even then it is generally not shown in *Exultet Rolls* or other pictures in Byzantine style.[23] It also becomes rare in Italy during the 13th century,[24] whereas it was the norm in most other parts of western Europe, and most 13th-century Italian bridles were shown with nose-bands. The appearance of this style on the Parma ceiling is thus a bit of a mystery as it is not particularly Italian and certainly not Byzantine.

13 – Round saddles with moderately raised cantles (Chedorloamer captures Lot, and Abraham defeats Chedorlaomer, figs. A and B)

In contrast to the bridles, the saddles on the Parma ceiling are more Byzantine than western European, at least in their overall outline. Most 13th-century saddles in French and German art have a squared outline whereas those at Parma are rounded, as was normal in Byzantine pictorial

---

[20] Wall paintings of huntsmen, c.1120–25 (*in situ* north-western tower, Cathedral of S. Sofia, Kiev).

[21] "St. Christopher", wall painting, Cypriot, 12th or 13th century (*in situ* local church, Moutaillas).

[22] Carved capital, Siculo-Norman, late 12th century (*in situ* Cloisters of the Cathedral, Monreale); "Petronas defeats the Saracens in Armenia", *Skylitzes Chronicle*, Sicily in Byzantine style, late 12th or early 13th century (Bib. Nac., Cod. 5–3. N2, Madrid).

[23] Carved wooden panels on the Episcopal Throne, southern Italian, late 12th century (Museo Abbaziale, Montevergine); "St. Eustace" and "St. George", bronze door panels, southern Italian, late 12th century (*in situ* Cathedral, Trani); "Cavalry of Verona" and "Vices and Virtues", carved stone reliefs, mid-12th century (*in situ* west front of the Church of S. Zeno, Verona).

[24] "The Milanese capture Napo della Torre at Desio", wall painting, end of the 13th century (*in situ* Rocca Borromeo, Angera).

sources of the 12th and 13th centuries. In Byzantine-style art, however, raised cantles behind the rider are either rarely visible, as in strictly Byzantine art, or are of a rudimentary form as seen in Bosnia, Turkish ruled Anatolia and Sicily.[25] All these areas are known to have been under a greater or lesser degree of western European military influence and the lack of raised cantles on war-saddles in strictly Byzantine art is likely to have been no more than an artistic convention by the 13th century. In western Europe such supporting cantles were closely associated with the couched lance system of fighting which is actually being used by the presumed figure of Abraham on the Parma ceiling. Saddles of rounded outline and having supporting cantles do, however, appear elsewhere in Italy[26] where they may have been a local fashion reflecting residual Byzantine influence. Other close but unexplained parallels may be found in illustrations of Muslim warriors in late 13th-century Spanish art.[27]

14 – Doubled girths securing a saddle (Chedorlaomer captures Lot, and Abraham defeats Chedorlaomer, figs, A and B)
A final feature of horse-harness that deserves attention is the doubled girths securing the two most visible saddles. No distinction is made between the forces of Abraham and Chedorlaomer in this respect and the doubled girth had been common on war-saddles throughout western Europe since the 12th century. It may even have originated in northern Italy where it was shown from the late 11th century onwards. Nevertheless such a system gradually became less common in the 13th century. On the other hand, by this time, it was appearing in the Byzantine world as a clear consequence of Western European influence on styles of cavalry

[25] "The Road to Damascus", wall painting, Bosnian, 1296 (*in situ* parish church, Arilje, Bosnia); "The Three Magi on horseback", wall painting, Christian art under Seljuk Turkish domination, 1190–1200 (*in situ* Chapel No. 19, Church of Elmali, Göreme, Cappadocia, Turkey); painted panel in Islamic style, c.1140 (*in situ* Cappella Palatina, Palermo); *Chronicle of Peter of Eboli*, Sicily or southern Italy, end of the 12th or early 13th century (Burgerbib., Cod. 120/II, Bern); *Skylitzes Chronicle*, Sicily in Byzantine style, late 12th or early 13th century (Bib. Nac., Cod. 5–3. N2, Madrid).

[26] Carved stone relief probably illustrating the "Siege of Jerusalem by the First Crusade", start of the 12th century (*in situ* north door, Church of S. Nicola, Bari); *Conquest of Jerusalem*, Venetian manuscript, late 13th century (Bib. del Seminario, Padua).

[27] *Cantigas of Alfonso X*, Castilian manuscript, end of the 13th century (Biblioteca, Cod. T.I.i, Escorial).

warfare, above all the introduction of the couched lance under the Comnenian Emperors.[28]

15 – Camel riders with clubs (Chedorlaomer captures Lot, plate A)
Clubs or cudgels apparently made from wood or only having heads of bitumen, and thus not rating as true maces, had long been the mark of the desert Arabs in Byzantine iconography.[29] How far they still reflected reality by the 13th century is immaterial because their presence on the Parma ceiling, as in other Italian art of the 12th and 13th centuries, is clear evidence of Italy's adoption of various Byzantine iconographic conventions.[30]

16 – Bell on a camel's neck (Chedorlaomer captures Lot, plate A)
The bell hung around one camel's neck at Parma may similarly be regarded as a borrowing from eastern iconography. Yet the situation is less clear-cut than it is with the camel-riders' cudgels. Such bells are not commonly found in Byzantine art, nor had they been in the art of the pre-Islamic Middle East at Palmyra or at Dura-Europos, nor in early Christian

---

[28] "Horsemen in combat", silver vase from Vilgort, Byzantine or Christian Caucasus, 12th century (State Hermitage Museum, St. Petersburg); "Mounted Saint", wall painting, Bosnian, 1296 (*in situ* local church, Arilje, Bosnia); "Kilij Arslan IV", stucco relief panel, Seljuk Turkish, mid-12th century (Museum of Turkish and Islamic Art, Istanbul); "Pharoah's Army", *Exultet Role* from Fondi, southern Italian, early 12th century (Bib. Nat., Nouv. Acq. Lat. 710, Paris).

[29] "Shepherds", wall painting, Byzantine, 850–60 (*in situ* Chapel of Anne and Joachim, Kizil Cukar, Cappadocia, Turkey); "Arabs" in the *Smyrna Octateuch*, Byzantine, 9th to 11th century (Vatican Library, Ms. Gr. 746, Rome); "Guards wearing turbans" in *Barlaam and Joasaph*, Byzantine manuscript, end of the 12th or early 13th century (Monastery of Iviron, Cod. 463, Mount Athos); "Joseph and the Midianite", embroidered textile, Coptic, 7 century (State Hermitage Museum, St. Petersburg). I am also grateful for Dr Shihab al-Sarraf for informing me that the mace with a bitumen head was known in 8th- to 10th-century Iraq, and that it continued to be used as a peasant weapon in that country until modern times when it was called a *mugwar* in Iraqi vernacular Arabic (from its original name, *muqayyara*, based upon the Arabic *qir* meaning bitumen).

[30] "Demons", carved stone relief, southern Italian, late 12th century (*in situ* on the exterior of the Cathedral, Barletta); "warrior on foot" on a bronze door panel, southern Italy, late 12th century (*in situ* Cathedral, Trani); "Arabs" on a mosaic, Venetian in Byzantine style, 13th century (*in situ* Basilica of S. Marco, Venice); "warrior on foot", carved capital, Siculo-Norman, late 12th century (*in situ* Cloisters of the Cathedral, Monreale); "armoured cavalryman", *Skylitzes Chronicle*, Sicily in Byzantine style, late 12th or early 13th century (Bib. Nac., Cod. 5–3. N2, Madrid); "traveller", *Chronicle of Peter of Eboli*, Sicily or southern Italy, end of the 12th or early 13th century (Burgerbib., Cod. 120/II, Bern).

Syria, nor in the early Islamic art of the Umayyad period. What then was the reality upon which this convention was built? One first has to look at the 8th to 10th century Middle East to find large open bells being worn by horses.[31] Bells had been, and remained, a characteristic of Turkish and Iranian military decoration but these were of the small spherical kind and were worn in greater numbers. The first example of a single large bell being worn around a camel's neck might be in the famous *Ashburnham Pentateuch*.[32] This rather mysterious manuscript is believed to have been made in Christian North Africa or Egypt in the 7th century. Other examples do not seem to reappear until the 13th century when they are almost exactly as shown in the *Ashburnham Pentateuch*. They are the same on the Parma ceiling, and in Islamic manuscripts from Egypt and the Fertile Crescent.[33] Perhaps one might conclude by taking this single bell on the Parma Baptistery ceiling as an example, not so much of traditional iconography borrowed from any particular source, but of artistic realism based upon a genuine fashion seen among the camel riding peoples of North Africa and the Middle East.

---

[31] "St. Mercurios", wall painting from the Cathedral at Faras, Nubian, late 8th century (National Museum, no. 149672, Warsaw); "St. Menas" in a Nubian manuscript, late 8th century (British Library, Ms. Or. 6805, London); silk textile from the reliquary of St. Cunibert, Syrian, 8th century (Erzbischofliches Museum, Cologne); fragment of decorated ceramic showing an elephant or a horse, Egypt, late 10th to mid-11th century (Benaki Museum, Athens). rt

[32] "Cain kills Abel",[8] *Ashburnham Pentateuch*, Egypt or North Africa, 7th century (Bib. Nat., Nouv. Acq. Lat. 2334, Paris).

[33] Inlaid bronze vase, Syria or Egypt, mid-13th century (Victoria and Albert Museum, inv. 740–1898, London); *Maqamat of al-Hariri*, manuscript from Iraq, 1242–58 (Suleymaniye Library, Ms. Esad Efendi 2916, Istanbul); *Maqamat of al-Hariri*, manuscript from Iraq, 1237 (Bib. Nat., Ms. Arabe 5847, Paris); *Maqamat of al-Hariri*, manuscript from Iraq, 1225–50 (Bib. Nat., Ms. Arabe 3929, Paris).

PLATE A. Abraham's brother Lot being captured by Chedorlaomer, leader of an
    alliance of Four Kings who rebelled against King Bera of Sodom and his
    alliance of Five Kings (Gen. 14: 12) on a painted panel on the first level below
    the Dome of the Baptistery. (photograph, Dott. Gianfranco Fiaccadori)

PLATE B. The army of the Four Kings is pursued by Abraham and his "servants" (Gen. 14: 15) on a painted panel on the first level below the Dome of the Baptistery. (photograph, Dott. Gianfranco Fiaccadori)

PLATE C. John the Baptist before King Herod (Mat. 1:3) on a painted panel on
the second level below the Dome of the Baptistery. (photograph, Dott.
Gianfranco Fiaccadori)

PLATE D. The beheading of John the Baptist (Mat. 14:9-10) on a painted panel on the second level below the Dome of the Baptistery. (photograph, Dott. Gianfranco Fiaccadori)

INDEX

'Abbasid dynasty: I 588; II 314; II 316–7;
IV 9–10; VIII 114; X 47, 79
'abid: X 50
abtal: I 593
Achaia, Principality: VI 334, 340
Acre: IV 14-15, 17; VI 327, 332, 340
Adab al-Harb wa'l-Shuja'ah: I 594
Adharbayjan *see* Azerbayjan
Aethiopica: IV 8
Afamiyah: VII 37, 39
afeutremens: V 21; VI 333
Africa, Africans: I 588; IX 90, 102; X 50,
Aght'amar: II 315, III 231, 233
agie: V 18
ahabish: IV 7
'ahdath: IV 16
'Ain Dara: III 226–30
alamdaran: I 595
Alans: II 313; VI 334
Albania: Introduction xi
Albanians (of Caucasus): IV 10
alemiele: V 17
Aleppo: III 226
Alexandria: X 72
alférez: I 598
allegiance: I 580,
Almoravid (*see* Murabitin dynasty)
Amalfi: X 48, 56, 62
aminan: I 596
'ammariyah: X 60
Anatolia: IV 13, VI 333–4; XI 3
Andalus, Andalusia, Andalusians: I 584–5,
590, 598; IV 10–11, 18, 31–2;
VI 333; X 51, 70
Andalusian influence: IX 87
Angevin dynasties: Introduction x; VI 331
Ansari, al-: IV 18, 31
anste: V 18
Antioch: III 227; VI 328, 330, 339–40
Principality of: VI 330–31; VII 39
Aphrodisias: II 304, 312
Apulia: V 25; X 48, 54, 56, 77
Aqsara'i, al-: IV 31–2
aquillon: V 21

Arabia, Arabs: I 582, 585, 589, 591; II 299,
302, 306–7, 311–2; III 230; IV 7,
8–10, 16; VI 327, 333; VII 34;
IX 90, 97, 101–2; X 49–51, 53–4,
68
Arab world: IX 96
Arab-Islamic culture: II 299
Roman province of: VIII 115
southern: IV 7
southern, pre-Islamic: I 594
Arabian Gulf: I 587
Arabs, early Muslim: VIII 116
arayish: I 595
archers, archery: I 591, 594–5; IV 9, 15,
34; IX 91, 98; X 58, 69;
infantry: X 58
Muslim: X 69
carcais: V 18
coivre: V 18
horse-archery: I 581, 589; IV 9, 11,
16–8; X 57
juwalduz: I 597
quiver: I 594; V 18; VI 332
Roman: I 584
saietes: V 18
tir andazan: I 594–5
'arifan: I 594
Armenia, Armenians: I 592; II 300–301,
306, 312, 315; III 227, 230–31,
233; IV 13; VI 327
Armenian artistic influence: VI 328–9
arming cap: V 19
armour
for hands: V 20
arm defences: Intro 3, V 20
laminated: III 231, 233
rerebrace: VI 334
armeure: V 20
auberc: V 20
auberc jaserant: VI 333
body: V 20
brogne: V 20
buff leather: X 50

Iberia: Introduction x; I 584, 586; II 300;
IV 32; VI 330, 332; X 64, 66,
77–8
Ibn al-Khatib: IV 32
Ibn Bassam: IV 8
Ibn Hawqal: IV 10
Ibn Hudhayl: IV 18, 31
Ibn Sa'id: IV 18
'idad: X 60
identification numbers: X 60
Ifriqiyah: X 51–4, 56, 79
Ikhshidid dynasty: IV 10
'Imad al-Din Zangi: IV 13; VII 38
India, Indians: I 584, 594; II 306; VII 33;
X 64
art: X 69
Islamic: X 68
infantry: I 594; II 306–307; IV 14; V 17,
22; VI 332; X 58, 74
Fatimid: X 52
light: X 57
Ingeborg Psalter: V 23
inheritance, as arms distribution:
Introduction xi
'iqlim: X 51
'iqta: IX 91; X 51, 56
Iran, Iranians (*see also* Persia, Persian):
Introduction xii; I 585, 589;
II 299, 301–302, 306–308, 311–2,
314–5, 317; III 233; IV 7–9, 10,
17; V 22; VI 334; IX 97; X 64, 70,
76–7; XI 6, 13
Iranian art: VI 333, X 64
Iraq: I 588, II 308–309, 317; IV 17, 331;
VIII 120; X 47
iron sources: X 61
Islam
classical period: IV 9
early period: VIII 114
armies: I 587
art: XI 6, 8, 13
civilization: VII 33
conquests: VIII 117
influence: I 586; V 20, 26; VI 328,
332, 335; IX 87; X 57
Middle East: I 583
military equipment: III 231
states: I 581
world: I 584; X 64, 66; XI 4, 9
world, during Crusader period: IV
16–8
world, western: II 303; VI 333
Isma'ilis: VII 35-6, 39

Italy,
Italians: Introduction x–xi; I 583–4,
586; II 313, 316–7; III 229, 231;
V 22, 25; VI 328, 330–4; IX 87,
91, 94; X 50, 54–7, 70–71;
Norman: III 231; VI 328
northern: X 57
art: X 47, 78

Jahiliya (*see also* Arabia, pre-Islamic): IV
7
Jahiz, al-: IV 9
jandaran: I 596
Japan: I 584; II 306
jarrahun, field surgeon: VII 35, 41
javelin: I 591; IV 7–8, 13, 16; V 18;
VI 333; VII 37; IX 91; X 49, 52,
60
dart: V 18
harbah: I 594, VII 37
khalanj: IV 10
khisht: VII 37
mitrad: I 595
mizraq: I 591
Jazirah (*see also* Mesopotamia): I 588;
II 301; VI 331, 335; VII 38;
IX 97, 99; X 65
Jean de Meun: IV 15
Jerusalem: VIII 116
siege of: V 25
jibs: VIII 122
jigar andazan: I 596
Jingling Johnnie: I 595
John Tsimiskes, Emperor: III 227, 230
John VIII Palaeologus, Emperor: IV 32
Jordan: II 301, 307; III 229
Jordan valley: VIII 114, 116–17
jund: IX 91; X 51, 58
Jund al-Urdun: VIII 116
Jund Dimashq: VIII 116
Jungfrauenspiegel: V 23

kamand andazan: I 596
kamand halqah andazan: I 596
kardha-yi buzurg: I 594
kettle-drums: I 588, 595
khadiman: I 596
khaftan: I 594
Kharajis: IV 9
khasak daran: I 596
Khazars: II 310, 313
Khirbat al-Mafjir: II 314
khizanah al-tajammul: X 60
khizanah al-malikiyah: X 72